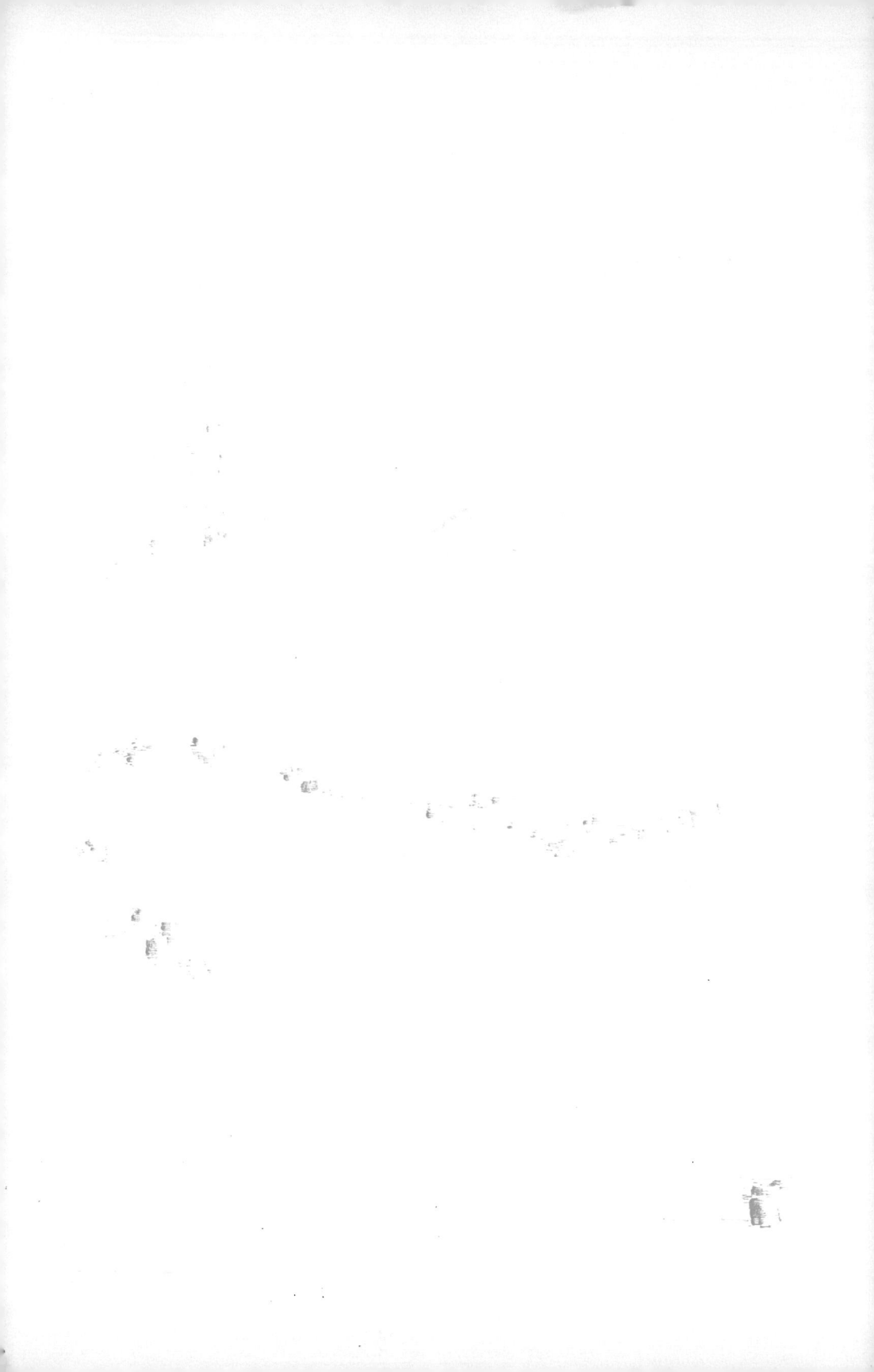

Hamlet | The Shakespearean Director

Shakespeare's statue at Weimar.

The statue was erected in the Park an der Ilm in 1904, the same year that Edward Gordon Craig came to Germany at the invitation of Count Harry Graf Kessler. In July 1904 Craig paid the first of many visits to Weimar, whose park offered hours of solitude for contemplation.

(Courtesy of Archiv für Kunst und Geschichte)

Hamlet | The Shakespearean Director

Mike Wilcock

Carysfort Press, Dublin

A Carysfort Press Book

Hamlet | The Shakespearean Director
By Mike Wilcock

First published in Ireland in 2002 as a paperback original by
Carysfort Press, 58 Woodfield, Scholarstown Road,
Dublin 16, Ireland

Typeset by Carysfort Press
Cover design by Alan Bennis

Printed and bound by Leinster Leader Ltd
18/19 South Main Street, Naas, Co. Kildare, Ireland

For Kay

'I could see in Hamlet the history of the theatre.'
Edward Gordon Craig

Contents

Acknowledgements

I wish to thank the following parties, who assisted in the funding, research and publication of the present study:
The Senate of the National University of Ireland for a generous grant in aid of publication; the Faculty of Arts at University College, Dublin for several travel grants as well as a post-graduate Arts scholarship, enabling extensive travel for reseach in both Europe and America; the Department of Education and Science for an enlightened policy of Study Leave allowing the pursuit, with few interruptions, of the project at hand – a huge advantage in anyone's book. Dan Farrelly, editor of Carysfort Press, who worked tirelessly on the text of this study; Lilian Chambers also of Carysfort Press; colleagues at UCD Centre for Drama Studies, several of whom read over and commented on the chapters in various stages of completion. In particular: Eamonn Jordan on the Guthrie chapter, and Enrica Cerquoni on the final chapter and conclusion; Professor Don Wilmeth of Brown University, Rhode Island whose advice, friendship and encouragement I very much value; Professor Richard Foakes for reading an early draft of Chapter 4 – his incisive suggestions were particularly helpful in clarifying the Hamlet theme. Edward Nolan of the Naugatuck Valley Community-Technical College, Waterbury who has helped for many years to research materials in the United States, his thorough efforts very much appreciated; supportive friends, young and old, past and present, at Newpark Comprehensive School, Blackrock – not least, Eileen O'Duffy and Gerry Murphy; staff of many libraries both in Europe and North America who have provided endless

valuable assistance, particularly the Birmingham Reference Library, the Shakespeare Centre Library, Stratford-upon-Avon, the Folger Shakespeare Library, Washington D.C., the Bristol University Theatre Collection; the New York Public library and the libraries of Trinity College, Dublin and University College, Dublin; Bernard Louglin of the Tyrone Guthrie Centre at Annagh-ma-kerrig; Seamus Hosey of Radio Teilifís Éireann; Olga Artemova for help in communicating with the Moscow Art Theatre; Heather Wilcock for assistance in translating French texts, and Charles Taylor for help in German research; the Rev. Canon Walter Crooks for valuable encouragement and support; Christopher Fitz-Simon, artistic director of the Abbey Theatre in the late 1980s, for discussing the challenges of directing and for sharing with me his memories of Tyrone Guthrie; Jonathan Williams for valuable and much appreciated advice on publishing; Father Peter Hiscock, my 'mentor' at Trinity College, Dublin in the late 1960s who first sparked my interest in Shakespearean staging by lending such books as Leslie Hotson's *Shakespeare's Wooden O*; the late Dick Cameron of 'The Group' in Monkstown, Co. Dublin, who many years ago gave me invaluable insights into the world of psychoanalysis, and introduced me to *Hamlet and Oedipus*; Professor Christopher Murray of the Department of English, UCD – a guiding spirit in much of the doctoral groundwork from which this book originates.

It hardly needs stating that none of the aforementioned bears any responsibility for errors, failings or omissions for which I must accept complete responsibility. My mother, Gwen, and sister, Julie, always have been a huge source of inspiration. Finally, I must thank my wife, Kay, for her patience and constructive criticism. Her unfailing support helped immeasurably in the completion of this work.

Illustrations

We have acknowledged, where appropriate, the source of the above illustrations. In several cases we were unable to trace the copyright-holders and would be grateful to receive any information as to their identity.

Foreword

The role and function of the theatre director are often misunderstood or misrepresented. Certain star directors, whose productions become better known than the plays they interpret, are worshipped this side of idolatry. The other extreme view is that the director is a peripheral figure whose job is to make sure that rehearsals start on time and that the actors don't bump into the furniture. While both the reverence and the scorn paint a false picture of the reality, it is often difficult to explain the complex series of responsibilities and relationships that directors have in each production. With a new play, the primary relationship is with the writer.

The director's responsibility is to ensure that the author's voice is heard clearly in the inaugural production. The future life of the play often depends on the clarity of thinking in that first production. For a director, it is an awesome responsibility to shepherd a new work into being and it is essential that the playwright and the director work closely together.

When dealing with classical texts, however, the opportunity for interpretation is greater and it is here that the influence and creativity of the director become evident. As twentieth-century Shakespearean productions became less concerned with re-creations of Elizabethan accuracy and began to reflect the universality of the themes and ideas expressed in the great texts, the role of the director became more crucial. Many great directors saw contemporary relevance in Shakespeare's genius truths. Principal among the pioneers who opened the work up to modern scrutiny was the great Tyrone Guthrie, who was never afraid to defy convention or to question received wisdom. His creation of both the Stratford Shakespearean Festival in Ontario and the Guthrie Theater in Minneapolis, Minnesota, greatly advanced the appreciation of Shakespeare throughout North America. By devoting an extensive chapter in his study of the Shakespearean director to Guthrie, Mike Wilcock reminds us of how innovative and influential this remarkable Irish director was in the middle years of the last century and how his work opened the way for many others who followed.

This study of the Shakespearean director as viewed through various interpretations of *Hamlet* is a welcome addition to our understanding of how essential it is for a director to have a clear vision of a great play. It also helps us to understand how each generation can see itself reflected in one of the greatest masterpieces ever written for the theatre. Mike Wilcock is an ideal witness to the lasting influence of *Hamlet*. When he was a young teacher in Dublin, I clearly remember a production he directed with teenagers in Newpark, Blackrock. While his performers were inexperienced, it was clear that a real directorial vision inspired them with a passion and a love of language that is rare and special. His subsequent research in Shakespeare and theatre has led to this present work.

It is an important study from which all of us who love Shakespeare and who understand the importance of continuing contemporary exploration may gain new insights.

Joe Dowling
Artistic Director
The Guthrie Theater.
Minneapolis, MN

Introduction | He who *is* there: the Hamlet director

All roads in the theatre, it is said, lead to Shakespeare. Equally – and paradoxically – all roads in the modern theatre lead to the director. It is that meeting place between the living and the dead, that crossroads, that *conflict*, which lies at the heart of this study and which provides its essential dynamic. If the idea of the director, as one critic puts it, 'is the most dominant feature of Western theatre in the twentieth century' (du Read 1988: 280), what, then, has happened to both Shakespeare and to the director in the great clash between that dominant figure and the most dominant playwright in Western theatre? In 'A Director's Theatre', written in the mid-1950s, Eric Bentley identified the core of the problem when he wrote:

> To speak of Shakespeare's *Hamlet* will soon be as unusual and eccentric as to speak of Schikaneder's *Magic Flute*. The playwright is just a librettist; the composer's name is Reinhardt, Meyerhold, Piscator, Baty, Logan, or Kazan. (1969: 269)

Although directors were a presence in Western theatre from the closing decades of the nineteenth century, what Bentley outlines is a fundamental change or evolutionary step in the role of the director – a change in the making from the early years of the twentieth century. It is ironic, perhaps more than mere coincidence, that Bentley should choose to set *Hamlet* along side his list of directors. For Shakespeare's play and its eponymous hero provide a compelling image of this new kind of director. Hamlet with his group of professional actors, with his detailed instructions to those players, and with his obsessive theatrical agenda – in other words, with his determination to be king in the theatre if nowhere else – is Shakespeare's *auteur* director par excellence. Nor is it surprising that Bentley should begin his list of directors with the names of Reinhardt and Meyerhold, both of whom are seminal influences in this story. In the evolution of the director's new role their names are inevitably linked with another key player: Edward Gordon Craig. Craig was born in 1872; Reinhardt in 1873; Meyerhold in 1874. Thirty years later – a significant age in *Hamlet* (III.ii.148; V.i.140-58) – these three figures would become a major force for change on the European stage. This study is about the revolution they began and the forging of a new role for the director – a role that can be defined most clearly through the image of Hamlet, Prince of Denmark.

To understand the significance of this new figure – the Hamlet director – it is necessary to examine how directors first entered Western theatre and began to shape Shakespearean production. In *The Producer and the Play* (1975: 15), Norman Marshall points out that the 'artist-director' first appeared in the nation states of France, Germany and Russia – the great European imperialist powers of the nineteenth century. There is a clear connection between these contending imperialistic cultures and the appearance of the director as a power within the theatre. As masters of world drama between 1650 and 1850 the French not surprisingly exerted an influence. The term régisseur (stage manager/director), so suggestive of political power, was exported by the French to the German and Russian theatres (although the French later developed their own terminology). German culture, too, has played a key role in the story of the Shakespearean director. It is hardly surprising that of the directors that Eric Bentley mentions at random (above), the first is an Austrian, the third a German and the second is a Russian – who had German parents.

The connection between cultural changes in the theatre and imperialist power is well illustrated in the figure who is so often credited with being the first director in the theatre: Duke Georg II of Saxe-Meiningen. In an article, 'From Political to Cultural Despotism: The Nature of the Saxe-Meiningen Aesthetic', John Osborne makes this connection clear. Frustrated long in his political ambitions, it was understandable that Georg, before becoming Duke in 1870, should have found the Arts an attractive alternative arena where he could exercise his energy and search for power. In time political and artistic concerns would be combined. 'Under [Duke Georg's] auspices,' notes Osborne, 'the political authoritarianism of the Second German Empire became transformed into a cultural authoritarianism' (1975: 41). In other words, when under Bismarck's controlling hand Georg finally replaced his father, Duke Bernhard, and began intensive work to develop the theatre in Saxe-Meiningen, he was in a position to fulfil both his artistic and, at least some of, his political ambitions.

Thus from the outset, the achievement of power has been a central preoccupation of the director's intention and nature. In that respect, at least, perhaps little has changed over the years. When in *Prospero's Staff* (1986: xv), Charles Marowitz asserted that the director is a 'self-obsessed colonizer', and that, with his group of actors, the 'underlying impulse and overriding aim of all these searches remain conquest', English-educated Marowitz, either consciously or unconsciously, was reflecting these origins of the directorial imperative among the imperialist powers of nineteenth-century Europe. In the year (1866) that Duke Georg took his first directorial steps in the theatre of Saxe-Meiningen, Bismarck wrote of the emerging German nation: 'We do not live alone in Europe but with three other Powers that hate and envy us.'[1] The statement is a striking reminder of the aggressive, indeed predatory, cultural atmosphere from which the director emerged. Such a mentality seeks strength and domination through a rigorously applied internal unity, and thus through the suppression of dissent. When Edward Gordon Craig, in the early years of the twentieth century, deplored the many voices of the theatre and spoke of the need for a stern, unifying ruler

(Napoleon was an idol), he was, in artistic terms, essentially echoing Bismarck's sentiments. 'Why did he not,' demanded Craig (in 1931) of Tolstoy, 'rise up and seize Russia by the scruff of the neck, and shake it and bring it to its sense, as Mussolini has done today with Italy?' (1989: 48). Thus Craig dismisses the writer and praises the ruthless dictator (Il Duce):

> Now, then, it is impossible for a work of art ever to be produced where more than one brain is permitted to direct; and if works of art are not seen in the Theatre this one reason is a sufficient one, though there are plenty more. (1957: 99)

Little wonder that Craig's ideas – inspired in part by that Wagnerian designer, the Swiss-German Adolphe Appia – received such a ready welcome on the continent of Europe where military despotism had long been a tradition. Only later would his ideas become influential in his own country, and even then, much to Craig's chagrin, only through foreign intermediaries such as Max Reinhardt.

Attention, then, in this study will be focused on directors and Shakespearean production in France, Germany, Russia and Britain. It is precisely in those countries where the director first emerged, and where there is a long and well-documented history of directorial achievement, that this changing role can be most clearly studied; even more so because it is in those societies that some of the most exciting and significant experiments in Western theatre have taken place. In the context of such European cultures of militaristic adventurism so long preoccupied with domination, power becomes a central consideration; essentially this matches the core, underlying question surrounding the struggle, the meeting place between Shakespeare and the director. Indeed traditional images of the director suggest this preoccupation with power and domination: dukes, princes, warrior kings – even gods. Who controls the production process is the key point. As French director Jean Vilar expressed it prophetically in 1946:

> Two conflicting methods confront each other, and will
> oppose each other just as resolutely in the decades to come
> so that one can summarize thus: Which one, the author or
> the producer, is today, the true creator of the dramatic work?
> (1975: 36-7)

No doubt both author and director contribute some part to the
production process – what Edward Braun describes as 'the co-
ordination of expressive means based on an interpretation of
the play-text',[2] but which of these two forces is the dominant
one? In the supposed contest between dead playwright and
living director the answer to that question, in this particular
case, might seem to be a foregone conclusion. As Tyrone
Guthrie – a man whose place in this story should not be
underestimated – puts it with characteristic gusto (1965: 177):
'The authors of most of the plays that really *demand* the author's
presence at rehearsal, are unavoidably prevented from being
there by a previous engagement, which not even the greatest of
mortals can decline' (Guthrie's emphasis).

Despite this, there is much in the ensuing pages to suggest
that the director's victory is not such a complete one. Nor is it
entirely clear that Patrice Pavis is correct, certainly in the case of
Shakespeare, when he pronounces that: 'We are now beyond
the quarrel between a semiology of text and a semiology of
performance. Each has developed its own analytical tools and
*we no longer attempt to analyse a performance on the basis of a pre-existing
dramatic text*' (1992: 2-3). Pavis, indeed, might well agree with
Peter Brook when he suggests that there is something
'infuriating' about the modern theatre being tied reverentially to
a sixteenth-century playwright. 'There are thousands of people,'
said Brook in conversation with Ralph Berry, 'for whom a
playhouse, in which the imagery is to do with kings and queens
and goddesses, is virtually intolerable' (Berry 1989: 130). Yet in
discussing the director's role it is precisely these images of gods,
princes and dukes that predominate. The term 'king', in fact, is
probably applied more frequently to Peter Brook than any other
living director – or playwright. And 'king' is only one of his
many titles. 'They have become charismatic figures, saints for a
secular age,' write Bradby and Williams (of Brook and

Grotowski), 'valued for their insistence on pursuing their own vision despite the normal criteria of theatre practice' (1988: 2).

It is a matter of historical accident that the first (commonly accepted) director was, in fact, a duke. To this coincidence there is some irony attached. In *Scene* (1923) Gordon Craig dwelt on the image of the sixteenth-century Italian duke who enjoyed a privileged seat in his theatre from which he enjoyed a perfect perspective. For Craig this provided an image of the modern director who has a clear overall view of production – in contrast to the Victorian actor-manager whose view, centred on his own performance, tended to be partial. Among Shakespearean characters one of the most frequently identified with the director is the figure of Prospero, Duke of Milan. Charles Marowitz, as already noted, entitles one of his books on directing *Prospero's Staff*. Peter Brook, not prone to repeating himself, has directed *The Tempest* four times, and is clearly haunted by the magical, fatherly figure of Prospero. In this figure, with some significance, playwright (Shakespeare as Prospero) and director (director as Prospero) challengingly meet.

Hamlet, we shall find, is a still more crucial figure in the story of the Shakespearean director. Among all of Shakespeare's characters, Hamlet (even more clearly than Prospero) arranges, orchestrates one might say, a real theatrical performance. Significantly he does it not because he is interested in entertaining people with a play. He uses *The Murder of Gonzago* as a vehicle for his own preoccupations and even audaciously adds 'some dozen or sixteen lines' to suit his own interpretation and agenda. In his directorial hands it becomes 'The Mousetrap'. In the changing role of the director in twentieth-century production, Hamlet emerges as the key figure. It is no wonder that the great iconoclasts of modern theatre, from Meyerhold and Craig to Brecht, Guthrie and Brook have been drawn to this fantasy warrior. Significantly they have often seen their own work in the theatre in terms of this Shakespearean character. *Hamlet: The Story of a Director* was to be the title of a book that Meyerhold long planned to write. That is part of a story that provides a particular focus to the opening chapters of this study.

The figure of Hamlet, then, provides a key to understanding the most fundamental shifts in the role of the director in Shakespearean production. 'I could see in Hamlet,' said Gordon Craig, 'the history of the theatre …' The early directors such as Duke Georg in Germany, Stanislavsky in Russia, and later Harley Granville-Barker in England as well as Jacques Copeau in France, saw themselves essentially as servants of the play. Fidelity to the Shakespearean text was a firm principle. They wished to distance themselves from the 'hacking and re-arranging' of the nineteenth-century actor-managers with their narrow view of the production. Duke Georg of Saxe-Meiningen, while authoritarian towards actors, revered the text of the author. Writing of the Meiningen *Julius Caesar* in London in May 1881, *The Times* critic wrote:

> As a subject for unqualified praise, we may first of all refer to the perfect reverence for Shakespeare's text which has been shown throughout, and which might serve as a model to English managers. The original is followed with minute fidelity as regards not only the sequence of the scenes, but also every stage direction. (31/5/1881)

In the years that followed that historic visit to London, William Poel and Harley Granville-Barker, rejecting the short cuts and textual distortions of actor-managers such as Henry Irving, would share the same enthusiasm for textual fidelity. In France, Copeau was inspired by Barker's example; in Russia, Stanis-lavsky too (despite some lapses) revered the author. Such figures firmly believed that their first duty as directors was to interpret faithfully the text before them. That meant usually not omitting lines – a practice for which Bernard Shaw gives Barker (a fellow playwright) particular credit: 'He would not cut a line to please himself.'[3] The first or Father directors made deference still to the Fathers of Dramatic Literature.

If these early directors were kings then they shared gladly the crown with the author. If any party was to be demonized, it was the actor. That early apostle of 'authentic Shakespeare', William

Poel wrote: 'It is owing to the despotism of the actor on the English stage, and consequently to the star system, that I attribute the mutilation of Shakespeare's plays in their representation' (1913:154). And that was just as pertinent a criticism of the Russian, the French and the German theatres as it was of the English. Indeed, what further narrows the scope of this enquiry is that these European monarchs of the theatre (like their real regal counterparts) are so closely related – in mind, if not in blood. Marking out the appearance of the anti-naturalist director in 1907, Meyerhold has no difficulty in relating himself to Gordon Craig in England and Max Reinhardt in Berlin.

'With the death throes of nineteenth-century naturalism, and the advent of the Hamlet director from Meyerhold and Craig onwards, the alliance between playwright and director began to break down. Symbolist and expressionist trends encouraged more daring forms of interpretation. As directors increasingly saw the play text merely as the raw material for their own preoccupations, as the concept of 'the author of the stage play' became more fashionable, the role of playwright – and thus of Shakespeare – became downgraded. Attitudes became less respectful. 'However much I love Shakespeare,' says Peter Brook, 'the moment I'm told that I'm serving Shakespeare, there's another instinct that says, "Fuck Shakespeare – why him more than anyone else?"' (Berry 1989: 142). Granville-Barker, at the turn of the century, would have been more reverential. 'Some part of the advance in the director's status,' wrote Tyrone Guthrie, 'has … been made over the dead body of the author' (1987:121). As Chapter 4 of this book makes clear, Guthrie stressed his own Hamlet role by defiantly writing 'Shakespearean' lines of his own and adding them to Shakespeare's text, 'without the slightest twinge of conscience' in so doing. In 1971, the year of Guthrie's death, Jonathan Miller wrote a long and influential letter to *The Times* (13/10/71), defending the directorial freedom of those such as Brook and Guthrie who refused to be awed by 'mandarin bardolatry'. Once out of the historical ambit of the author, the 'subsequent performance' (as Miller put it in a later book) must always have a life of its own quite independent of its original creator and his 'intentions'.[4] Indeed, like Guthrie, Miller casts doubt on whether we can know for certain what those intentions were. Yet these ideas were in themselves hardly new. 'Our standard,' said Max Reinhardt, 'must not be to act a play as it was acted in the days of its author … How to make a play live in our time, that is decisive for us' (Bradby and Williams 1988: 17).

However, the director's freedom to interpret and invent can never be unfettered. As Charles Marowitz puts it (1986: 44, 61):

> A despot imperviously imposes his own will and is the sole arbiter of all events, but the director imposes his will for the sake of the tyranny imposed upon him by the play. Try as he may, he can never escape the stranglehold of the play … Hamlet, for instance, can be many things, but he cannot be decisive, inarticulate, and unreflective and still inhabit Shakespeare's play. (Marowitz's emphasis)

From a man who 'collaged' Hamlet that is an interesting statement. It is an admission that helps us to see the weaknesses as well as the strengths in the director's position. To some extent he must defer, even if reluctantly, to the writer. And yet many directors are still happy to accept the play on the author's terms. 'In every actor,' writes Steven Berkoff in I am Hamlet (1989: vii), 'is a Hamlet struggling to get out. In fact, in most directors too.' In most, perhaps – but not all. This study will demonstrate that the trend towards an increasing encroachment on the territory of both actor and writer is not the only one. Not all directors are rebel princes. Of these Jean Vilar, with his strict repudiation of directorial invention, is a prime example.

Above all this book is an examination of power – its use and abuse – in the theatre. 'Once he can persuade the state to fund him adequately,' note Bradby and Williams, 'the modern director enjoys almost total control' (1988: 22). Since Shakespeare is concerned often with the machinations of the powerful, his plays will provide us with important clues in our search and our examination of these modern theatrical kings. It is not without significance, for example, that the image of the cuckoo – that imperialist bird – is a recurring one in Shakespeare:

> That ungentle gull, the cuckoo's bird … did oppress our nest. (*1Henry4* V.i.60)

The cuckoo referred to, in this instance, is Henry IV, a king who advises his son, Harry 'to busy giddy minds/With foreign quarrels' (*2Henry4* IV.iii.341-2). Does one admire the cuckoo for its cheek, cunning (slyness?) and ingenuity, or does one despise 'that ungentle gull' for its invasion? Opinions will differ.

All roads in the theatre may lead to Shakespeare, yet all roads in Shakespeare lead to (and from) *Hamlet*. Shakespeare wrote great plays before 1600, but his greatest, including *Hamlet*, date from that time. What in Shakespeare's personal life may have brought about that sea change must remain a matter of speculation. What cannot be disputed is that Shakespeare created his most famous character two or three years before the death of Queen Elizabeth I in 1603, at a time of still smouldering civil discord. By 1600 the immediate danger of civil war had receded. Yet for some time in Shakespeare's younger days the spectre of political instability, and even total civil breakdown, hung menacingly in the air. That relationship between private anguish and a sense of impending political disaster is well expressed in *Hamlet*:

> The single and peculiar life is bound
> With all the strength and armour of the mind
> To keep itself from noyance, but much more
> That spirit upon whose weal depends and rests
> The lives of many. The cess of majesty
> Dies not alone, but like a gulf* doth draw   (* whirlpool)
> What's near it with it… (III.iii.11-17)

Questions of authority (Who rules, How and Why?) are at the heart of Shakespeare's play. Hamlet finds a power base to confront these (and other) questions in the theatre. This is one area where he can be decisive. With his overwhelming personal agenda, he pushes others, not only to excellence, but also, in a sense, to one side. He becomes a theatrical king, albeit a cuckoo one. That is why he stands as a potent and questioning symbol for a certain kind of modern director. As Hamlet himself says of another aspiring, rebellious prince:

For by the image of my cause I see
The portraiture of his. (V.ii.77-8)

In other words, in the pages that follow, we shall view not only Shakespeare through the eyes of the directors, but also – and just as importantly – the directors through the eyes of Shakespeare. For all the world's a stage ... and in his time Hamlet has played many parts. In the deranged Prince of Denmark, trained in Wittenberg but now transformed beyond recognition, Ophelia sees not only an estranged lover, but also a courtier, a *soldier*, a scholar (III.i.154). Now let that shifting, changing figure find his twentieth or twenty-first century counterpart.

[1] See Gordon A. Craig, *Germany 1866-1945*, (Oxford, 1981), p.4. G.A.Craig's introduction to this book gives a sense of the German cultural fascination with *Hamlet*.

[2] Edward Braun, *The Director and the Stage*, (London, 1982; repr. 1992), p.7. Even the title of Braun's excellent book reflects the change of emphasis from earlier in the century. In the 1950s Norman Marshall entitled his book on directors, *The Producer and the Play*. For good or ill, the movement has been from *play*(text) to *stage*.

[3] George Bernard Shaw, 'Barker's Wild Oats', *Harper's Weekly*, 19/1/1947, reprinted in *Drama*, No.173, (Dec.1989): 32.

[4] See Ralph Berry, *On Directing Shakespeare*, (London, 1989), pp.1-3; also, Jonathan Miller, *Subsequent Performances*, (London, 1986), p.77. I have used the term 'Hamlet director' throughout this study because I believe that (with the exception of the father figure, Stanislavsky) all the directors share certain key characteristics, namely: (a) an Oedipal obsession, and thus a *rebellious* demeanour (b) a masculine entrancement with Mars, the God of War (c) an overwhelming desire to create power through theatre – an attempt to re-define both self and others through the dramatic re-writing of texts: an underlying desire to be king in and through theatre. As W.D. Howarth puts it in *Molière: A Playwright and his Audience* (Cambridge, 1982, p.252): 'It is not so very unusual for us to think

of people we know as "a Falstaff" or "a Harpagon": convincing
proof that *these characters possess some quality or other that transcends the
boundaries of time and place.'*
Quotations from Shakespeare in this and other chapters, unless
otherwise stated, are taken from *William Shakespeare: The Complete
Works*, edited by Stanley Wells and Gary Taylor (Oxford, 1988).
Quotations from the Bible, unless otherwise stated, are taken from
The Good News Bible (London, 1976).

**Emphasis within quotations in this and in other chapters,
unless otherwise stated, is my own.**

1 | Playing Hamlet at the Moscow Art Theatre

'With martial stalk hath he gone by our watch.' *Hamlet* I.i
(Epigraph to Meyerhold's article 'The Solitude of Stanislavsky' (1921))

'Russia,' commented Soviet academic and critic Alexander
Anikst, at a conference shortly before his death in 1988, 'is like
Germany, a very Shakespeare-ized country.'[1] In fact, as Anikst
also points out, some of the first translations of Shakespeare
into Russian were from German, not English. In both countries, moreover, are found key developments in the story of the
Shakespearean director. If it is true to say that the director
originated in Germany, then it is in the Russian theatre that the
modern director comes of age.

In the daring theatricalism of Vsevolod Meyerhold (1874-
1940) and the contrasting psychological realism of Konstantin
Stanislavsky (1863-1938) is forged a theoretical basis for the
practical work of the director in the modern theatre. The
influence and importance of both Meyerhold and Stanislavsky
can hardly be overstated, a view reflected in contemporary
scholarship. Samuel Leiter, for example, begins his thorough
survey of the modern director (1991) by devoting more than a
third of his first volume to these dominant figures. In *The
Director and the Stage*, Edward Braun, apart from a chapter on
Stanislavsky and Chekhov, devotes two chapters of his thirteen-
chapter book to Meyerhold – the only director to be so

honoured. Of Meyerhold's experiments at the Studio of the
Moscow Art Theatre, Braun writes: '[They] led to the
establishment of a new movement in the Russian Theatre, a
movement to which the Moscow Art Theatre itself remained
committed and to which it was soon to contribute with a series
of productions culminating in 1912 with the *Hamlet* of Edward
Gordon Craig' (1982: 114).

This chapter, and the one following, will consider that 1912
production and will assess the lasting but differing influences of
both Meyerhold and Stanislavsky. The contrasting styles and
theories of these two directors we will examine in the context
of Russian Shakespearean production generally, but also in
terms of their personal fascination with certain plays by Shakespeare. Inevitably the overview will consider also the huge
social and political upheavals that Russia experienced in the first
half of the twentieth century. It will ask what relationship exists
between revolutionary fervour in society at large ('Something is
rotten in the state of Denmark' I.iv.67) and revolutionary
changes in dramatic practice within the theatre ('The play's the
thing ...' II.ii.606) – particularly as these changes reflect on the
role of the director. Predominantly, then, but not exclusively,
this changing role will be illuminated through the figure of
Hamlet.

Playwright versus Director

The story of the Shakespearean director in the Russian theatre
begins some time earlier in the closing years of the nineteenth
century; and the figures that dominate that history are
inextricably bound up with the Moscow Art Theatre (MAT),
founded in 1897/8 by Konstantin Stanislavsky and Vladimir
Nemirovich-Danchenko (1858-1943). In the first year of the
Art Theatre (1898), after the crowd-pulling *Tsar Fyodor*, *Antigone*
('a production that will create a complete illusion of the ancient
world') was not successful. Two similarly conceived Shakespearean revivals *The Merchant of Venice* and *Twelfth Night* also
proved embarrassing failures. Only Chekhov's *Seagull* at the first
year's end rescued the theatre and established the new

enterprise's reputation and house style. In time, in recognition of this, the symbol of the Moscow Art Theatre would become a seagull.

Illustration 1

Anton Chekhov reading *The Seagull* to the actors and directors of the Moscow Art Theatre (1899)

Indeed the photograph, (illus.1), suggests much about both the personalities and the central conflicts whose imprint is so often felt not only in Russian but in much of twentieth-century Western theatre. At the centre of the picture, holding court, sits Chekhov, the still regal author. In the coming age of the director that commanding central presence of the author would increasingly be questioned. To his left, seated, is the brooding directorial figure of Stanislavsky, perhaps dreaming of his infamous naturalistic *mise-en-scène* for *The Seagull* replete with dogs, cuckoos, owls, nightingales, clocks, harness bells and crickets. The founding principles of the Art Theatre made axiomatic unity of ensemble, directing and design in the *mise-en-scène*. In his 'Programme and budget for the first year of the Moscow Art Theatre, May 1898,' Stanislavsky's co-director and close collaborator, Nemirovich-Danchenko had written: 'In forming the company the most important attention will, of course, be paid to the directorial aspect, *which ought to be the strongest element in the whole affair.*' In the photograph Nemirovich-Danchenko is standing on the extreme left while seated on the far right is the rather disaffected-looking figure of Vsevolod Meyerhold (then a student actor) seemingly distancing himself, like some disillusioned Hamlet, from the whole proceedings. The motherly Olga Knipper, Chekhov's leading lady and future wife – she was later to play Gertrude in the Craig *Hamlet* (1912) – sits beside Stanislavsky in profile.

Indeed the figure of Hamlet seems to haunt those early years at the Moscow Art Theatre. One of the theatre's basic aphorisms was: 'Today Hamlet, tomorrow a supernumerary, but even as a supernumerary you must be an artiste' (Senelick 1991: 412). Chekhov, himself, believed that *Hamlet* was a quintessentially Russian play. It was in the eighteenth century the first Shakespearean play to be translated into Russian. In nineteenth-century Russia the political undertones of the play were deeply felt. Liberals were impressed 'because a Hamlet [Mochalov's] so obviously capable of cleansing the Augean stables of Elsinore suggested other stables, nearer home, which could also do with a cleaning ... In fact, to be "*anti*-Shakespearean" became a mark of political respectability' (Speaight 1973: 114). Alexander Anikst suggests that the character of Hamlet was always present in Chekhov's mind.[2] 'To play [your] characters,' Meyerhold wrote to Chekhov, 'just as seriously and interestingly as Shakespeare's *Hamlet* ...' (Rudnitsky 1981: 13).

The great playwright's ambition had always been to write – not an adaptation – but a true Russian *Hamlet*. When that project proved impossible (*Ivanov* failed), Chekhov turned to a satirical treatment. Konstantin Treplev, Chekhov's modern 'Hamlet' in *The Seagull*, is an anti-hero in an age when heroes are, seemingly, no longer possible. Yet Oedipally-fixated like Hamlet he stages a play within-a-play (Act I) and gives instructions to the player(s) – but, as can be seen from the following extract, with noticeably less satisfactory results than in Shakespeare's play. The scene is worth reproducing at some length for a number of reasons. It shows not only the crucial underlying conflict between naturalism and symbolism so central to this chapter but also the remarkable influence of Shakespeare on Chekhov's mind; it also raises fundamental questions about 'the author of the stage play' (i.e. the Hamlet director). Above all it is worth remembering the personalities involved in that 1898 Art Theatre production. Apart from the Shakespeare-inspired Chekhov, Stanislavsky was the director and took the part of the writer and surrogate-father ('Claudius') Trigorin. Olga Knipper (later Craig's Gertrude) played 'Hamlet' Treplev's mother, Arkadina. Perhaps most significant of all, Vsevolod Meyerhold, played the young rebel and theatrical innovator, Konstantin Treplev.

> KONSTANTIN (*comes out from behind the improvised stage.*)
> ARKADINA. (*to KONSTANTIN*) 'Come hither, my dear Hamlet, sit by me...' My precious, when's it going to begin?
> KONSTANTIN. In a minute. If you would just be patient.
> ARKADINA. 'O Hamlet, speak no more/ Thou turn'st mine eyes into my very soul; / And there I see such black and grainèd spots / As will not leave their tinct.'
> KONSTANTIN. 'Nay, but to live / In the rank sweat of an enseamed bed / Stew'd in corruption, honeying and making love / Over the nasty sty ...'
> (*A horn sounds behind the improvised stage.*)
> Ladies and gentlemen, the performance is about to begin. Your attention, if you please. (*Pause.*) I'm going to start. (Knocks with a stick and speaks in a loud voice.) You honoured ancient shades that hover in the hours of night above this lake, make our eyes grow heavy, and let us dream of what will be in two hundred thousand years from now! ...
> (*The curtain rises. The view over the lake is revealed, with the moon above the horizon and its reflection in the water. On a large stone sits*

NINA, all in white.)
NINA. Men and lions, partridges and eagles, spiders, geese,
and antlered stags, the unforthcoming fish that dwelt
beneath the waters, starfish and creatures invisible to the
naked eye; in short – all life, all life, all life, its dismal round
concluded, has guttered out … Cold, cold, cold. Empty,
empty, empty. Fearful, fearful, fearful. (*Pause.*) The bodies of
all living creatures have fallen into dust, and Everlasting
Matter has turned them into stones, into water, into clouds;
while all their souls have merged into one. And this one
universal world soul is me … me … **In me are the souls of
Alexander the Great, of Caesar, of Shakespeare, of
Napoleon**, and of the least of leeches … All I'm allowed to
know is that in this stubborn, bitter struggle with the Devil,
marshal of all material forces, I am fated to be victor; and
that matter and spirit will thereafter merge in wondrous
harmony to usher in the reign of Universal Will. But that will
come about only after long tens of thousands of years, when
moon and bright Sirius and earth alike will gradually turn to
dust … (*Pause. Two red spots appear against the background of the
lake.*)
Here comes my mighty adversary, the Devil, now. I see his
fearful crimson eyes …
ARKADINA. There's a smell of sulphur. Is there supposed
to be?
KONSTANTIN. Yes.
ARKADINA. (*laughs*) I see – it's an effect.
KONSTANTIN. Mama!
NINA. He pines for human company …
POLINA. (*to DORN*) You've taken your hat off. Put it on –
you'll catch cold.
ARKADINA. He's taken it off to the Devil, the Father of
Eternal Matter.
KONSTANTIN. (*out loud, losing his temper*) Right, the play's
over! That's it! Curtain!
ARKADINA. What are you getting cross about?
KONSTANTIN. That's it! Curtain! Can we have the curtain,
please? (*Stamps his foot.*) Curtain!
(*The curtain is lowered.*)
I'm sorry! I was forgetting that playwriting and acting are
reserved for the chosen few. I've infringed their monopoly!

It …I … (*He tries to say something else, but then flaps his hand and goes off left.*) (Frayn 1988: 68-71)

Unlike Hamlet whose directorial experiment is a stunning success in catching the conscience of the king ('O, my offence is rank' III.iii.36), Treplev's play is a disastrous failure. Apart from acting, Treplev is both director and author. Although Hamlet refers to 'my lines' (III.ii.4), he is only author of 'The Mousetrap' in a limited, and perhaps quite modern, sense. By arranging *The Murder of Gonzago*, by introducing 'some dozen or sixteen lines' into the script (thus changing the meaning), by instructing the actors on how they should perform, Hamlet has become 'the author of the stage play'. Treplev, on the other hand, combines the roles of actor, of author (in the traditional sense) and 'author of the stage play' – that is *metteur en scène* (Nina in white, the symbolic rock, the two red spots representing the 'Devil-Father', are all part of that). Both Shakespeare's Hamlet and Chekhov's Treplev are determined 'authors' of their respective stage plays; but the modern Hamlet, Treplev, as director, is fascinated by stage effects.

Thus it is ironic to note that Vsevolod Meyerhold, arguably the greatest modern exponent of theatrical innovation and experiment, should have begun his acting career playing the anti-hero 'Hamlet' Treplev in *The Seagull* of 1898. 'The casting of Meyerhold as Konstantin in the Art Theatre's historic production,' writes Edward Braun, 'was a foregone conclusion, and predictably he played the part to the life' (1979: 25). That early experience of playing 'Hamlet' in a 'court' inspired by a benevolent fatherly author, Chekhov, whom Meyerhold hero-worshipped and adored, and an increasingly intrusive and dominant director, Stanislavsky – of whom Meyerhold, *at that time*, was deeply suspicious – must have had a profound effect on the young man. It remains a fact that throughout his long career this director was to dream of staging *Hamlet*. Although it remained an unfulfilled dream, he later planned a book about *Hamlet* in which detailed directions might help some other director to stage the play. His book was to be called *Hamlet: The Story of a Director* (Leiter 1991: 78).

The phrase 'other director' is significant. Astonishingly for one so prolific, and so ruthless in converting lesser writers to his bold designs, Meyerhold never staged Shakespearean tragedy. Late in life, half-jokingly he said, 'Engrave on my tombstone: Here lies an actor and director who never played and never staged *Hamlet*' (Senelick 1982: 185). He even envisaged a theatre where that play alone would be performed in the versions of Stanislavsky, Craig, Reinhardt and himself. Yet in reality, unlike Stanislavsky who had little difficulty in that regard, Meyerhold found it impossible to wield the knife against the king of all playwrights: 'And, like a neutral to his will and matter, / Did nothing' (II.ii.484-5). David Magarshack refers to Meyerhold as 'the great assassin of the art of the dramatist' (1950: 4), but when it came to 'assassinating' Shakespeare, he faltered. Like Hamlet, too, he both *identified with* and profoundly rejected the new 'Claudius' director (I.ii.152.3 and III.ii.232-52). Meyerhold himself admits: 'I began as a director by slavishly imitating Stanislavsky. In theory, I no longer accepted many points of his early production methods, but when I set about directing myself, I followed meekly in his footsteps' (Braun 1979: 30).

Life imitated art still more accurately in that Meyerhold, like Treplev, would soon grow tired of naturalism, the form of production then favoured by the Moscow Art Theatre. Although he began his directing career by imitating Stanislavsky's realism, like Treplev he was soon to reject the kind of theatre where 'when the curtain goes up, and there, in a room with three walls lit by artificial lighting ...' is revealed, 'how people eat and drink, how they love and walk about and wear their suits' (Frayn 1988: 63). Instead, by rejecting 'the fourth wall', Meyerhold would move towards a theatre of stylization where there would be no attempt to ape the mundane details of people's lives:

> We, too, will show you life that's real – very!
> But life transformed by the theatre into a spectacle most
> extraordinary! (Mayakovsky trans. Daniels 1968: 46)

If it is true that all mirrors both reveal and deceive, then this, too, would be a theatre where the mirror held up to nature would be a distorting mirror – but where the rhythmic movements of actors might be a liberation from the strictures of the everyday. In the early years of the twentieth century Meyerhold abandoned naturalism; instead, he attempted in each production to reveal the heart of the play through imaginative, non-illusionistic means. From Chekhov he had learned that the theatre must be a place for 'essences, allusiveness, restraint, and selectivity', not for the photographic reproduction of offstage reality (Leiter 1991: 48). In his diary (11 September 1898) Meyerhold quotes A.P. (Chekhov): '... the stage demands a degree of artifice. You have no fourth wall. Besides, the stage is art, *the stage reflects the quintessence of life* and there is no need to introduce anything superfluous on to it' (Braun 1969: 30).

Eugene Vakhtangov, one of Stanislavsky's protégés at the Moscow Art Theatre, was later to describe the differences between the older and the younger director in striking terms:

> Meyerhold understands theatricality as a performance at which the audience does not forget for a single moment that it is in a theatre. Stanislavsky demanded exactly the reverse: that the audience forget that it is in the theatre, that it come to feel itself living in the atmosphere and milieu in which the characters of the play live. He rejoiced in the fact that the audience used to come to the Moscow Art Theatre to *The Three Sisters*, not as to a theatre, but as if invited to the Prosorov house. This he considered to be the highest achievement of the theatre. (Cole and Chinoy 1964: 185)

In time Stanislavsky, despite his own very different approach, was to recognize the importance of Meyerhold's work by appointing him, in 1905, head of the experimental Studio attached to the Art Theatre. Yet Meyerhold's style at that time still horrified Stanislavsky. As Robert Leach says of the dress rehearsal for *Schluck und Jau*:

> Only Stanislavsky's dramatic intervention itself at the dress rehearsal, shouting 'Lights! Lights!' like Claudius during Hamlet's play, perhaps showed Meyerhold what spectator-performer 'fusion' might mean. (1989: 5)

Even after the failure of that initial exercise, Stanislavsky throughout his career would attempt to find means of reconciling his ideas with those of his young rival. On his deathbed Stanislavsky was to describe Meyerhold as his 'sole heir in the theatre – here or anywhere else.'[3] ('For let the world take note/You are the most immediate to our throne' I.ii.108-9.) However, this conflict between the psychological realism of Stanislavsky and the theatricalist, anti-illusionist approaches favoured by Meyerhold would soon become a central question in Russian Shakespearean production, a conflict most clearly illustrated in the Stanislavsky/Craig *Hamlet* of 1912. To put that production more fully in context we must return to the source of Stanislavsky's ideas, his early work in directing Shakespeare – and to the beginning of Meyerhold's rebellion against Stanislavsky's ruling ideas.

Stanislavsky's Early Shakespeare

'The stage is a scaffold,' wrote Anton Chekhov, 'on which the playwright is executed.' The comment suggests that the writer probably had certain directors in mind, for Chekhov's major plays were written at a time when – for good or ill – the stage director was becoming a dominant force. 'Chuck the theatre,' was his advice to a fellow writer, 'with a few exceptions it is nothing but an asylum for megalomaniacs' (Magarshack 1972: 9). No doubt these comments were coloured by Chekhov's renowned brushes with Stanislavsky. It is commonplace to recall Chekhov's complaint that Stanislavsky had turned his characters into 'crybabies'. More than just this, Stanislavsky's inability to see that Chekhov had moved beyond realism and to recognize the symbolist elements in Chekhov's plays was a potent source of conflict between author and director. It was, perhaps, not quite the ideal marriage to which Marc Slonim refers (Slonim 119; Rudnitsky 1981:14).

In criticizing Stanislavsky's directing style, Meyerhold shows clearly how between 1898 and shortly before Chekhov's death in 1904 the Moscow Art Theatre moved increasingly towards literalism and an extreme realism on stage. More and more, according to Meyerhold, the audience's imagination was being thwarted and stifled. 'A work of art,' argues Meyerhold quoting Schopenhauer, 'can influence only through the imagination.' In support of this Meyerhold goes on to quote Tolstoy's *On Shakespeare and the Drama*:

> One should reveal little, leaving the spectator to discover the rest for himself, so that sometimes the illusion is strengthened even further; to say too much is to shake the statue and shatter it into fragments, to extinguish the lamp in the magic lantern. (Braun 1969: 26-7)

These comments might apply, as Meyerhold suggests, to staging Chekhov but their enduring relevance to Shakespeare is even more striking. By the time of his successful, if controversial, productions of Chekhov, Stanislavsky was also producing Shakespeare: *Othello* (1896), *Much Ado About Nothing* (1897), *Twelfth Night* (1897), *The Merchant of Venice* (1898), and *Julius Caesar* (1903). In style these productions were heavily influenced by Duke Georg's Meiningen company which had visited Russia in 1885 and 1890. In particular, the latter visit had proved crucial in influencing Stanislavsky – at that time family wealth allowed him the luxury of experiment in theatre. In Russia during the 1880s the Imperial theatres, which had a virtual monopoly, still placed enormous emphasis on the central character in Shakespearean production, rather than on developing an overall view of the play; the star actor dominated the stage. Audiences went to see Hamlet, Othello and Macbeth, not *Hamlet*, *Othello* and *Macbeth*. Reacting against this trend Stanislavsky had identified, in several important respects, with the Meininger and had imitated their approach to Shakespeare. 'Productions,' as he put it, 'that were historically true, with mass scenes, splendid outer form and amazing discipline' (Vining Morgan 1984: 17).

The obsession with historical detail and meticulous work with crowd scenes were obvious examples of Meiningen influence. Meyerhold would later identify this trend as one of his chief disagreements with 'Devil-Father' Stanislavsky: 'The principles of the Meiningen school became our chief enemies, and since in one area of its activities the Art Theatre followed the Meiningen principles, I was forced to recognize it, too, as my enemy in the struggle for new dramatic forms' (Braun 1969: 48). The following description of Stanislavsky's *Othello* (1896) for the Society of Art and Literature, set in Renaissance Venice and Cyprus, is given by Joyce Vining Morgan. It provides a clear picture of the extraordinary lengths to which the director was prepared to go to create 'real life' on stage. In preparation for the production the company had visited Cyprus (Slonim 1963: 116). The comparison with the contemporaneous actor-managerial productions of Henry Irving and Herbert Beerbohm Tree, with their naturalistic scenography, is unavoidable:

> The interior sets were striking, historically accurate represen-tations of the Venetian and the Moorish. More striking were the exteriors. When the first curtain rose to the sound of the distant striking of a tower clock, there was a far-off splashing of oars. A floating gondola stopped on the stage; with a clang of chains it was fastened to a painted Venetian pile, after which it rolled gently in the water. (To intensify the realism of the set, Iago was directed to dip his hand into the canal, into noticeably real water – available in a hidden washtub next to the gondola.) Roderigo and Iago began their scene sitting in the gondola, then disembarked under the colonnade of a house which resembled the Palace of the Doges. After the alarum was raised and Desdemona's abduction was known, the entire house came to life: casements opened; sleepy figures looked out; servants put on their armor as they emerged from the house, picked up their weapons, and ran off to seize the Moor. Some jumped into the gondola and rowed under the bridge; others crossed the bridge on foot. The careful build-up to this frenzied activity caught the audience at once, and the realism of the set gave it all an irresistible immediacy. (1984: 21)

In watching the Meininger, Stanislavsky had been deeply impressed by, and had begun to imitate, Duke Georg's artistic director, Ludwig Chronegk, who behaved in the theatre as a total artistic autocrat working with *military* discipline to create a polished ensemble effect. Thus the central control exerted in a similarly uncompromising way by Stanislavsky resulted in productions of a certain kind. At that time, such minute planning was new in Russia. All the actors had to do was follow the instructions to achieve a satisfactory performance. Such tyrannical control led to a total unity of production, but it was a unity inspired almost solely by the director, with little contribution from the actors (Leiter 1991: 38). During the *Julius Caesar* production (1903), the whole Moscow Art Theatre was placed under 'martial law' and every actor and administrator and stage hand were mobilized. No one dared refuse work, on any pretext whatsoever. Thus Chekhov's comments about megalomania may have reflected his distaste for this new tendency in the Russian theatre towards an all-powerful, autocrat-director. Even Meyerhold (whose later practices were often seen as autocratic) refers to the dangers of the new trend: 'Once everything became subordinated to "the ensemble", the creativity of every actor was stilled' (Braun 1969: 33).

By 1903, when Nemirovich-Danchenko and Stanislavsky directed *Julius Caesar,* the growing trend towards total realism and historical accuracy was reaching a climax. Stanislavsky's recent successes at the Moscow Art Theatre encouraged him to approach Shakespeare with his own productions of Chekhov in mind. 'We must play Shakespeare differently than other theatres do,' he told the actors, 'we must stage *Caesar* in Chekhovian tones' (Vining Morgan 1984: 17). If the attempt to create a complete illusion of reality was problematic in staging Chekhov, then in presenting Shakespeare on stage it was an even riskier gamble. When in the prologue to *Henry V*, for example, Shakespeare refers to 'this unworthy scaffold … this wooden O', and promises his audience to 'on [their] imaginary forces work', he is hardly intent on creating a complete illusion of real life. When in *Julius Caesar* Cassius ponders over the body of the slain emperor: 'How many ages hence/ Shall this our lofty scene be acted over/ In states unborn and accents yet unknown!' and Brutus replies, 'How many times shall Caesar *bleed in sport*' (III.i.112-115), Shakespeare is clearly reminding his audience (if they needed reminding) that they are in a theatre; he is diverting his audience's attention from a real historical 'tragedy' to a present theatrical experience. However, the play's

stormy history with the censor in Russia makes it seem remarkable that *Julius Caesar* was being staged in any shape or
form. Denied a production years before, one theatre practit-
ioner, P.P.Gnedich, had argued with the censor: 'When I said
that the Meininger *Caesar* was allowed, they answered, "it's
possible in German, but regicide must not be shown in the
Russian language"' (Vining Morgan 33). The ban, in fact, was
lifted in 1897.

Meyerhold, who was already urging a theatre of non-illusion,
was quick to point out the absurdities to which this 1903 *Julius
Caesar* gave rise: 'Nobody believes that it is the wind and not a
stage-hand which causes the garland to sway in the first scene
of *Julius Caesar*, because the characters' cloaks remain still ... The
hills on the battlefield ... may be constructed so that they
decrease in size towards the horizon, but why don't the
characters become smaller, too, as they move away from us
towards the hills?' Meyerhold's critique went deeper than
pointing out these absurdities which included the inherent conflict between two-dimensional scenery and three-dimensional
actor:

> *The technique of copying historical styles* was born in the
> naturalistic theatre. With such a technique it is natural that
> the rhythmical construction of a play like *Julius Caesar* with its
> precisely balanced conflict of two opposing forces is
> completely overlooked and so not even suggested. Not one
> director realized that a kaleidoscope of 'lifelike' scenes and
> the accurate representation of the plebeian *types* of the period
> could never convey the synthesis of 'Caesarism'. (Braun
> 1969: 24 and 31; Meyerhold's emphasis)

'The Meininger lessons had been thoroughly – too thoroughly –
digested,' comments Robert Speaight, 'there was the same
search for antiquarian detail at the expense of artistic truth'
(1973: 117). In the manner of an early Reinhardt *regiebuch,* the
promptbook for the production was a masterpiece of detail. As
Leonidov (Cassius) recalled: 'it tells you not only what and
where Julius Caesar, Brutus or Antony does or says, but also
what the twenty-eighth legionnaire does in the last act, what he
shouts and to whom.' Nemirovich-Danchenko (who was

director-in-chief with Stanislavsky as assistant director) even
headed a special mission to Rome to assemble the topograph-
ical and archaeological data. 'We were staging "Rome in the
time of Julius Caesar,"' wrote Nemirovich-Danchenko later,
'not just Shakespeare's tragedy. The principal character was
Rome' (Vining Morgan 38 and 54). In emphasizing the power
of the ordinary citizens, 'the rabblement' and 'rag tag people'
(I.ii.243 and 258) as well as the central characters, Nemirovich-
Danchenko was giving the play a decidedly modern slant: it
spoke directly to the contemporary Russian situation (a point
which Soviet scholars would later stress). But the directors were
leaving nothing to the imagination. Towards the end of Act I:

> The force of nature represented by the storm seems to
> parallel the power of the people. It begins with strong winds,
> which eventually blow objects about on the stage, breaking
> pots and beating at people. As it assumes hurricane force,
> lightning and thunder are heard – the sky has been overcast
> from much earlier on. The sounds of wind and thunder,
> shrieks of buffeted people and the metallic clanking of bolts
> being closed cry warning of a horrible darkness filled with
> thunder created in front, then over and around the audience,
> then fading out in back of the house. With this effect, the
> audience is forcibly included in the action. (Vining Morgan
> 67)

Great fun – one imagines – but all this effort was in vain
because the audience's imagination was fettered rather than
liberated by the obsessive realist verisimilitude. The critics
understandably objected when the brilliance of the stage environment kept the audience gawking at life in Julian Rome
instead of following Shakespeare's play.

Meyerhold had some years earlier seen Stanislavsky's *Othello*
(1896) and had been impressed by the actor-director's portrayal
of the Moor (Just as Irving's Shylock had grown out of a
chance encounter in Tunis, so Stanislavsky modelled his
Othello on an Arab he met in Paris). 'Stanislavsky is highly
gifted,' he wrote in his diary in January 1896 (Braun 1979: 20), 'I
have never seen such an Othello, and I don't suppose I ever
shall in Russia'; but as Brutus in *Julius Caesar*, Stanislavsky failed

to impress. In part this failure was due to a disagreement between the directors. Stanislavsky saw Brutus as essentially decisive and strong-willed, whereas his co-director perceived him as akin to Hamlet. Like Hamlet, Brutus takes on the superhuman task of cleansing his world of evil, of restoring past purity to a corrupt age. Nemirovich-Danchenko's view prevailed but Stanislavsky was never happy with the interpretation and soon developed an almost pathological dislike for the whole production and, in particular, his part in it. Edward Braun sees the production as the 'nadir' of the Moscow Art Theatre's reliance on external realism and refers to 'a leaden, historicist version of *Julius Caesar*, in which Stanislavsky suffered acute personal embarrassment in the role of Brutus' (1979: 36). '*Julius Caesar* won't take us as far as Chekhov will,' a downcast Stanislavsky wrote to Olga Knipper (Senelick 1982: 11). And to Chekhov himself, he wrote: 'I feel like finishing with *Caesar* as soon as possible and taking on some Chekhov.' Later Olga Knipper, having seen one of the dress rehearsals, wrote to her husband: 'They're all crazy about Kachalov [Caesar] ... No one likes K.S. [Stanislavsky] and that's a tragedy for the theatre.' Apart from Kachalov's (universally praised) performance which portrayed Caesar as an astute leader, the acting, as Stanislavsky later admitted, 'was all wrong. We were inferior to our décors' (Speaight 1973: 117). In fairness to Stanislavsky he was a reluctant partner in the production which was staged at the insistence of Nemirovich-Danchenko. Undoubtedly, too, there was a certain irony: for, in this instance at least, Stanislavsky, *the actor,* had become the victim of Nemirovich-Danchenko, *the* (Hamlet obsessed) *director.*

This failure began to impress on Stanislavsky what might become a creeping death for the Art Theatre from the dire effects of a disease Meyerhold scathingly calls Russian 'Meiningenitis' (Braun 1969: 35). Meyerhold's appointment as director of the new MAT 'Theatre-Studio' in 1905 was a reflection of Stanislavsky's anxiety to find novel directions for the theatre. Selective naturalism, Stanislavsky was now forced to conclude, while it can create an effective stage environment, does not necessarily inspire the inner truth of feeling found in the Art Theatre's experience with Chekhov. Significantly, too, in 1907 Stanislavsky staged two *anti*-naturalistic productions at the Moscow Art Theatre that encouraged Meyerhold to view him in a much more favourable light. Indeed, in a footnote to a 1907 article Meyerhold remarkably lists Stanislavsky among anti-naturalist directors. Meyerhold's footnote listing the leading anti-naturalist directors reads:

> The Theatre-Studio (Moscow), Stanislavsky (from *The Drama of Life* onwards), Gordon Craig (England), Max Reinhardt (Berlin), myself (Petersburg). (Braun 1969: 61)

The idea that the 'Devil-Father' had become, in time, the 'Ideal-Father' is reinforced in a later article by Meyerhold entitled 'The Solitude of Stanislavsky' (1921). The epigraph to that article (referring to the ghost of Old Hamlet) reads (*Ibid.* 175):

> With martial stalk hath he gone by our watch. (*Hamlet* I.i)

The Moscow Art Theatre productions in 1907 of Hamsum's *The Drama of Life* and Andreev's *The Life of Man,* both directed by Stanislavsky, clearly derived much from Meyerhold's experiments in stylization. 'So a founding father of psychological realism,' Marjorie L. Hoover records, 'Stanislavsky, managed completely to depersonalize the characters of *The Life of Man*' (1988: 44).

The following year, Stanislavsky succeeded with a classic symbolist production of Maeterlinck's *Blue Bird* – a fantasy seen through the eyes of a child. Just as, earlier in his career, Meyerhold had been influenced by 'Father' Stanislavsky, now the positions were reversed: now it was the older director learning from the younger. Significantly this concept of the Father and Son figures changing places, reversing roles, is central to Chekhov's *Seagull*: 'Here comes the man with the real talent,' says Treplev (Meyerhold in the 1898 version) about the older Trigorin (Stanislavsky), his mother's lover, 'entering like Hamlet, even down to the book. (*Mimics him*) "Words, words, words ... "' (Frayn 1988: 86); but it is also central to Meyerhold's later dream of staging *Hamlet*:

Seashore. Sea mist. Frost. A chill wind chases silver waves up on to a sandy, snow-free beach. Hamlet, wrapped from head to foot in a black cloak, is waiting for the Ghost of his father. He looks impatiently out to sea. The minutes drag unbearably. Peering into the distance, Hamlet sees his Father (the Ghost of his Father) amidst the waves breaking on the shore; he is emerging from the mist, dragging his feet with difficulty from the clinging sandy bottom of the sea. He is clad from head to foot in silver: silver cloak, silver chain-mail, a silvery beard. Water is frozen on to the chain-mail and on to his beard. He is cold and he moves with difficulty. He reaches the shore and Hamlet runs to meet him. Hamlet pulls off his black cloak to reveal silver chain-mail. He wraps his father from head to foot in the black cloak and embraces him. During the brief scene we see the father in silver and Hamlet in black, then the father in black and Hamlet in silver. Having embraced, father and son leave the stage. (Braun 1969: 279-80)

In considering the events betweem 1908 and 1912 at the Moscow Art Theatre, Meyerhold's dream, for the moment at least, must be sidelined; but later, in Chapter 2, we will return to the strange and significant story of his involvement with the play.

Hamlet at the Moscow Art Theatre (1912)

By 1907, when Stanislavsky was making significant steps in the direction of stylization, the relationship with his co-director and co-founder of the Art Theatre was in disarray. Nemirovich-Danchenko had long disliked Meyerhold's influence at the theatre and particularly resented the young director's appointment to the MAT 'Theatre-Studio' in 1905. Two years later the long-standing working partnership between Stanislavsky and Nemirovich-Danchenko was effectively over. In part their disagreement had been fuelled by their conflicting attitudes to Meyerhold's rebellion against the prevailing ideas of the Moscow Art Theatre. Nemirovich-Danchenko had been Meyerhold's original teacher and mentor at the drama school of the Moscow Philharmonic Society. Initially, Nemirovich-

Danchenko had spoken highly of Meyerhold and had recommended his star student to Stanislavsky.

At first some of Meyerhold's rebellious hostility to the prevailing practices of the Art Theatre had been directed at Stanislavsky's conservatism. In 1899, in a letter to Nemirovich-Danchenko, he suggested that 'the director-in-chief' (Stanislavsky) tended to ignore the social issues in drama. By 1905, however, when he was appointed to direct the Theatre-Studio, Meyerhold had reconciled himself with the Father of the Moscow Art Theatre. Concerning that appointment, Stanislavsky wrote: 'I decided to help Meyerhold in his new work which, it seemed to me, *accorded largely with my own dreams*' (Braun 1979: 37). We have also noted how in 1907 Meyerhold, somewhat surprisingly, lists Stanislavsky with Craig and Reinhardt as an anti-naturalist director. In contrast, Meyerhold's relationship with Nemirovich-Danchenko had deteriorated. Laurence Senelick dates their growing disaffection from 1902 (1982: 6). In Edward Braun's words: 'The hostility between him and Meyerhold continued to smoulder for many years, fuelled at intervals from both sides. Nemirovich frequently condemned Meyerhold's innovations as mere modishness, whilst Meyerhold blamed Nemirovich for stifling Stanislavsky's innate theatricality by confining him within the bounds of psychological realism' (1979: 38). The ending of Stanislavsky's close collaboration with Nemirovich-Danchenko was no doubt connected with this antagonism.

His new theatrical experiments left Stanislavsky more amenable and open to other influences particularly the 'school' of directing whose chief representatives at that stage were Meyerhold, Reinhardt and Craig. The challenge for Stanislavsky was to continue his investigations into the satisfactory fusion of theatricalist staging and profoundly truthful acting. In 1906, although physically exhausted and close to a nervous breakdown, he had begun to make serious progress toward developing his famous 'system' while on a recuperative summer vacation in Finland. Two years later when Isadora Duncan visited Moscow, she suggested to Stanislavsky that he might collaborate with Gordon Craig on a production in Moscow

(Senelick 1982: 12-14). Although a pirated version of *The Art of the Theatre* had been circulated in 1906, Craig's name was virtually unknown in Russia until 1907 when Meyerhold visited Berlin and heard about Craig's experiments in stylisation and his influence on Reinhardt. Shortly after this Meyerhold translated from German two articles by Gordon Craig but, while warm in his praise of the Englishman, was careful to point out that his own crucial experiments at the Theatre-Studio were realized without knowledge of ideas expressed in Craig's book *The Art of the Theatre* (1905). On her visit to Moscow Isadora Duncan gave Stanislavsky a copy of the German translation of *On the Art of the Theatre* and some copies of Craig's journal *The Mask*. Entranced by her dancing, Stanislavsky was touched by Isadora Duncan's charm (although he righteously resisted her attempted physical seduction of him), and that autumn Craig came to Moscow to discuss plans for a production of *Hamlet*.

Craig's experience of the Art Theatre at that time increased his admiration for Stanislavsky's talent. For example, Stanislavsky's portrayal of many parts, even of a country doctor (Astrov) in *Uncle Vanya*, revealed 'true theatrical style' which, according to Meyerhold, 'didn't escape Edward Gordon Craig's notice' (Braun 1969: 176). Apart from his desire to work with Stanislavsky, particularly at the Moscow Art Theatre, financial considerations – he needed money to finance his projects in Florence – may have encouraged Craig to undertake the work at the Art Theatre. In his later book *On the Art of the Theatre* (1911), Craig mentions that he undertook the production of *Hamlet* in Moscow because he felt a need to practice as a director, which he had not done for some years (1957: 285). In the light of subsequent events, this latter reason, while it contains an element of truth, does not seem entirely credible. For his part, Stanislavsky, although he now rejected the 'scientific' excesses of naturalism, was not relinquishing his realist principles but rather seeking for ways to make realism subtler, more psychological than visual in orientation. He explained to the critic Gurevich: 'That is why we have invited Gordon Craig. We are questing once more, and we shall enrich our realism again. I have no doubt that every abstraction on the stage, stylized or impressionistic, can be achieved by a more refined and more profound realism' (Vining Morgan 89).

It is clear that despite Stanislavsky's new openness to theatricalism there were still glaring discrepancies between the approaches of the two directors, and thus to their effective collaboration. Particularly crucial was their approach to actors. By 1909, when a *Hamlet* production was agreed finally – Stanislavsky being named as director and Craig as designer – the older director's approach to directing had begun to take a very different pitch to that employed in his earlier Meininger-inspired Shakespearean productions. In his 'Report on Ten Years of Work by the Moscow Art Theatre' (1908), he admitted that the Chekhovian style did not prepare the actors to experience, genuinely and simply, the strong emotions and 'noble ideas' of Shakespeare. In one sense this change made his collaboration with Craig easier. Alluding to the original Meininger artistic director, Ludwig Chronegk, Meyerhold speaks of 'his [Stanislavsky's] recovery from the ailment of "Chronegkitis"' (Braun 1969: 176). Further Stanislavsky realized that to free the actor from the tyranny of the naturalistic set, the symbolist approach seemed promising.

Yet there is no doubt that from 1906, as Stanislavsky developed his 'system', he put increasing emphasis on the actor and the actor's discovery of his role. In this new system, collaboration with actors – in theory, at least – became the norm rather than a mere dictation from director to actor. This move towards actors and away from the autocrat-director seemed to put Stanislavsky at odds with Craig. In *The Art of the Theatre*, Craig had written: 'You expressed astonishment that the acting – that is to say, the speaking and actions of the actors – was not left to the actors to arrange for themselves. But consider for an instant the nature of this work. *Would you have that which has already grown into a certain unified pattern, suddenly spoiled by the addition of something accidental?* In directing Shakespeare, the contrast in approach was no less marked. Here, for example, is Craig imagining in his mind's eye a production of *Romeo and Juliet*:

> Therefore, whoever is chosen to move and speak as Romeo
> must move and speak as part and parcel of the design – this
> design which I have already pointed out to you as having a
> definite form. He must move across our sight in a certain
> way, passing to a certain point, in a certain light, his head at a
> certain angle, his eyes, his feet, his whole body in tune with
> the play, and not (as is often the case) in tune with his own
> thoughts only, and these out of harmony with the play. For
> his thoughts (beautiful as they may chance to be) may not
> match the spirit or the pattern which has been so carefully
> prepared by the director. (Cole and Chinoy 157)

When it is objected, 'Are you not asking these intelligent actors
almost to become puppets,' Craig admits (in 1905), 'for a
theatre we need more than a doll'; yet justifies his approach by
comparing the theatre to a ship where 'the captain of the vessel
is the king, and a despotic ruler into the bargain' (*Ibid.* 156). In
contrast for Stanislavsky, even the mature Stanislavsky who has
absorbed theatricalist influences, the actor's inner wealth of
experience is all-important in establishing how the part of
Romeo is to be played (*Ibid.* 111):

> The business of an actor is to act. You play Romeo. *If* you
> were in love *what* would you *do?* Take your notebook and
> write 'Met her at some spot, she did not look at me, I turned
> away offended.' In this way you can fill a whole volume. You
> recall your life, you transfer your emotions to your role. This
> passion, *love*, you analyze into its component moments of
> logical action. All of them together constitute *love* ... To all
> the stages in the unfolding of the emotions there will be
> corresponding logical sequences. Along these stages you will
> step into your role, because you took from your own life
> everything that concerns love and you transfer it to your
> role. These are not merely *bits of Romeo*, they are *bits of yourself.*
> (Stanislavsky's emphasis)

At first sight these attitudes might seem irreconcilable. But as
one critic puts it: 'Stanislavsky never shied away from
contradictions or refused the paradoxical' (Benedetti 1982: 2).
As for Craig, when he finally came to explain his ideas to the
assembled *Hamlet* cast of the Art Theatre, he said: 'I contradict

myself at every moment, as everyone does in life ... even Shake-speare himself is contradiction ... and Hamlet is total contra-diction' (Senelick 1982: 17).

One prevailing attitude, however, seemed to leave little room for misunderstanding or contradiction. In July 1908, while negotiations with the Moscow Art Theatre were still underway, Craig had written to Stanislavsky:

> I am really in love with my Art ... and with the Theatre, vile and mad as it is I have no other interests in the world than to remain true to the Art, and I am not able to continue a work in a theatre where there is more than one master. I studied under Henry Irving who rules [*sic*] his theatre sternly and justly. I have not had the pleasure of meeting any such ruler since he died.
>
> In the European theatre intrigue rules and the director is merely a figurehead. I understand this is not the case in your theatre. I should be glad of this assurance from you, and in this event glad to work under you. (Senelick 1982: 17)

Stanislavsky, although his system, as previously noted, tended to emphasize the inner role of the actor, seemed at pains to reassure Craig on this point. A year later when rehearsals for *Hamlet* were in progress, Craig enquired, during a train journey to Moscow, about Stanislavsky's methods:

> 'How do you deal with your actors' – I asked. He grimaced – then he smiled: his whole face puckers up at all points – the lips always closed.
>
> He puts up his hands.
>
> We take the actor like this (his left hand took him) we take his part like this (his right hand took it up and closed to a fist) and we bang it into him thus and one two three went his right fist in to his left palm with slow thuds – I thought – 'how humane'. (*Ibid.* 82)

Craig always found it ironic, notes Laurence Senelick, that he, the feared proponent of the Super-marionette, should be more indulgent to actors than their mentor Stanislavsky (*Ibid.* 81). Thus it is possible to overstate the differences between the two men. Not only were they both natural autocrats but Stanis-lavsky's elaborately wrought *mises-en-scène* sometimes tended to

undermine the written words of the author just as surely as
Craig's wild fantasies. If Craig, with his obsessive personal
vision, is a prototypical Hamlet director, it cannot be denied
that the fatherly Stanislavsky bears within himself the seeds of
this new role.

Particularly in his early encounters with Craig, the Russian
director adopted an open and flexible attitude. Stanislavsky's
initial thinking about the *Hamlet* production was a blend of his
traditional realist approach and the stylized form of theatre that
Meyerhold had demonstrated so impressively in St. Petersburg.
Elsinore was a stone cold prison, a place ravaged by repeated
Norwegian invasions and governed by a brutal militarism. On
the other hand, some scenes were highly suggestive and symbolic rather than realist. In the second scene of the play, for
example, the impression of the individual being subsumed by
the collective will of the court was conveyed:

> On a golden throne sit the King and Queen ... The problem
> is to show the throne, the three characters, and the retinue,
> the courtiers, merge into one generalized background of
> gold. Their mantles flow together, and they cannot be per-
> ceived to have individuated faces. They are rough brush-
> strokes, saturated with majesty, a *background.* (Senelick 1982:
> 40)

This conception remarkably prefigured Craig's vision for the
play and in the final production was partially retained. It certainly reflects Craig's reverence for the regal, and his overwhelming sense that the lesser actors are totally subservient to
that 'despotic ruler', the director-king. This impression is
reinforced by Stanislavsky's description of the lesser members
of the Moscow Art Theatre company as: 'The rest – the mob –
the background' (*Ibid.* 118).

However, when Craig returned to Moscow in April 1909
with his design sketches and discussion began in earnest on the
production, it became clear just how radically the two directors
differed in fundamental approaches to the play. For example,
Craig insisted that the play was a monodrama, to be seen
through Hamlet's eyes alone. Hamlet, thought Craig, might be

on stage throughout the production. Unlike Stanislavsky who conceived of an historical Denmark, a stone cold prison, Craig argued that Shakespeare was unconcerned with real life or historical accuracy. Instead the central conflict was of a struggle between matter and spirit; Hamlet's fixation on death being an obvious manifestation of this. The underlying conflict between Craig's ethereal visions and Stanislavsky's more practical psychological realism is conveyed clearly in the following interaction, recorded by assistants at the theatre, in which Craig speculates about keeping one character on stage all the time (in addition to Hamlet?) as a contrast with 'the criminality of the characters taking part'. Craig suggests that one might put on the stage instead of Ophelia – in the scene between Laertes and Polonius, for instance – some very realistic workman, working at something, in order that by his presence, and 'his honest, genuine labor' he might show the falsity of the world in which Polonius and Laertes live:

> STANISLAVSKY. We have tried this, but nothing ever came of it. Perhaps we did not know how to set about it, and you will succeed, but we never succeeded. All the theory of Meyerhold rests on this. The audience lost all the beauty of the play because all the evening they were wondering and asking: 'What is the meaning of this workman?'
> CRAIG. I think that as a matter of fact one could act Hamlet without the text, but I don't suppose anyone would like it.
> (Senelick 1982: 65)

The latter comment – a tangential speculation – illustrates well the difficulty that Stanislavsky would encounter whenever he attempted to make Craig face the practical difficulties of staging highly imaginative but often unrealizable concepts.

Significantly, Stanislavsky makes the connection between the problems being faced and the theory of Meyerhold. This reference to Meyerhold was noted 'astutely' by Craig, who jotted down the name of the Russian innovator in his copy of *Hamlet*. Surprisingly, however, the paths of these two like-minded Hamlet directors would not cross for many years; they seemed fated to miss one another narrowly throughout their careers. Laurence Senelick outlines some of the striking similarities between the two directors as opposed to the glaring discrepancies between Stanislavsky and Craig (*Ibid* 72). What Meyerhold found so attractive in Craig's writings and sketches was support

Illustration 2

Promptbook page from Craig's *Hamlet* (1912). (Courtesy of the Bibliothèque Nationale, Paris.)

for the idea of the conventionalized essence of stage art, the
need to create an enriched and monumentally poetic theatre, a
theatre which had engendered the new techniques of stage
expression. Craig's desire to begin *Hamlet* without a curtain and
with actors setting the stage corresponded exactly with Meyerhold's contemporaneous projects for staging. On the philosophical level, Meyerhold was impressed by Craig's directorial
extremism, his striving to become the one and only 'author of
the spectacle', who subjugated everything on stage to the
'almighty law of rhythm'. He also shared Craig's distrust of the
everyday, his fondness for abstraction, and his concept of the
theatre as a *mysterium*, in which man the marionette is governed
by the power of occult 'unseen forces'. Had Craig and Meyerhold cooperated in a production, Senelick suggests, they would
have spoken a common language and avoided the conflicts in
which Craig and Stanislavsky invariably landed. In any circumstance, Craig would probably have found it hard to share his
artistic prerogatives with another artist – most particularly on a
production of *Hamlet* with which he was obsessed. Yet since
Meyerhold was himself obsessed with *Hamlet* and shared certain
key ideas with Craig, not least that one must be playful to
achieve tragedy, it is fascinating to speculate what a fusion of
their talents might have brought about in staging the play.

Adding to other difficulties were ongoing problems of
language and translation. Stanislavsky's conversations with
Craig 'were apparently held in a mind-bending mix of English,
pidgin German and the occasional French phrase' (Vining
Morgan 92). Apart from their underlying differences in approach, Craig and Stanislavsky clashed on their interpretation of
character. The Russian found it difficult to accept Craig's
dismissal of Ophelia as stupid and unpleasant – if beautiful
(Bablet 1966: 147). Nor could Stanislavsky accept Craig's view
of the mother figure, Gertrude:

> CRAIG. Do you think the queen took part in the murder?
> STANISLAVSKY. I think not.
> CRAIG. How is one to show that even the mother whom
> Hamlet greatly loves, that she also, together with all the
> world, is his enemy ... though I have seen many per-

formances of Hamlet … both the queen and Ophelia, are as
a matter of fact very bad women, very worthless. I want this
to make itself felt. I want that between Hamlet and all the
rest of the world there should not be one single point of
agreement, not the smallest hope as to the possibility of a
reconciliation. *I could see in Hamlet the history of the theatre.* In
Hamlet all that is living in the theatre is struggling with those
dead customs that want to crush the theatre. (Senelick 1982:
69)

It is evident that Craig sees Hamlet (sees himself?) as a figure
struggling against all the tired, worn-out conventions of the
theatre. In this he is coming remarkably close to Meyerhold's
heart-felt portrayal of Chekhov's Treplev in *The Seagull.* Just as
Konstantin Treplev reproves the 'bad' mother, Arkadina, so
Hamlet, too, provided a perfect vehicle for Craig's misogyny.
'Hamlet', he said, 'is for extremes. Once it was *"Mother"*, now it
is *"Harlot"*, once *"Angels"* now, alas! *"Devils"*'. Craig even
imagined Death as a separate character, a beautiful (wo)man,
who during the 'To be or not to be' soliloquy attempts to
seduce Hamlet (*Ibid.* 68-9). Kachalov (Hamlet), who was the
only actor party to the discussion between the directors,
objected strongly to the idea of this 'duet with Death'. Later, in
Craig's absence, the idea was dropped. In terms of 'the system',
this incident may be particularly revealing. As David
Magarshack explains: 'The task of defining the ruling idea of a
play and so making sure that the through-action follows the
course the author had intended for it, becomes even more
tricky than it is if the [director] wishes to introduce some
tendentious interpretation into it' (1950: 72). For Stanislavsky it
is Hamlet's desire to expose and punish the murderer(s) of his
father that provides a clear line of 'through-action' (Slonim
168).

Despite these disagreements and the underlying discrepancy
in their approach, Stanislavsky was deeply impressed by Craig's
imaginative concept of *Hamlet.* While he differed fundamentally
with certain interpretations, particularly of character, he was
fascinated by Craig's desire to spiritualize *Hamlet* and create a
mystical inner drama. In conversation with Craig, Stanislavsky

would agree that, *'the chief, ruling idea must be the collision of two antagonistic objects – spirit against material'*. Shortly after these discussions on 21 May 1909, a general meeting was called and, to the surprise of the company, Stanislavsky announced that Craig would be given complete control of both the directing and designing of *Hamlet*. The saga of Craig's involvement with the Moscow Art Theatre, his comings and goings from then until the performance in January 1912, has been too well documented to need detailed recounting here. It is part of 'a tale,' as Dennis Kennedy puts it, 'on both sides of misunderstandings, childish affronts and imagined treacheries, coupled with the usual Craigian demands, delays, and damnations' (1993: 50). However, this clash between the Father of the Art Theatre, Stanislavsky, and the iconoclastic Craig provides an important key to understanding the nature and changing role of the modern director – and thus is worth further consideration. As we shall see in the second chapter, Stanislavsky's ongoing relationship with Meyerhold (whose ideas so closely mirrored Craig's) is part of the same story.

In fact after the Englishman's departure, to Florence, to work on his screens and models, in June 1909, Stanislavsky was to find Craig's ideas difficult, if not impossible, to realize on stage. The moving screens which were crucial to the production concept – Craig envisaged them being twenty-eight feet high and made of aged wood – also proved impractical. Craig was convinced that *Hamlet* was the ideal testing ground for his screens, especially since the Art Theatre stage-frame was rectangular. The designer was to be further encouraged in 1911 when W.B.Yeats, who was using designs by Craig for two plays at the Abbey in Dublin, wrote to him: 'Your work was always a great inspiration to me. Indeed, I cannot imagine myself writing any play for the stage now, which I did not write for your screens' (Vining Morgan 88). According to Craig, *Hamlet* would commence with a symphony of screens in motion and come to rest only when the play ended. Although numerous combinations of materials were tested, none of them proved reliable. Thus the collapse of the screens (the 'crack of breaking wooden frames, the sound of ripping canvas') just hours before the opening performance was a telling reminder of Craig's inability to provide practical solutions to his deeply imaginative notions.

Unfortunately, as Norman Marshall points out, Craig had given little thought to the technical problem of how the screens were to be made to stand up safely and yet still be mobile. Like Stanislavsky, who later abhorred 'those terrible and dangerous walls', Marshall had personal experience of Craig's screens – and of the director's vagueness in their use. He recalls (1975: 38) how when Craig visited the Cambridge Festival Theatre (where Marshall was a director), 'we tried in vain to discover how he had envisaged them being moved in view of the audience. I remember him standing on the stage peering in puzzled silence through his pince-nez at these screens, as if he were surprised and pained by their obstinacy in remaining so immobile'. (It is worth noting that Terence Gray, the director of that theatre, also introduced the winding staircase characteristic of Meyerhold's theatre; and that Tyrone Guthrie, who in turn influenced the highly theatrical Laurence Olivier, was trained in this theatre). Although Stanislavsky retained the screens in performance, they had to be moved behind a curtain, which ran quite contrary to Craig's intention. Eventually the screens were used more or less according to plan despite the cumbersome changes. In one of the highlights of the production, the Mouse-trap scene, the line of the screens was pulled back so that the full depth of the stage was revealed. Ultimately the aim was to blend actors, screens, lighting, painting and music (by Ilya Sats) into a symphonic unity (Slonim 158).

When Craig returned to Moscow in February 1910 he was generously supplied with both workshop and office. In one room was an exact model of the theatre and this model was equipped with eight banks of lights which duplicated the electrical system used on the main stage. One of the Russian assistants, Mardzhanov, describes Craig's working method and how he conveyed his intentions to Stanislavsky and Sulerzhitsky (assistant director) by means of wooden figurines. Yet although Craig was working on *Hamlet* for the second year now 'one peculiarity of this clever artist was his inability to set a stopping point, to break off and move on to a realized concept – and this brought us no nearer to production'. If the directors were baffled and confused by Craig's procedures, the actors were still more alienated. The lack of communication between director and cast was not helped by difficulties of translation (Craig's Russian was non-existent) and his aloof demeanour. As one actor Konstantin Khokhlov put it: 'He worked in total isolation from us, the actors, and behaved like a conspirator.' Another young actress Serafima Birman believed that, 'we may not have understood Gordon Craig because he never talked to us personally.' At best the actors could read his published statements 'and worry about being metamorphosed into Übermarionetten'. On a rare visit to his workshop, he boasted to the actress Gzovskaya – later cast as Ophelia – of his misanthropy; she soon would become the object of Craig's usual 'amorous *Blitzkrieg*' (Senelick 1982: 104). Craig, she reported, 'merely pointed out everything to me like a director, a master of stagecraft, yet said of actors that the only actor was Irving and the only actress Ellen Terry, his mother, and all the rest rubbish, and he would like to turn them all into puppets.'

Yet in his Daybook Craig privately expressed very different and quite contrasting feelings, especially about Stanislavsky, 'a despotic ruler' – to use Craig's phrase – whom the Englishman appears, in part at least, to have identified with Irving. After two years at the Art Theatre, Craig felt that he had found a man with an even worse opinion of actors than his own: Stanislavsky.

> How to conjure a Hamlet out of Kachalov – an Ophelia out of Koonen or Gzovskaya – Stanislavsky's answer is with his hands – his left hand closes tight – he inserts a finger into it & then pretended [*sic*] to hammer it in with his right palm. Bang bang bang. 'We three regisseurs' he says 'can do it' & he laughs his jolly yet grim laugh. There is much sense in what he says *yet he dooms the actor to everlasting servitude – an impossibility if great things are to pass from actor to spectator.* (*Ibid.*112)

Not only is the imagery here profoundly sexual (director – 'masculine'; actor – 'feminine'), but the whole description tends to confirm Charles Marowitz's contention that directors are colonizers, albeit cultural colonizers, whose main preoccupation is conquest (1986: xvi). Craig's other (better?) self sees how wrong it all is: '... *he dooms the actor to everlasting servitude – an impossibility if great things are to pass from actor to spectator.*' Yet elsewhere in Stanislavsky's stated scheme of things, if the 'mother' of the creative part is the actor, then the 'father' is the writer:

> In the normal course of pregnancy and delivery... the inner creation of the actor assumes a physical form naturally, and is then nursed and brought up by his 'mother' – the actor. But there are also in our business premature births, mis-carriages, and abortions. It is then that unfinished and malformed monsters make their appearance on the foot-boards. (Magarshack 1950: 77)

Here Stanislavsky casts himself (the director) in the role of matchmaker or midwife. He does not admit that the director might be an interloper (a Claudius?) who has crept into the 'mother's' (i.e. actor's) artistic 'bed'. Indeed imperialist and sexual forms of conquest are linked in Senelick's notable phrase 'amorous *Blitzkrieg*'. In rehearsal actors were caught between Stanislavsky's demands for truthful, realistic acting and Craig's dissatisfaction with that style of acting, coupled with his demands for impossible acrobatic feats. 'I am more thoroughly convinced than ever,' Craig would state later, 'that the plays of Shakespeare are unactable – that they are a bore when acted – but also that the crowd loves nothing so well as a good confusion of principles' (1957: 285).

After Craig's departure from Moscow in April 1910, huge efforts were made by Stanislavsky and his assistants to fulfil Craig's specifications and dreams, but Craig seemed unaware of these Herculean efforts. Instead, he made new and unreason-able demands for more money. Indeed Craig's dictator-like lack of sympathy for his embattled theatrical minions, his tendency to give unrealizable instructions from afar and to wave aside all objections, is strangely reminiscent of the following description of Adolf Hitler's behaviour when directing (from afar) the German forces at the Battle of Stalingrad:

> In discussing plans Hitler continued his airy habit of waving his hand over the map in big sweeps, although the advances were now so slight that they were hardly discernible. As he became less able to sweep aside the Russians he became more inclined to sweep obstructive counsellors out of his office. He had always felt that "the old generals" were half-hearted about his schemes.[4]

Indeed, it appears that Hitler only became a military dictator after he had failed to become a theatre designer (Fuegi 1994: 58). 'Megalomania,' David Magarshack claims, 'is an endemic disease of the theatre' (1950: 4). Dr. Chekhov diagnosed the modern version of this disease in its early stages. Arnold Wesker has designated it 'the Führer complex' (Delgado 1996: 8).

When in 1910 Stanislavsky became seriously ill with typhoid fever (linked possibly to the *hectic* pressure), the production already delayed was further postponed for a year. Craig's sympathy was muted. 'He is ill,' he wrote to Lilina, Stanislavsky's wife, 'it is too bad – so am I.' At this stage the Art Theatre board might well have cancelled the whole expensive project but since Stanislavsky still fondly dreamed of producing the play, *Hamlet* would therefore be postponed until he was capable of resuming work. Just as Stanislavsky had invested his dreams in Meyerhold at the MAT Theatre Studio only to be disillusioned, so also in following Craig's visions he was to find limited satisfaction. In both cases he seemed to turn back from these exploratory theatricalist journeys with renewed determination to develop his own ideas. The feelings of alienation between the two directors were growing. By this stage Craig felt: 'This work in Moscow is old work. I have passed it all – gone on into places where I have really seen *something* – a glimpse of something wonderful. And now I have to return and work at this nothing – this "producing HAMLET"' (Craig's emphasis).

But by February 1911 Stanislavsky had had enough: from now on *Hamlet* would be solely his responsibility. The cast of *Hamlet* would be chosen from the younger generation of actors and therefore would be more adaptable; they would in future, follow Stanislavsky's new 'system'. From this point on Craig's *mise-en-scène* would be limited to the realm of design: the inner life of the play, its essential interpretation, now became the focus of Stanislavsky's quest for a deeper reality. Stanislavsky's *method* was to analyse each scene into sections and assign tasks or 'inner wants' for each scene. The actors were to write in these internal desires next to the lines, and these would become the pattern for the role that was to be learned by heart after each rehearsal. It has since become standard procedure for 'method acting' but this may be the first occasion on which it was compulsory. 1911, in fact, marks the date when Stanislavsky finally overcame the resistance of many actors and directors at the Moscow Art Theatre and the first stones of the foundation of his 'system' were laid (Vining Morgan 100).

In important respects Stanislavsky's interpretation of *Hamlet* began to differ from Craig's. Gzovskaya (Ophelia), watching a rehearsal of Act III from the stalls, thought that Kachalov's was a brilliant Hamlet — Hamlet the artist, teacher and preacher, who knew more than anyone around him. This was far from Craig's abstract Hamlet, illuminated by death lights, striving to overcome his despised earthly existence; Stanislavsky, rather, showed Hamlet to be virile, full of human nobility and restrained passion. If Nemirovich-Danchenko in the 1903 *Julius Caesar* had been determined to turn Brutus into Hamlet, Stanislavsky now seemed determined to reverse the process. Finally, by December 1911, as the production grew to maturity, Kachalov (Hamlet) was not only exhausted physically but deeply confused. He complained that he was oscillating between Stanislavsky's interpretation and Craig's approach. He longed to give up the part to his understudy Leonidov who was a faithful disciple of Stanislavsky's system. However, Stanislavsky still tried to keep some contact with Craig. It would be a mistake, he told Nemirovich-Danchenko, to break off all relations with him: 'I can only remember that at the present time Craig is the greatest talent in our art' (Senelick 1982: 145). This concurred with Stanislavsky's earlier positive judgement that 'he [Craig] *is half a century ahead of us.* He is a superb poet, a remarkable artist, and a director of the most refined taste and knowledge' (Vining Morgan 94).

Well away from the scene of the action, Craig, 'simultaneously a child, after all, and an artist' (as Sulerzhitsky described him), kept up a steady correspondence with Lilina, Stanislavsky's wife. He was delighted when Lilina wrote to say that Olga Knipper (whom Craig had seduced) would now take the part of Gertude. He wrote a postcard to 'Mrs. Temple - Queensky': 'I cannot say how happy I am that you are to act the Queen. *You know how much I wished for that* and now *I have my wish!* ... say to Kachalov that I will not disturb him until the work is done. I am sure he will *be noble* and that he will be *the first STRONG HAMLET* the world has seen' (Craig's emphasis). In fact, Craig had illustrated his mother-fixation and fear of women in an earlier letter to Knipper when he tried to explain why he could not pursue their relationship:

> I too send you love ... but I will not keep my cynicism to
> myself either. You are so charming – and so much more –
> something so mysterious that I can say once
> I love you very much –
> I fear you very much –
> You tell me 'not to think that you have forgotten me'... of
> course I don't ... I never do. I am so concieted [*sic*] that I
> know men and women never forget me. (Senelick 1982: 32)

As widow to Anton Chekhov – one of the Fathers of the Russian theatre – and as a leading, now celebrated, actress, she must in Craig's mind have corresponded almost perfectly to his actress mother, Ellen Terry (stage partner, if not wife, to Henry Irving, 'Father' of the English theatre).

To understand Craig's monodramatic interpretation of Hamlet it is essential to remember how personally he identified with the central character of the play. 'A Hamlet-intoxicated man' is Laurence Senelick's depiction of Craig; 'the identification of Hamlet with idle and rebellious young men, thus with himself became Craig's *idée fixe*' (1982: 24). Dennis Kennedy accuses Craig of being 'as obsessed with treachery as Hamlet' (1993: 54). For Enid Rose: 'the Hamlet daemon in him made him help to create the legendary Craig' (48). Craig himself was later to record that 'Hamlet almost seemed to be myself. Hamlet was not only a play to me nor a role to be played – *I somehow or other lived Hamlet day by day*'. Laurence Senelick explains:

> If the Ghost was his father, E.W. Godwin the scene-designer, Hamlet was also in part his surrogate father, Henry Irving, whose subtle and refined interpretation was the authoritative one on the late Victorian stage. And Craig had a chance to supplant this father figure by assuming the role himself. In 1897 he played it for six performances in place of Nutcombe Gould, with Ben Greet's company at the Olympic Theatre. Irving, as if acknowledging Craig as his heir apparent, lent him the dagger and costume from his own wardrobe. (1982: 129)

The writer does not consider the possibility that Craig might also have identified Irving with Claudius – a not unlikely scenario since the actor-manager had largely replaced his own real father. Surprisingly, too, Senelick does not mention Ellen Terry. The fact that Craig desperately wanted Knipper – so easily identified with Terry – to play Gertrude, fits into this pattern. What reinforces this impression is an association of Craigian images. If Gertrude is seen as a fallen woman ('once ... "*Mother*"... now "*Harlot*", once ... "*Angels*" ... now "*Devils*"') then the London theatre (once inextricably associated with Terry and Irving) Craig would also, in time, depict as 'a fallen woman' (Rose 88-9).

Craig's understanding was entirely solipsistic and self-centred: 'I'd say that everything is not quite clear to you concerning *my* Hamlet,' he wrote to Stanislavsky in May 1910, '*excuse me speaking of Shakespeare's play as mine* ['my lines'? III.ii.4] ... I do not ask that my plan for production shall meet the approval of anyone. I am responsible for that ... it is enough that I approve.' Yet Craig's monodramatic dream, his insistence that the struggle between matter and spirit lay at heart of *Hamlet*, strangely paralleled the teachings of Russian symbolists such as Vladimir Solovoyov, whose ideas Chekhov had satirized in Treplev's play of *The Seagull*. (Life, Life, Life ... Cold, Cold, Cold. Empty, Empty, Empty. Fearful, Fearful, Fearful ... *Me* ... *Me* ... *Me* ...). In the play-within-the-play, Nina, speaking as 'The World Soul', (Treplev's voice of symbolist truth), says: 'all I am allowed to know is that in this stubborn, bitter struggle with the Devil [Father], marshal of all material forces, I am fated to be victor.' Just as Meyerhold, in his symbolist rebellion against Stanislavsky, had rejected Russian 'Meiningenitis', Craig too had rejected surrogate-father Irving's materialistic stage settings (also partly inspired by the Meininger).

If it was astonishing that the revolutionary Meyerhold had been fated to play the visionary theatrical innovator, Treplev, in Stanislavsky's version of *The Seagull* in 1898, then surely it was equally remarkable that Craig himself was fated to play a real life 'Hamlet' Treplev in the days preceding the first performance of the Art Theatre's *Hamlet* in January 1912. His rebellious (and ineffectual) directional tantrums indeed might have come straight from Chekhov's play. As the production came to fruition in December 1911 the board of the theatre cancelled all performances from 25 December to 4 January so that *Hamlet* could rehearse on the main stage day and night and open on time. The first run-through began at 11 am on 26 December on the main stage and had reached the middle of the Mousetrap scene, and Hamlet's line 'Go let the strucken deer go weep', when something unheard-of in the history of the Art Theatre occurred. In the auditorium where no one had ever before raised his voice during a rehearsal, the word 'Stupid' was shouted in English. Gordon Craig, who had just arrived from the railway station, was furious to find they had begun without him and created a huge disturbance. Politely but firmly he was asked to leave and not to return until the final dress rehearsals. In the days that followed Craig saw further rehearsals and wrote: 'It is hard to remain patient and silent while my imaginings are being messed about.' During one rehearsal Craig's patience, fragile as it was, crumbled completely during the Mousetrap scene. The lighting was diffused, whereas Craig had specified shafts of light and a sharply defined chiaroscuro to emphasize the height and massiveness of the palace. The two directors argued vehemently in French, and Craig ended by storming out of the stalls. The rehearsal was ended abruptly (Vining Morgan101).

> In his rage and his wrath
> Cries 'Ah ha' to the devil
> Like a mad lad
> 'Pare thy nails, Dad'.
> Adieu, goodman devil.[5]

The fact that the 'Devil-Father' (The Father of Eternal Realism) Stanislavsky had so clearly overruled his wishes infuriated Craig. 'If Stanislavsky wanted to turn Shakespeare into Gorky,' he complained to Alisa Koonen – another actress (ex-Ophelia) lover with whom Craig had dallied in Moscow – 'Why did he invite me and put up my screens?' If Craig had visualized Claudius as a fiercesome tiger, it was his turn to imitate the beast Father: in a final act of defiant fury he picked up his inkwell, threw it at the stage and demanded that his name be removed from the programme (Vining Morgan 102). The English Gentleman, as one observer recollected, had turned into a raging lion. But Craig's concept of Hamlet as some kind of theatrical crusader (like Treplev) is deeply relevant. 'I could see in Hamlet,' he had insisted to Stanislavsky, 'the history of the theatre. In Hamlet all that is living in the theatre is struggling with those dead customs that want to crush the theatre' (Senelick 1982: 69).

There was little however that the Craigian lion could do about Stanislavsky's 'monkeying' ('Even the Russians are nothing but "clever monkeys",' Craig said to Count Kessler in 1922, 'when they are let loose on the stage. There is nothing genuine behind their optical tricks').[6] In his absence much of what had been arranged was a *fait accompli,* although some lighting changes were made under his direction. In truth the final production was a strange hybrid of Isadora Duncan's 'two favourite geniuses' – Craig and Stanislavsky; and the basic problem was a conflict in style between the playing and the scenography. 'What else would we expect,' asks Dennis

Kennedy, 'when the champion of the interior actor met the advocate of the *Übermarionette*?' (1993: 57).

Yet Hamlet, for all Kachalov's reluctance to play the part, was impressive. His was a contemplative, low-keyed interpretation. Although he felt that his was a boring Hamlet, too Chekhovian and understated, the reflective tone in his soliloquies startled an audience accustomed to romantic ranting. Rarely emotional Kachalov's Hamlet was not mad but quietly determined to see that justice was restored to Elsinore. One of the Art Theatre's most hostile critics A.R. Kugel, editor of *Theatre and Art*, was unusual in his praise:

> I have never seen such a Hamlet, although I have seen many times over ten famous actors in this part. Craig's production also made for great attention and, with all its gaffes, I found it brilliant and totally unappreciated by our theatre critics ... After Kachalov, all Hamlets will seem made out of theatrical cardboard. (Senelick 1982: 176)

Although his acting was considered too naturalistic, V.V. Luzhsky as Polonius also impressed. Yet the king played by Massalitinov was disappointingly wooden; archdeacon-like and far from beastly, he looked too drab ever to seduce the queen, and Knipper, with her Chekhovian tones, Craig had to admit, 'a disaster'.

Critical opinion on the production, as Kugel's previously quoted comment suggests, was deeply divided but much of it was negative. 'No light, no air, it's stifling,' wrote one critic, 'screens, screens and more screens. Screens without end.' Another declared 'Stanislavsky and Nemirovich are head and shoulders above this swell-headed Englishman. Let him learn from them, not they from him.' Although the first-night audience reacted enthusiastically with Craig, Stanislavsky and Kachalov all being called on stage for encores, Kachalov himself noted in his diary: 'Dubious success of Hamlet.' Craig, too, was dissatisfied although pleased with some scenes including the finale; he felt it had not reached the heights of some of his previous productions. Kachalov's lack of theatricality and Stanislavsky's refusal to use Craig's seductive Death figure rankled. The following day Craig wrote rather sourly to his sister, Edy: 'it will do its best under the disadvantage of having cost the management over £14,000.'[7] In the letter he included a sketch of himself jumping through Stanislavsky's hoop. Years later (in 1935) interviewed by a young student Nikolay Chushkin, Craig passed a final damning judgement on the affair:

> They slaughtered me! Kachalov played Hamlet his own way. It was interesting, even brilliant, but it wasn't mine, not *my* Hamlet, not at all what I wanted! They took my 'screens', but discarded the production of my soul! (Craig's emphasis)

The parting shot of this *enfant terrible* to the directors of the MAT was an injunction to close the theatre immediately (Craig 1957: 285) – another piece of Craigian advice that Stanislavsky appears to have ignored completely. Yet for all their differences Craig and Stanislavsky, at times, were able to find common ground. There was a meeting of minds in the second scene of Act III, where Stanislavsky and Craig were able to indulge their love of backstage activity by depicting the players putting on make-up and costumes, practising vocal exercises and gestures, and tuning up the instruments. Hamlet was able to deliver the speech on acting with conviction, for it related closely to the aesthetic programme of the Moscow Art Theatre.[8]

---

[1] See *Is Shakespeare Still Our Contemporary?* edited by John Elsom (London, 1989), p.43.

[2] *Ibid.* p.62.

[3] Edward Braun, *The Director and the Stage* (London, 1982), p.14.

[4] B.H.Liddell Hart, *History of the Second World War* (London, 1973), p.268.

[5] *Twelfth Night*, IV.ii.130-4.

[6] See Laurence Senelick, *Gordon Craig's Moscow 'Hamlet' : A Reconstruction* (Westport, CT., 1982), p.188.

[7] *Ibid.*, p.174.

[8] *Ibid.*, p.166. See, for example, Meyerhold's article, 'The Solitude of Stanislavsky' (1921) in *Meyerhold on Theatre*, ed. E.Braun, (London, 1969), pp.175-180.

Illustration 3 | Vsevolod Meyerhold in 1898

'Here comes the man with the real talent, entering like Hamlet, even down to the book'. (*Mimics him.)* "Words, words, words."' *The Seagull*, Act 2.

2 | Reforming It Altogether

'O, reform it altogether.' (III.ii.38)

Certainly, at the time of production, Stanislavsky believed that the 1912 *Hamlet* justified his approach to acting Shakespeare. Stanislavsky not only defined his own art as realist, he also judged Shakespeare to be a realist. 'Realism as Stanislavsky understood it, was rooted in the complexity of life' (Vining Morgan 1984: ix). When, reviewing the (1896) *Othello*, Lucien Besnard poured scorn on Stanislavsky for ignoring important theatrical traditions in playing Shakespeare, Stanislavsky replied firmly by citing Hamlet's advice to the players (III.ii.1-45) as contradicting the traditions of nineteenth-century theatre. 'They' have now invented so many traditions, so many different rules, he argued, that the ordinary public can no longer understand Shakespeare. Nor is it accidental, he continued, that Hamlet says of the actors in the second act: 'They are the abstracts and brief chronicles of the time' (II.ii.527).

These points invite the question: Is Hamlet's advice to the players the voice of Shakespeare the director ('my lines'), uniquely engaging with the audience, and the actors, on a subject that surely must have concerned him deeply – the first principles of acting? Hamlet's speech might, of course, be viewed as a light-hearted piece of cheek: Hamlet, in that case, an opinionated amateur talking to professionals who know better than he does but who are bound to indulge the royal personage by at least not interrupting. For Patrice Pavis in *Theatre at the Crossroads of Culture* (1992: 190) such speculations are largely irrelevant. The Elizabethan performance style, in his view, has not been preserved by a living tradition and is difficult to reconstruct, 'all the more because this form, now dead, would appear both out of place and too mimetic and simplistic'. Clearly for Pavis what matters is adapting Shakespeare's work to a performance style suitable for the contemporary theatre; he goes on to cite Ariane Mnouchkine's experiments with Shakespeare which were inspired in important respects by Meyerhold's 'biomechanics' – in which actors learned a highly disciplined, acrobatic system of body control. For Terry Eagleton, too, Hamlet's advice to the players raises as many problems as it solves:

> Hamlet's advice to the Players, to suit the action to the word and the word to the action, begins to look ludicrously utopian; instead, language devours and incorporates reality until it stands in danger of collapsing under its own excess. (1986: 34)

Doubtless this is a necessary warning concerning the 'imperial word' and its 'verbal colonialism'. Yet, perhaps, the problem lies less in the words than in the people who use them. Sliding the signifier becomes an art form for those intent on corruption, deception or, at least, on concealing their true feelings. The great enemy of clear language, as George Orwell puts it in 'Politics and the English Language' (1962: 154), is insincerity. Words such as 'pacification', and the more recent additions to the Orwellian glossary of horror such as 'friendly' and 'cleansing' have one objective in common: to shield the listener or reader from a grisly and unbearable reality. The spin doctors contrive to combine word and action in 'sugar[ing] o'er the devil himself' (III.i.48-9). 'Quid est veritas?' becomes a convenient evasion for the power-loving Pilate. Truth is the first casualty, not only of war, but of those whose chief motivation is of running verbal rings around their (supposedly) less able opponents. In attempting to match words, actions and feelings, Stanislavsky sought for a new truthfulness and sincerity in acting (to watch a David Suchet or a Meryl Streep in action is to realize that the quest was not entirely a vain one). And it is this belief in suiting the action to the word – and further employing the action to inspire feeling – that lies at the heart of Stanislavsky's 'system'. Unfortunately for Stanislavsky, his 'system' was being refined at a time of such brutal political upheaval that insincerity of speech and action, both inside the theatre and out, became almost a necessity, if only as a means of ensuring survival. As Meyerhold's story confirms truthfulness in speech and action was a pricey commodity in Stalin's Russia.

In Meyerhold's anti-illusionist theatre words and gestures also have a certain correspondence. In *Bubus the Teacher* (1925), for example, Meyerhold for the first time introduced a technique that he termed 'pre-acting' whereby the actor employed mime before he spoke his lines in order to convey his true state of mind. As Marjorie L. Hoover explains:

> 'pre-acting' (predygra) ... Meyerhold derived from the Oriental theatre and Shakespeare. Specifically he found it exemplified in *Much Ado About Nothing* when Benedick, having overheard that Beatrice loves him, exchanges a gloating grin with the audience before he even begins to speak. (1988: 145)

This style of acting is suggested in *Hamlet*:

> KING. There's matter in these sighs, these profound heaves;
> [*to Gertrude*] You must translate. 'Tis fit we understand them.
> (IV.i.1-2)

The arguments for these two contrasting views of theatre have always been well balanced, it seems; yet Stanislavsky would never cease to experiment or to seek means of reconciliation with Meyerhold, 'the Prodigal Son'. This chapter will pursue further the contrasting fortunes of these very different but equally influential directors.

The influence of the rebel 'son' figures, Meyerhold and Craig, was further illustrated in 1917 when Stanislavsky returned to direct Shakespeare with a highly theatricalist *Twelfth Night* at the First Studio. On this occasion he employed minimum sets and a simple auditorium in which players and audience were in (what amounted to) a shared space (Vining Morgan 129). The highly successful production soon transferred to the main Moscow Art Theatre stage – a fact which tends to qualify Robert Speaight's caustic comment that Stanislavsky 'never had much luck with Shakespeare' (1973: 117). When in time the First Studio evolved into the Second Moscow Art Theatre *Twelfth Night* became an integral part of its repertory. In the First Studio production the beautiful Olga Baklanova played Olivia; Boleslavsky, Sir Toby; Kolin, Malvolio. The character of Malvolio, the isolated authority figure, always fascinated Stanislavsky himself. 'I have always,' he once confided to Isadora Duncan, 'felt alone'[1] *(With martial stalk?)*. Malvolio's isolation and mental torment, as well as his disputed sanity ('Are you not mad indeed, or do you but counterfeit?' IV.ii.116-7), provide several thematic links with *Hamlet*, both plays being written in the same period (c.1599-1600). Records of that 1917 production are limited: only memoirs, a few photographs and reviews sketch the event; yet, arguably, it was with this production that Stanislavsky came closest to finding a suitable performance style for Shakespeare, certainly the comic Shakespeare with which he seemed most at home. The whole play, in fact, was interpreted as a challenge to boredom and pessimism, as 'an explosion of gaiety and free spirit' (Slonim 188).

So dramatic, indeed, are the changes in Stanislavsky's style of directing at this point that it is difficult not to view them against the background of revolutionary changes in society. Unlike Meyerhold, Stanislavsky did not actively seek a new role for himself in the developing revolutionary situation but he can hardly have been unaffected by the events leading up to, and beyond, October 1917 – not least because the Art Theatre was already the subject of revolutionary scrutiny and criticism. Casting a wary, fatherly eye over the fortunes of the Moscow Art Theatre (that 'long hoped-for, long-promised child' as Stanislavsky referred to it is his inaugural address) he may have feared for its future in troubled times. Safety might well lie in proving that his theatre could match the spirit of those times.

As it turned out, the Moscow Art Theatre was lucky to survive in a recognizable form during the years after 1917; but by the mid-1920s it had accommodated itself to the new political situation. It would (in Lunacharsky's words) 'be allowed to develop in [its] own way in a revolutionary atmosphere' (Braun 1969: 164).

Although in his own role at the Art Theatre there was always something of the autocrat about Stanislavsky, as he grew older the tendency increasingly was to reject his earlier dictatorial methods and to allow the actor greater freedom. In February 1925 he wrote to Sergei Balukhaty:

> In other words, the method of the old *mises-en-scène* belongs to the despotic director, against whom I now battle, while the new *mises-en-scène* are made by directors who depend upon the actor. (Benedetti 1982: 40)

This new trend in Stanislavsky's thinking (combined with his reverence for the author) provides an important contrast – and challenge – to the concept of the Hamlet director who inevitably centres power in himself. In gradual opposition to this, Stanislavsky came to believe that the most important director in the theatre was – life. Was it possible then, that the revolution which in Moscow had produced 'The First Symphony Orchestra without an Oppressive Leader' founded 'to liberate musicians from the fetters of the conductor'[2] might also some day produce a theatre in which actors would work without a controlling director? Marc Slonim describes the Moscow Art Theatre as being 'like a symphonic orchestra under a brilliant conductor' (1963: 167), but certainly in his final years Stanislavsky would sometimes leave actors for a period to work without direction. In art, he would argue, it is impossible to give orders. In Stanislavsky's career one can trace a radical shift in the role of the director: from Meininger-inspired autocrat to enlightened observer; but in an age that lauded great dictators Stanislavsky would never rid himself entirely of a patriarchal tendency to pronounce and control. Ultimately he believed that if the director of a theatre does not enjoy proper authority, the work of the theatre will sooner or later come to a standstill (Magarshack 1950: 289).

Stanislavsky made a more systematic application of his ideas to Shakespeare between 1926 and 1930 with preparation for an ill-fated production of *Othello* at the Moscow Art Theatre. At this stage Stanislavsky (it may be argued in response to the prevailing political atmosphere in Russia) was stressing the importance of *physical action* in exploring a role rather than psychological techniques such as 'emotion memory'. Despite this shift, the Bolshevik authorities were uneasy with the work in progress at the theatre. Seemingly under great stress, Stanislavsky's health broke down and his direction notes were sent from Nice where he had gone to recuperate. Ironically, at the time of the production, Stanislavsky found himself in a situation analogous to that of Gordon Craig two decades earlier. Like Craig, he was deeply dissatisfied with what the directors of the Art Theatre were presenting to the public, but was powerless to do very much about it. He was convinced that his promptbook had not been followed as instructed and was ashamed that his name was being used on the programme. 'I blush,' he wrote, 'when I think of it' (Vining Morgan 133). Yet more importantly for posterity, the notes he wrote for *Othello* reveal much of the theory which Stanislavsky had recently incorporated in his three part *An Actor's Work on Himself (An Actor Prepares, Building a Character* and *Creating a Role*). Although certainly not definitive *Stanislavsky Produces Othello* remains the fullest statement of Stanislavsky's mature approach to directing Shakespearean tragedy. This essentially involved a move away from the earlier overwhelming emphasis on emotion ('the psychological task dissolves like smoke') towards a greater exploration of tragic character through physical action: 'the physical task is more easily nailed down' (Trans. Nowak 1948: 184).

The Moscow Art Theatre weathered this minor Shakespearean storm and its future was not jeopardized by the short-lived production whatever hostility it may have caused initially in official circles. Moreover, Stanislavsky's return to the Soviet Union smoothed the way to greater personal success for the director. Things were moving his way. In 1934, at the Congress of Soviet Writers Stalin's close associate, Zhdanov – in a ritual appeal to Lenin's authority – had endorsed socialist realism while condemning 'formalist' experiments in the arts (Eagleton 1989: 40). Thus Stanislavsky's style of production received official approval. Indeed two years earlier both Stanislavsky and Nemirovich-Danchenko had come out with severe criticism of 'formalistic innovators', and defended realism on the stage as the only sound and healthy method, and as a 'national tradition' (Slonim 317). Perhaps Stanislavsky was fortunate. Apart from the troubled waters surrounding *Othello*, his production of *The Days of the Turbins* (based on Bulgakov's *The White Guard*) had caused such hostility in some circles that at one point in 1929 it was removed from the repertory of the theatre. It controversially took a critical and somewhat unsympathetic view of the revolutionaries in 1917. However in a manner reminiscent of the fate of Gogol's *The Government Inspector* in nineteenth-century Russia, the production had been saved by one highly significant factor. Just as the Czar had revived the fortunes of *The Government Inspector* against official disapproval, so Stalin had saved this play. It became part of the repertory again in 1932 when it was discovered that Stalin had liked it enough to have seen it fifteen times.[3] Stanislavsky was well on his way to becoming, in John Fuegi's words, 'Stalin's favourite director' (1994: 256).

But what was good for Stanislavsky was not so good for Meyerhold.

Before considering Meyerhold's fate at the Moscow court of Joseph Stalin in the late 1930s, it is necessary to return to the formative years of that director's controversial career. In the first chapter we began to trace Meyerhold's fundamental rebellion against naturalism, his determination to experiment with symbolist stage settings and to discover new stylized, non-representational forms of acting: 'working to match moods and symbolic colours, characters and fixed gestures, and applying it even to Ibsen' (Styan 1977: 81). The new movement initiated by Meyerhold was to have far-reaching effects in the Russian Theatre, and at the Moscow Art Theatre in particular.

In 1907 Meyerhold had visited Berlin, and while there had been able to study the work of Max Reinhardt. With him had gone Fyodor Kommissarzhevsky, brother to the celebrated actress-manager, Vera Kommissarzhevskaya. She had played Nina in the original (and supposedly unsuccessful) production of *The Seagull* at the Alexandrinsky Theatre in 1896. Although the first night *had* been a disaster, her performance as a strong Nina had subsequently captivated audiences and her portrayal of Chekhov's heroine – unlike Stanislavsky's tearful creature in 1898 – had accorded with the playwright's vision of the part (Senelick 1991: 410). After the triumphant second performance she wrote to Chekhov (21 October 1896) declaring the 'Victory is ours': 'Your – no – our *Seagull* [Nina], *because I have merged with her forever heart and soul* – is alive; her sufferings and faith are so ardent that she will compel many others to have faith' (Heim 1973: 283). Her partnership with Meyerhold had begun in 1906, but their co-operation in the theatre was short-lived. She felt her own talents were being diminished and this modern Ophelia (Nina) had no intention of becoming a perpetually crushed victim of a Hamlet-inspired director. It is alleged that she disapproved of his interest in marionettes and his tendency to turn the actors into puppets – a charge that was to haunt Meyerhold's reputation as a director. Clearly, in this case at least, Meyerhold's experiments systematically reduced acting to such a strict pattern that the personality of Kommissar-zhevskaya was definitely sacrificed (Slonim 198). Nina's re-bellion against Trigorin's oppression in *The Seagull* may well have inspired her to challenge Meyerhold.

In Berlin Meyerhold was understandably fascinated by what he heard of Craig's *Übermarionetten* and his theories of staging. When he returned to Russia he helped to foster the growing interest in the Englishman's work. The subsequent anti-naturalist slant in Stanislavsky's directing, as we have noted, was due in part to Meyerhold's influence. Although it may be true to say that it was Isadora Duncan who had to some degree engineered the entire extravaganza, Stanislavsky's willingness to co-operate with Gordon Craig on *Hamlet* between 1908 and 1912 was in no small measure attributable to Meyerhold's influence on the older director. 'When Craig first began work at the MAT,' notes Laurence Senelick, 'his most fervent champion in Russia was Meyerhold' (1982: 72), and after the excitement of the Craig *Hamlet* had died down the effects of this epoch-setting production slowly began to filter through to other theatres in Russia. Although Craig and Meyerhold did not meet at this time, Meyerhold was the first to adapt the *Hamlet* model to a modern play; in 1914 he used cubes and rectilinears as the basic structural components in Pinero's *Mid-Channel*, at the Alexandra Theatre, with settings by Golovin. In the same year in producing Alexander Blok's symbolist-poetic play *The Unknown,* he used a construction instead of a decorative set for the first time. A year before this (using the pseudonym Dr. Dapertutto) the director had founded his own 'Theatre-Studio' to continue his experiments and to begin building up a permanent company conversant with theatrical techniques such as those of the *Commedia dell'arte*. About this time, also, he began to break with the symbolist belief in aesthetic unity or 'synthesis'. Now he began to use open theatricalization: 'eccentric accessories, jugglers, Chinese boys throwing oranges among the audience, quaint things and human figures were interwoven in a fantastic manner' (Gassner 1966: 196).

Meyerhold Rehearses *Hamlet*

During the 1915-16 season Meyerhold launched the first of several abortive attempts to stage *Hamlet*. The tentative nature of his plans, however, is suggested by comments that he wrote at the time:

> The Studio has set itself the task of staging *The Tragedy of Hamlet, Prince of Denmark* without any cuts, either of complete scenes or of individual lines. Such a production can be achieved only if we succeed in finding the key to the performance of Shakespearean tragedy by experimenting with two or three extracts from the play, studying its form and then re-creating it on the stage. (Braun 1969: 152)

His plan for an 'uncut' *Hamlet* is notable but for a man whose whole career was based on taking risks and breaking accepted norms his initial comments seem remarkably cautious.

First exercises towards producing *Hamlet* ignored the dialogue entirely (note Craig's speculation about *Hamlet* without dialogue). In the Mousetrap scene, for example, 'any dramatic work which is imbued with the quality of true theatricality is amenable to total schematization, even to the extent of temporarily removing the dialogue with which the skeleton of the scenario is embellished'. After this attempts were made to progress from exercises in stage movement to work on dramatic extracts with dialogue – in particular Ophelia's mad scene. In approaching Shakespeare, Meyerhold rejects outright the Stanislavskian method of 'experienced emotion'. 'You must not forget,' he reminds the actors, 'that you are speaking verse and that there can be *none of the freedom enjoyed by the actor* who "lives" his part and is subject to no formal discipline.' In portraying Ophelia's mad scene, Meyerhold is determined to break old moulds and confound expectations. The actress playing Ophelia – presumably at the director's behest – 'is trying to recapture the naïve simplicity of the original strolling players'. What must be created is a very new style of acting which matches the essentially non-realist verse.

> The tenseness caused by so-called 'experienced emotions' has been replaced by the free play of imagination and a stage technique has been liberated which brooks no obstacles. We cannot hope for a successful rendering of this extract until we have eliminated all traces of Duncanesque balleticism, until the actor takes the stage with all the dexterity of a juggler, manipulating his lines as the juggler does his balls, which fly back and forth above his head in intervals and patterns similar to the rhythm and rhyme of spoken verse. (Braun 1969: 151-2)

In fact, Meyerhold's distaste for 'experienced emotions' may be traced to an occasion (24 August 1895) when he had performed A.N. Apukhtin's monologue, *The Madman,* at a student gathering. He became so absorbed in the part: 'I felt myself becoming mad.' Thereafter he viewed such performances with suspicion as 'a narcotic' (Leach 1989: 4). Heinrich Notman who played Hamlet in those fragmentary rehearsals in 1915/16 was coached to be the diametric opposite of Kachalov in the 1912 production: 'impulsive, dynamic, musical and buoyant' (Senelick 1982: 186). Not only is the contrast with Stanislavsky's 'system' glaringly obvious, but this attempt to return 'to the naïve simplicity of the strolling players' – the imagery is of the circus and the music hall – was to be deeply influential on later directors such as Bertolt Brecht, Ariane Mnouchkine and Peter Brook. Quoting a description about a theatrical success in the London of the 1560s (Thomas Preston's tragedy, *Cambyses*) as a 'lamentable tragedy mixed full of pleasant mirth', Meyerhold lays down his basic approach to Shakespeare's play:

> May one not consider the tragedy of *Hamlet* as a play in which the tears are glimpsed through a series of traditional theatrical pranks? Should we not forget once and for all the arguments of scholars about the strength or weakness of Hamlet's will, ignore all the various intentions which are attributed willy-nilly to the author? (Braun 1969: 152)

In questioning the concept of 'author's intention', Meyerhold is establishing another key principle for the Hamlet director. However 'the strength or weakness' of this director's 'will' to stage *Hamlet* could itself be called in question: 'That we would do / We should do when we would.' The abatements and delays on this occasion were caused by war; in consequence Meyerhold's dream of staging a full-length production of *Hamlet* with his pupils was never realized, and after one further season the Studio closed in Spring 1917 (Braun 1969: 118). In fact the theme of war has a particular relevance not only to *Hamlet* but to Meyerhold's own personal biography; and to understand Meyerhold's reservations about producing Shakespeare it is a theme worth pursuing.

Courtier, *Soldier*, Scholar

In 1874 Meyerhold was born in Pensa, a small but flourishing trading centre some three hundred and fifty miles to the south-east of Moscow. (Pensa is where in Gogol's *The Government*

Inspector the young Hlestakov is cheated by the infantry captain; it was also, according to Meyerhold, the place which he used as a model for the seedy provincial town in his own (in)famous production of *The Government Inspector* (1926)). His family were affluent, middle-class Germans and Meyerhold was the youngest in a family of eight children, where he was considered of little account by his father – the father being concerned more about the proper schooling of the two eldest sons, the likely successors to the family business. 'In consequence, *Karl grew up under the influence of his mother Alvina Danilovna*, and came to share her passion for music and the theatre. He circulated freely in the varied society of the busy little town, being on easy terms with his father's workmen and more than once falling in with "socialists" who offended *his father's Bismarckian rectitude*' (Braun 1979: 19). The strong influence of, and attachment to, his mother as well as the distance and hostility of the father perhaps explains why Meyerhold would later find *Hamlet* a particularly fascinating play. 'Meyerhold's father,' notes Robert Leach, 'seems to have been something of a weight round his son's neck' (1989: 2). Well before he came to play 'Hamlet' Treplev in Chekhov's play, he no doubt realized the relevance of Shakespeare's tragedy to his own life.

Hamlet may have had resonance in Meyerhold's immediate circle for another and more general political reason. A cultured middle class German family in the latter part of the nineteenth century would have imbibed the German cultural fascination with *Hamlet* and might well have known of Ferdinand Freiligrath's celebrated poem which begins: 'Deutschland ist Hamlet' [Germany is Hamlet] and later continues its commentary on the woes and missed opportunities of the Fatherland:

> At best he did nothing but think
> He stayed too long in Wittenberg
> In the lecture hall and the pubs
> And therefore he lacks determination. (G.A.Craig 1981: vii and 765)

Indeed Gordon A. Craig (to be distinguished from Edward Gordon Craig) begins his thorough history, *Germany 1866-1945*, with the words: 'This book tells of the reign of Fortinbras and his successors and it is a tragic story.' Like Russia, Germany is a very Shakespeare-*ized* country. Three years before joining the Art Theatre in 1898, Meyerhold had renounced his father's Lutheran religion in favour of the Orthodox faith and took the Russian name and patronymic, Vsevolod Emilievich. This, it seems, was not so much a decision of conscience as a means of avoiding conscription into the Prussian army. It also made possible his marriage the following year to a Russian girl, Olga Munt (Braun 1979:19). In seemingly trading war for love – Fatherland for Motherland – Meyerhold was tracing a pattern or dichotomy evident in *Hamlet*. For according to the Clown/ Gravedigger it was on *the very day* that Old Hamlet struggled in belligerent combat with Old Fortinbras that Gertrude gave loving birth to Hamlet (V.i.140-5). In thus avoiding the militarism of the Prussian state, Meyerhold might not have recalled the scene in *Hamlet* where the hero watches the army of Fortinbras embarking on its journey to the war zone: 'While to my *shame* I see/The imminent death of twenty thousand men/That for a fantasy and trick of fame/Go to their graves like beds' (Signet ed. IV.iv.59-62). But, by 1939, – in a Russia where *Hamlet* (for obvious reasons) was officially banned – he must have been struck by the irony that the 'little patch of ground', the 'plot/whereon the numbers cannot try the cause' was set in Poland.

Yet the young director's 'instincts' were far from pacific. Indeed Meyerhold's enthusiasm for the new Bolshevik state was grounded in militarism as much as in ˙social commitment. In 1899 Meyerhold had criticized Stanislavsky for his failure to confront the social issues in drama (Benedetti 1991: 45). In March 1901 the young director during a visit to St. Petersburg with the Art Theatre had observed the brutal suppression of a student demonstration by the police and military. In a letter to Chekhov he described his reaction. He wanted, he told the older man, to burn with the spirit of the times. He wanted all servants of the stage to recognize their high destiny. He was irritated by 'those comrades of mine' who had no desire to rise above the narrow interests of their caste and respond to the interests of society. 'Yes,' he concluded, 'the theatre is capable of playing an enormous part in the transformation of the whole of existence!' (Braun 1969: 159). Despite these early hints of an enthusiasm for a theatre of social change and revolution, Meyerhold until 1917 showed little interest in such an approach, even suggesting (in 1913) that the theatre was a world apart: 'The stage is a world of marvels and enchantment, it is breathless joy and strange magic' (*Ibid.*).

Significantly, in relation to earlier comments about Meyerhold's avoidance of war and militarism, an event which seems to have shaken the director out of this escapist mould was the visit to one of his Theatre-Studio rehearsals in 1914 of a group of wounded soldiers. He was enthusiastic about their reaction to his *Commedia dell'arte* style players and believed that they constituted the very audience for which 'the new theatre, the truly popular theatre, is intended'. Shortly after the fall of the Russian monarchy, Meyerhold attended a debate entitled, 'Revolution, Art and War'. He criticized the silent, passionless parterre where people come for a rest cure and demanded: 'Why don't the soldiers come to the theatre and liberate it from the parterre public?' If some inner voice had once cried '*shame!*' – or even '*coward!*' – when Meyerhold had evaded conscription into the Prussian army (a not unlikely scenario given his father's stern Bismarckian demeanour), it is interesting to note the now-maturing director's enthusiasm for things military. When, after the revolutionary struggle of 1917, all theatres came under close state supervision, Meyerhold was quick to offer his services to the new Bolshevik rulers. This was not necessarily opportunism. Indeed 'Bolshevik power was far from secure at that time and a declaration of solidarity amounted to a hazardous act of faith. This act Meyerhold committed and soon affirmed it in 1918 by joining the Bolshevik Party' (Braun 1969: 160).

Like Hamlet, Meyerhold could admire real soldiers but would prove much better at *playing* war and death than enacting them in reality. This is borne out by an almost theatrical appearance of militarism which he adopted in the new Soviet Union as his own personal power increased. The actor Igor Ilinsky described Meyerhold's appearance at about the time he had been appointed – after imprisonment and a fortuitous, Hamlet-like, close brush with death at the hands of 'The Whites' – as director of the Theatrical Department for the entire Soviet Republic:

> He was wearing a soldier's greatcoat and on his cap there was a badge with Lenín's picture ... In spite of its apparent simplicity, his appearance was somewhat theatrical, because although he was dressed modestly and without any super-fluous 'Bolshevik' attributes, the style was still *à la* Bolshevik: the carelessly thrown on greatcoat, the boots and puttees, the cap, the dark red woollen scarf – it was all quite unpre-tentious, but at the same time effective enough. (Braun 1969: 162)

Meyerhold's growing enthusiasm for the military soon took dramatic form. In one production, *The Dawn*, staged to mark the third anniversary of the October Revolution, the audience, composed in many cases of soldiers, was showered with propagandist leaflets in the huge, unheated, derelict auditorium. The highlight of one memorable performance was the an-nouncement of news from the Civil War front. Meyerhold's highest aspirations were realized on the night when the Herald announced the Red Army's decisive break into the Crimea at the Battle of Perekop, which prompted someone to sing 'As Martyrs You Fell' while cast and audience stood still in silence (Leach 1989: 36). Although such a unified response was not typical the production was altered to placate Lenin's wife, Nadezhda Krupskaya, who complained that it was a sheer insult 'to cast the Russian Proletariat as a Shakespearean crowd that any self-opinionated fool can lead wherever the urge takes him' (Braun 1982: 135). So successful was this interruption in stirring up the audience that Meyerhold began planning seriously a production of *Hamlet* as a modern political satire. Mayakovsky was to re-write the grave diggers' scene and all the other prosaic scenes of the tragedy and update them politically (Rudnitsky 1981: 273). *Earth Rampant* staged in 1923, marking Meyerhold's twenty-fifth anniversary in the theatre, was dedicated 'to the Red Army and the First Red Soldier of the RSFSR, Leon Trotsky'. The destruction of the audience/ stage divide was emphasized in one performance attended by Trotsky himself. According to Yuri Annenkov (Leach 1989: 19):

> During one of the acts, happening to glance towards the seat of Trotsky, I saw that he was no longer there. I assumed that the production was perhaps not to his tastes and that he had decided to leave the theatre. But after two or three minutes Trotsky suddenly appeared *on the stage* and, in the same setting which contained the actors, delivered a short speech regarding the fifth anniversary of the founding of the Red Army which fit right in with the action of the play. After thunderous applause the action on stage continued as if without interruption and Trotsky again returned to his seat. (Leach's emphasis)

As part of the mass spectacle, real military vehicles were driven up on the stage where the uniforms of the soldiers were authentic and the actors wore no make-up. In the same year celebrating his jubilee, Meyerhold would be made an honorary soldier of the Moscow Garrison. In *Tarelkin's Death* (1922) Meyerhold would employ once again the knockabout tricks of circus clowns and strolling players, but in case the audience got too comfortable, an assistant director seated in the front row announced the intervals by firing a pistol (one presumes a blank was used) in the direction of the audience and shouting 'Entrrrr-act !' (Braun 1969: 186).

In his methods clearly Meyerhold was waging war against the old bourgeois culture with its comfortable theatres and 'aesthetic values'. Yet Chekhov's fear that the theatre was fast becoming an asylum for megalomaniacs might have been confirmed by Meyerhold's behaviour when he was appointed Head of the Theatre Department of the Soviet Commissariat for Enlightenment. In that capacity he assumed virtual dictatorship over the entire Russian theatre. It was his turn to play Devil-Father ('I am very proud, revengeful, ambitious.' III.i.126-7):

> Hell-bent on breaking the hegemony of the commercial managements and the former Imperial companies, not to mention settling a few old scores, Meyerhold proclaimed the advent of the October Revolution in the theatre, and sought

to initiate a ruthless redeployment of manpower and material resources. (Braun 1982: 131)

In 1921, for example, Meyerhold recommended closing the celebrated Maly theatre, 'this reactionary museum or old-age asylum' (Slonim 285). Luckily for the more established 'museum' theatres such as the MAT and the Maly, the State – in line with its policy of preserving artistic traditions – frustrated the director in his quest for total power. Disgusted, Meyerhold soon resigned from his position. Old Father Chekhov might well have turned in his grave at the antics of his protégé; but the lines: '... Let four captains / Bear Hamlet like a soldier to the stage, / For he was likely, had he been put on, / To have proved most royally.' (V.ii.349-52) had a somewhat ironic ring in the circumstances. There may be in every person a Hamlet (Hazlitt), but in every Hamlet there is also a potential megalomaniac ('We are arrant knaves, all. Believe none of us.' III.i.131).

In the same year, 1920, that Meyerhold was exercising his megalomaniac tendencies over the Russian theatre, Bertrand Russell, after a visit to the Soviet Union, published *The Practice and Theory of Bolshevism*. In it, with commendable prescience, he wrote: 'Marxians never sufficiently recognize that love of power is quite as strong a motive, and quite as great a source of injustice, as love of money; yet this must be obvious to any unbiased student of politics' (68). The truth of Russell's warning would be chillingly demonstrated in the life's work of that ultimate Devil-Father, Joseph Stalin. Yet if Russell was later to see Stalin as a goblin damn'd, Bernard Shaw was to see him as an angel blest. 'We have rebuked her ungodliness,' Shaw said, after visiting the Soviet Union in 1931, 'and now the sun shines on Russia as on a country with which God is well pleased ...'[4]

Shakespeare, Chekhov and the Theatre of Revolution

What relationship, then, does Shakespeare (or Chekhov) have to such a revolutionary theatre? The answer to that question can best be gleaned from a series of speeches and articles that Meyerhold himself delivered and published in the years 1920 and 1921. In these, Shakespeare sometimes is identified with a reactionary bourgeois theatre that must be swept away. Likewise the director identifies Chekhov with the backward-looking practices of the 'museum' theatre, the Moscow Art Theatre: 'I don't think there is much likelihood of the Red Army taking its banners along to *Uncle Vanya* when it can come to productions which it looks on as its own. More than anyone, the Moscow Art Theatre is to blame for the passivity of the spectator whom it held in thrall for so long; at one time he was not even allowed to applaud when a surge of enthusiasm demanded applause' (Braun 1969: 174). As this, and other, evidence suggests Meyerhold could not abide a quiet unresponsive audience – or a theatre that encouraged such unresponsiveness. He would use any strategy to provoke a response, the aim being not to unify the spectators but to challenge and divide them into progressive and reactionary factions. Thus Meyerhold in these speeches demands a political theatre ('our theatre') which involves the spectator as much as the actor: 'No man [no actor] has ever been a-political, a-social; man is always a product of the forces of his environment.' He argues that Chekhov at the turn of the century was successful, because the mood of the performers corresponded to the general mood of the intelligentsia at that time. Equally, then, the only theatre that can become exemplary in 'this age of mighty revolution' is a revolutionary theatre. Yet, he insists, the repertoire of such a theatre does not have to consist exclusively of Verhaeren's *The Dawn* or Vermishev's *Red Truth* (*Ibid.* 168-9):

> It could just as easily include Wilde's *Salome* and Shakespeare's *Hamlet*; everything depends on the interpretation … After all, Mochalov conveyed a hint of Bakunin in Hamlet. In the same way, before running the King through, the New Actor could flick the crown from his head with a deft movement of his slender, steel rapier.

If until 1917, Meyerhold told his company, we behaved with a certain caution and care for the literary work, then today we are no longer fetishists, we do not kneel down and call in prayer:

'Shakespeare, Verhaeren! ...' *Now we no longer defend the interests of the author, but those of the audience* (Rudnitsky 1981: 269). It is clear that Meyerhold proposes to make of every notable play ever written propaganda for a class (Bentley 1991: 144).

After these comments, mostly delivered at the beginning of October 1920, Meyerhold proposes in his 'Inaugural Speech to the Company of the R.S.F.S.R. Theatre No 1' that the repertoire will include: *The Dawn* (Verhaeren), *Mystery-Bouffe* (Mayakovsky), *Hamlet* (Shakespeare), *Great Catherine* (Bernard Shaw), *Golden Head* (Claudel) and *Women in Parliament* (Aristophanes): 'But since all this is merely literature, let it lie undisturbed in the libraries. We shall need scenarios and we shall often utilize even the classics as a basis for our theatrical compositions. *We shall tackle the task of adaptation without fear, fully confident of its necessity*' (Braun 1969: 169-70). Rejecting totally Stanislavsky's 'system', he establishes fundamental axioms for his theatre and, in a later article, confidently awaits the moment when the master (Stanislavsky) exhausted with work alien to him, will 'follow Gogol's example and hurl the oft-amended pages of his "system" into the stove'. There must be, he argues, no pauses, no psychology, no 'authentic emotions' either on the stage or whilst building a role. 'Here is our theatrical programme: plenty of light, plenty of high spirits, plenty of grandeur, plenty of infectious enthusiasm, unlaboured creativity, the participation of the audience in the corporate creative act of the performance' (*Ibid.* 170).

However, despite the brave directorial assertion, 'We shall tackle the task of adaptation without fear, fully confident of its necessity', still there was to be no production of *Hamlet*:

> Yet I,
> A dull and muddy-mettled rascal, peak
> Like John-a-dreams, unpregnant of my cause,
> And can say nothing. (II.ii.568-71)

Like Hamlet pausing beside the praying figure of Claudius ('Now might I do it pat, now a is praying, / And now I'll do't. [*He draws his sword*]'), Meyerhold once more was able to find an excuse, for this 'now', seemingly, was never the correct 'now':

Now, whether it be
Bestial oblivion, or some craven scruple
Of thinking too precisely on th' event –
A thought which, quartered, hath but one part wisdom
And ever three parts coward – I do not know
Why yet I live to say, 'This thing's to do,'
Sith I have cause, and will, and strength, and means
To do't. Examples gross as earth exhort me.
Witness this army ... (Signet ed. IV.iv.39-47)

Yet, at times, Meyerhold came tantalizingly close to realizing his dream. According to Marjorie L. Hoover:

> In the 1920s Meyerhold seemed more than once about to stage *Hamlet*, that capstone classic of every director's career. In January 1921 he ordered a model for the set of *Hamlet* from Dmitriev – soon, that is, after the opening of the designer's show *Dawns*. Not Meyerhold, however, but Valerii Bebutov carried on preparatory discussion of the model – Bebutov, co-director at the Theater RSFSR I, where *Hamlet* was to be the next production in the repertory. Then before talking to Meyerhold himself Dmitriev had to return to Petrograd because of an obligation there for military service. (1988: 201)

Dmitriev's biographer informs us that the *Hamlet* set was to be 'abstract' and to achieve its effect by the 'play' of various textures, masses and surfaces and rays of silver wire stretched in different directions to remind of light beams.

No doubt one difficulty faced by the director was the prevailing attitude to tragic drama in the new communist state. Lunacharsky, the first Soviet Commissar of Education, proclaimed that one of the defining qualities of a communist society would be the *absence* of tragic drama. The communist press, for example, was infuriated by Mikhail Chekhov's portrayal of Hamlet in 1924/25 as a man so crushed by the growing sense of grief and so despairing of himself and of mankind that he approached insanity, and displayed many signs of mental and emotional derangement (Slonim 274). Because he is convinced that the powers of reason can master the forces of 'blind fate', a communist will no longer see meaning in tragedy

– or will dismiss it as some relic from 'the museum of the moral past'. As George Steiner puts it in *The Death of Tragedy*:

> [For the Marxist] The tragic theatre is an expression of the pre-rational phase in history; it is founded on the assumption that there are in nature and in the psyche occult, uncontrollable forces able to madden or destroy the mind ... He knows that there is no such thing as *Anangké*, the blind necessity which overwhelms Oedipus ... Tragedy can occur only where reality has not been harnessed by reason and social consciousness. When the new man of the communist society comes to a crossing of three roads, he will encounter a factory or a hall of culture, not enraged Laius in his cart ... Marxist literature, therefore, is joyous affirmation or a cry to battle. Stalin was perfectly consistent with the aims of a communist society when he demanded that all plays and novels should have a happy ending. (1961: 342-3)

In producing *Othello,* this was a principle that Stanislavsky singularly failed to appreciate; but after 1930, 'Stalin's favourite director'[5] (unlike Meyerhold) steered well clear of Shakespearean tragedy.

If Marxist optimism was the real reason for Meyerhold's inability to fulfil his intentions, it is strange that he should have continued to plan *openly* productions of Shakespeare during the nineteen-thirties. As late as 1937, as Meyerhold showed visitors around his practically finished new theatre, he enthusiastically described his plans for *Hamlet* – possibly with settings by Picasso. Indeed, one might have expected a low profile from a director who only a few years before had dedicated one of his highly popular dramas to Stalin's most loathed and feared opponent: The First Red Soldier of the RSFSR, Leon Trotsky. But even at the height of Stalin's power, when it was not unusual for the innocent to disappear overnight merely for an unwitting expression of yesterday's 'wrong' opinion,[6] Meyerhold continued his duet with death. He defied augury:

> If it be now, tis not to come. If it be not to come, it will be now. If it be not now yet it will come. The readiness is all. (V.ii.166-8).

In 1929 Meyerhold had directed an amusing but highly controversial satire, Mayakovsky's *The Bedbug,* which ridiculed Soviet bureaucracy. The play was produced with a characteristic emphasis on spectacle and physical energy. Life in the communist future was mocked for the play told of a NEP (New Economic Policy) man frozen in ice and restored to life in 1979. To exemplify the two eras, two contrasting scenic conceptions were used: in the first half a semi-realistic set, in the second a modernist-constructivist set (Leiter 1991: 65). When in the early years of the Russian revolution, Lunacharsky had promulgated the slogan 'Back to Ostrovsky', he was countered with the riposte 'Forward to Meyerhold!' The contrast between the two sets in *The Bedbug* was an affront to he orthodoxies of social realism. It (amongst other things) cheekily suggested that the future lay with the modernist-constructivist theatre of Meyerhold. Yet the inspiration for all this may have been far from futuristic: Meyerhold himself described how in *The Bedbug* there are a number of striking shifts from one episode to another 'in which we feel *the best rhythmic modulations of Shakespeare'* (Leach 1989: 164). Meyerhold and Mayakovsky developed this futuristic theme even more daringly in *The Bathhouse* (1930), where 'Meyerhold displayed with dazzling dexterity the while gamut of styles of theatre, from naturalism through dance to agitprop. Each served as an attraction in itself, but as a sequence it became a stinging challenge to critical and therefore ideological and therefore political complacency' (*Ibid.* 165). As though his advocacy of and undisguised admiration for Trotsky had not been enough, his rebellious mockery must surely have sealed Meyerhold's fate in the court of Joseph Stalin. Mayakovsky's end was swift for he committed suicide – or 'committed suicide' – less than a month after the performance, and Meyerhold lost not only a friend but one of the few writers with whom the director had a good working relationship. Meyerhold himself did well to survive; the wonder, perhaps, is that he survived so long:

How dangerous it is that this man goes loose!
Yet must not we put the strong law on him.
He's loved of the distracted multitude. (IV.iii.2-4)

Meyerhold's awareness of the ever-growing presence of
death was reflected powerfully in his dramatic work. Maybe
remembering Craig's unrealized 'Death figure' in the 1912
Hamlet, Meyerhold incorporated such an ominous figure into
Camille (1934). American director Lee Strasberg describes how
Meyerhold had a marked actor dressed in black and standing
against a black background suddenly appear from nothingness.
As frightened as the other characters, Camille screams:

> Then the man takes the mask off, and it is one of the people
> whom we had seen previously at the party. The shock and
> the theatricality is so impressive that later on in the scene,
> when Camille tells Armand that she is afraid of death, so are
> you – afraid for her because you have just seen it,
> experienced it (1973: 109).

Black, it should not be forgotten, is a colour characteristic of
Hamlet. 'Good Hamlet,' says Gertrude, 'cast thy *nightly* colour
off' (I.ii.68). Apart from his inky cloak and customary suits of
solemn black, when he chooses lines to quote to the actors that
word predominates:

> He whose *sable* arms,
> Black as his purpose, did the night resemble
> ... black complexion ... (II.ii.455-8)

If Meyerhold was reluctant, except indirectly, to tackle
Shakespeare, then he seems to have felt a similar reticence in
staging Chekhov. After his early productions in the manner of
the Art Theatre, he left that father figure well alone. Then
suddenly in 1935, after a gap of more than thirty years, he
produced, not one of the major Chekhov texts, but an adaptation based on some short one-act plays called *Thirty-Three
Fainting Fits*. A description of Meyerhold at the first rehearsal of
this is surely significant. He began by defining his approach to
theatre: to find the author's idea and clothe it in an appropriate
form, 'a sequence of *jeux de théâtre*' (Clyman 1985: 214). In this

production he told the actors, he had chosen the idea of thirty-three fainting spells (the swoons supposedly exemplified the neurasthenic legacy of the prerevolutionary intelligentsia) suffered by the characters of the three one-act plays. He then read the script to the company, noting as he did when the fainting occurred. However, if we remember the photograph of Chekhov reading *The Seagull* to the actors and directors of the Moscow Art Theatre in 1899, (illus.1), the scene as described takes on a particular significance. At the opening rehearsal of the production the director sat at a table on stage surrounded by the entire company; seemingly filled with superhuman energy he appeared, *'to be almost in a state of spontaneous combustion!'* (Houghton 1936: 117). In the original picture Chekhov, the playwright, is placed at the centre reading the play to the cast and directors; Meyerhold sits marginalized, a seemingly alienated figure. In this present description it is Meyerhold, the director, filled with dynamic energy 'almost in a state of spontaneous combustion' who has taken centre stage and who now reads (and controls) the Chekhovian text. The son has finally replaced the father; the director has replaced the playwright.

1935 was a remarkable year in another respect. For it was in that year that Gordon Craig visited Moscow and the two directors met at last. Craig claimed in an article for *The London Mercury* that given the opportunity 'he would haunt Meyerhold's rehearsals exclusively, to gain an understanding of such an exceptional theatrical genius' (Senelick 1982: 72). Craig was not the only Hamlet director who came to Moscow in 1935 to learn, wonder and admire: *Verfremdung* (alienation) would shortly be born. As John Fuegi expresses it:

> Despite a growing undercurrent of fear that it was essential to publicly ignore, Brecht was to find Moscow wonderfully exciting in many ways during his stay there from mid-March until mid-May 1935. It was a watershed moment in history. The stages and screens glowed with the last rays of a sunburst of creative activity that had dawned in the first brilliant years of the twentieth century. In the physically grubby Moscow theaters of the twenties and early thirties, Meyerhold, Stanislavsky, and Tairov rubbed shoulders with

Mei lanFan from China, Piscator, Gordon Craig from England, French writer André Malraux, and a host of Americans
including Joseph Losey, Hallie Flanagan, Harold Clurman,
Lee Strasberg, and Stella Adler – all visibly dazzled by what
they saw and heard.

The Soviet Union, it seemed, was in the vanguard of the
arts. It seemed also to be on its way to the triumphant un-
folding of the human spirit and a classless, nonracist, and
nonsexist society. This was a dream still widely believed in
1935 both inside and outside the Soviet Union.
(Fuegi 1994: 323)

Yet as *The Bedbug*, and even more clearly *The Bathhouse*,
showed, Meyerhold was no longer entirely convinced by this
dream; and *Hamlet* provided a perfect vehicle for his doubts
about life under the new director-in-chief, Stalin. Still he continued to dream of staging *Hamlet*. Indifferent to the growing
Stalinist orthodoxies, his scenic conceptions reflected the need
to banish the stuffiness of the old theatre and to include
settings inspired by the most modern artists. In 1920 he had
praised artistic innovators such as the Cubists: 'The modern
theatre wants to move out into the open sea or something
constructed by the new man.' In the 1930s his plans to work
with Picasso on designs for *Hamlet* – according to Alexander
Gladkov, in summer 1936 Meyerhold discussed this project
with Picasso in Paris – were in line with this (Braun 1969: 244).
In 'The Queen of Spades' (a talk given in Moscow in 1934),
Meyerhold in envisioning a scene from *Hamlet* had remained
true to his scenario of the 'open air'. The description (quoted
more fully in the first chapter) begins:

> Seashore. Sea mist. Frost. A chill wind chases silver waves up
> on to a sandy, snow-free beach. Hamlet wrapped from head
> to foot in a black cloak is waiting for the Ghost of his
> Father. (Braun 1969: 279)

Dennis Kennedy is surely missing the point when he writes:
'Classic drama had little place in that Soviet dawn and Shakespeare had none at all for Meyerhold, who was one of the few
major directors of the century to *ignore* him' (1993: 93). The
great Russian innovator even contemplated casting his wife,

Zinaida Raikh, as the Prince, and also (in a manner similar to that later employed by Friel in *Philadelphia, Here I Come!*)[7] imagined two Hamlets on stage representing warring aspects of the character's nature (Leiter 1991: 78).

He had come closer to realizing these conceptions in Yuri Olesha's *List of Benefits* (4 June 1931), a production remarkable not least because he made no attempt to stretch the resources of the traditional stage. The play details the story of a fictitious Soviet tragic actress, Yelena Goncharova, who finds her creativity stifled by rectilinear, schematized plays devoid of imagination; she emigrates to Paris, the city of her dreams, 'only to find herself propositioned by lecherous impresarios and invited to perform pornographic sketches in a music hall' (Braun 1969: 242). Significantly, Meyerhold incorporated into Olesha's play some incidents ('some dozen or sixteen lines'?) from the biography of actor Mikhail Chekhov (nephew of Anton and one of the greatest of modern Russian Hamlets) – incidents which the actor had recounted to him in Berlin a year before. In one scene Goncharova auditions for Hamlet – the scene she plays is from Act III, Scene 2. Meyerhold directed her to say her lines first sarcastically, then calmly, but to burst out in rage on the lines: 'Why look you, how unworthy a thing you make of me. You would play upon me: you would seem to know my stops …' Meyerhold, says Rudnitsky, used Raikh's lips to answer many people. 'It was not without reason that he dreamed of staging *Hamlet* in those days.' (1981: 493).

The whole mood of the play typified the dilemma facing many Russian artists in the twenties and thirties. The title of the play refers to how the heroine, the actress Goncharova, keeps a balance sheet of benefits and crimes performed by the Soviet government, and comes to the conclusion that the new regime, despite a number of good points, is not propitious for free creation (Slonim 300). Although her subsequent experiences in France lead to a condemnation of Western decadence, so ideologically ambivalent a production was bound to inflame further Stalinist suspicions of Meyerhold.

Soon, however, the abatements and delays in dealing with Meyerhold would cease. For the one who had identified the disease of 'Chronegkitis', who had warned against the fever of Russian 'Meiningenitis', had himself been identified as a dangerous virus in the body politic. In the stark and sterile wards of socialist realism, the scourge of 'Meyerholditis'[8] would soon be identified as a serious threat to public health. This hectic in the blood of Stalin must soon be purged and cured:

> I like him not, nor stands it safe with us
> To let his madness range ...
> Diseases desperate grown
> By desperate appliance are relieved,
> Or not at all. (III.iii.1-2; IV.iii.9-11)

The murmur of criticism in the Press, often a precursor to a victim's arrest and death, grew louder. On 17 December 1937 *Pravda* published a particularly ominous article entitled 'An Alien Theatre' which included the following damning charge against the director: 'It has become absolutely clear that Meyerhold cannot (and, apparently, will not) comprehend Soviet reality or depict the problems which concern every Soviet citizen' (Braun 1969: 250).

The following year, already a political pariah, his theatre now closed by the authorities, Meyerhold was given sanctuary at the Moscow Art Theatre by Stanislavsky; but this respite was short-lived. In August Stanislavsky died and with that brief protection removed, Meyerhold's days were numbered. Yet two months later when Meyerhold became director of the MAT 'Opera-Studio', ('...think of us / As of a father'), it was powerful proof of the rapprochement between Stanislavsky and the younger director. Not only had Stanislavsky come to recognize and to imitate his rival but Meyerhold, for his part, had moved more in the direction of realism and the inner exploration of character. That said, Meyerhold's new theatre, if it had survived, might well have been true to Mayakovsky's axiom:

> Theatre
>   is not a reflecting mirror
> but –
>   a magnifying glass. (Rudnitsky 1981: 461)

If Chekhov urged that the stage must reflect *the quintessence of life*, then Meyerhold, it might be said, *magnified* to reflect life more accurately. Yet, as Edward Braun suggests, the dialogue would inevitably have resumed between the mask of Meyerhold and the face of Stanislavsky (1969: 251).

In one of his final (reported) speeches in April 1939 Meyerhold spoke of a lengthy dialogue with Stanislavsky shortly before his death. First Stanislavsky spoke for an hour and a half, then Meyerhold spoke for the same time. 'I listened to him,' Meyerhold told his audience, and took in what he said:

> Konstantin Sergeevich said: 'Don't you want to reform me?' I said I wanted to reach agreement with him and he replied: 'I thought you were planning a revolt. I've taken over a Mozart-style auditorium. It would be a good idea to start staging intimate Mozart operas there. The productions there may be run-of-the-mill and cliché-ridden, but we'll blow some fresh air through the theatre.' He used to say: 'We'll perform without a front curtain ...' He said that just to please me. This shows that Konstantin Sergeevich *needed a rebel near him* who was prepared to roll up his sleeves and work. (Braun 1969: 300)

Clearly the differences remained although the friendship between these two contrasting figures is evident:

> During the brief scene we see the father in silver and Hamlet in black, then the father in black and Hamlet in silver. Having embraced, father and son leave the stage.

Soon it was time for the 'son' as well as the 'father' of this modern Russian drama to leave the stage. On 15 June 1939 Meyerhold addressed the All-Union Conference of Stage Directors. His recantation was either too late or too little.[9] Immediately after the conference he was arrested and it is believed that he was shot in a Moscow prison on 2 February 1940. To add a final authentic touch to this 'Shakespearean' tragedy, his actress wife, Zinaida Raikh, would shortly meet a similar fate. 'Don't leave me,' he had written to her in October 1938, 'I love you, you – my wife, sister, mother, friend, darling. *You are golden like this nature which creates miracles.* Zina, don't leave me!' (Meyerhold's emphasis). Ten days after his arrest Zinaida Raikh was savagely stabbed to death in their Moscow flat. Apart from a few papers little was taken and the 'mystery' assailants were never caught. 'Call me what instrument you will, though you can fret me, you cannot play upon me' is the epigraph to one English collection of Meyerhold's writings (Braun 1969). Thus there is a characteristic touch of ironic, self-mocking humour in the epitaph that Meyerhold chose for himself. 'Engrave on my tombstone,' he told his friends: 'Here lies an actor and director who never played and never staged Hamlet.[10]

'Just as Stanislavsky and Meyerhold were utterly complementary in their own time,' Charles Marowitz has commented, 'so are the theatrical styles they spawned. In classical productions by companies such as the Royal Shakespeare, Le Théâtre du Soleil, and the Piccolo Theatre of Milan, they often march hand in hand.' (1986: 103). In these opening chapters those two figures have rightly taken centre stage, but that half-child, half-artist, that 'spoilt child in artistic Europe', Gordon Craig has also illuminated their changing relationship in the drama of life. Indeed, one seemingly trivial dispute between Stanislavsky and Craig seems, in hindsight, particularly significant. Craig was keen to see Olga Knipper play Gertrude in the 1912 *Hamlet*, but Stanislavsky resisted Craig's pressure. 'I do not see, and cannot understand how Knipper will play the Queen,' Stanislavsky wrote to Craig, 'the more so, as I do not believe that she really very much wishes to play this part.' In the end, however, Craig – the Son figure who became the Father of all the Hamlet directors – got his way. As it turned out the casting was a mistake; it seemed the director-in-chief of the Moscow Art Theatre had been right all along. Yet Craig's (mad/megalomaniac?) prophetic soul may have seized upon a more profound truth, a hint of which is suggested in the postcard he sent when Knipper (once Arkadina to Meyerhold's Treplev) finally took the part (Senelick 1982: 142):

> I cannot say how happy I am that you are to act the Queen. *You know how much I wished for that* and *now I have my wish.* (Craig's emphasis)

Thus Craig wrote to Anton Chekhov's leading lady and former wife; she was an interesting choice for Gertrude since with his determined amorous *Blitzkrieg* he had already played Claudius with her 'honeying and making love' (*Hamlet* Act III ; *Seagull* Act I). 'Craig's first step,' observed T.S. Eliot, 'in wading through seas of theatrical blood to grasp his crown, is to dismiss the poet' (1989: 36): 'My crown, mine own ambition and my queen' (III.iii.55). For Craig ('half a century ahead of us', as Stanislavsky described him) was not only signalling the replacement of the Father by the Son; he was – more significantly for the theatre – signalling his fervent wish for the replacement of the old Playwright King by the new Devil-Father, the director (*in me are the souls of Alexander the Great, of Caesar, of Shakespeare, of Napoleon*).

I could see in Hamlet the history of the theatre.[11]

---

[1] See Joyce Vining Morgan, *Stanislavski's Encounter with Shakespeare: The Evolution of a Method* (Ann Arbor, Mich., 1984), p.84.

[2] *People's Century*, '1917 Red Flag,' BBC I (TV), 27/9/95.

[3] See Samuel Leiter, *From Stanislavsky to Barrault: Representative Directors of the European Stage* (New York, 1991), p.28. For more on the Czar's attitude to Gogol's play, see Janko Lavrin's introduction to *The Government Inspector* trans. by D. J. Campbell (London, 1953), p.10.

[4] *People's Century*, 27/9/95.

[5] John Fuegi, *The Life and Lies of Bertolt Brecht* (London, 1994), p. 256. For a more sympathetic interpretation of Stanislavsky's role in Stalinist Russia, see Marc Slonim, *Russian Theater* (London, 1963), p.316.

[6] See, for example, Malcolm Muggeridge's essay 'Many Winters Ago in Moscow' in *Tread Softly For You Tread On My Jokes*.

[7] Brian Friel's play is, in fact, infused with the spirit of Hamlet – Friel wrote the play after watching Guthrie direct *Hamlet* in Minneapolis (See Chapter 4).

8 For commentary on this term (in relation to Tyrone Guthrie), see Samuel Leiter, *From Belasco to Brook: Representative Directors of the English-Speaking Stage* (New York, 1991), p. 104.
9 Commentators seem to disagree on whether or not the director's comments were conciliatory or provocative. In reality it probably mattered little: by that stage Meyerhold's fate was sealed.
10 Laurence Senelick, *Gordon Craig's Moscow 'Hamlet'* (Westport, CT, 1982), p.185.
11 *Ibid.*, p. 185. The previous line in parenthesis is from Treplev's play in *The Seagull* (See Chapter 1).

3 | General Intendant

> LITTHENNER. The Boss wants to show that Coriolanus isn't indispensable.
> PODULLA. Singlehanded, he storms Corioli.
> LITTHENNER. *A military specialist…*
> LITTHENNER. Say what you please, the Boss has found his style again.
> PODULLA. Frayed leather and denim.
> LITTHENNER. The work clothes of *a military specialist…*
> BOSS. That's how I see him, artisan of battle,
> Blackmailing a nation until it believes
> No one can ever replace him, Coriolanus –
> Oh cult of personality! – Unless we
> Delete him. Do we really need him?
> (from Günter Grass, *The Plebeians Rehearse the Uprising: a German tragedy.* Act 1)

In *The Theatre Advancing* (1921) Gordon Craig complained – with some justification – that his ideas had influenced English theatre, but only after they had been adopted abroad and then reintroduced as 'foreign'. In particular this seemed to be true of the work of Max Reinhardt (1873-1943) some of whose productions were greatly inspired by Craig. Numerous Craigish elements, whether or not derived directly from him, were to be found in Reinhardt's pre-war productions and critics were not slow to pick them up. Reinhardt frequently, but without success, tried to lure Craig to direct for him. Of a 1911 London production of *King Oedipus*, in which Reinhardt acted as adviser, Craig wrote belligerently:

> The piece was lighted in a way, if not familiar at all, quite familiar to me. It was dressed differently from the usual productions, the movements were different from what we are used to, and all this done by Mr. Martin Harvey *because Professor Max Reinhardt had been enabled by his countrymen to test English ideas in Berlin*. (1921: 215-6; Craig's emphasis)

Undoubtedly Harley Granville-Barker was influenced by the German impresario, and, after the First World War, Tyrone Guthrie and many British directors were impressed by Reinhardt's spectacular productions of Shakespeare and other classics which aimed not only to remove the spectator completely from the realm of everyday, but also to involve the audience in a ritual of 'total theatre'. Guthrie recalled how profoundly he was affected by *Jedermann* (Everyman) at Salzburg unforgettably staged by Reinhardt on the steps of the Cathedral against its baroque west front (1963: 29). Reinhardt's conception of the Everyman production was grandiose in the true sense of the word. Craig and a few others in the modern theatre may have imagined theory of this scale but only Reinhardt dared to risk the presentation of full-scale ritual. In *Max Reinhardt and his Theatre* (1924), Hugo von Hofmannsthal wrote:

> He [Reinhardt] has learned much from Gordon Craig, that lonely pioneer, whose dream was to control the scene by means of changing light, and to create 'an ever shifting maze of colour, form and motion'. He learned much from him, but only in order to create out of what he learned something newer, more powerful, better suited to the practical theatre. (Sayler 1968: 22)

If this latter statement was true of Reinhardt, it was also applicable (but, as we shall see, in a different way) to that other towering figure among modern German directors: Bertolt Brecht (1898-1956).

Yet to appreciate the varied approaches of Reinhardt, Brecht and other German directors to Shakespeare some historical frame of reference is necessary. Indeed these instances of interaction, of cross-fertilization between German and British theatre were nothing new. This had been a recurring pattern from the sixteenth and seventeenth centuries when touring companies of the Englische Komödianten (English Comedians) brought contemporary Elizabethan drama to a land which, as yet, had little native drama of its own. For much of the seventeenth and eighteenth centuries, under the pressures of war and political upheaval, German theatre remained dormant, but by 1765 Gotthold Ephraim Lessing (1729-81) was praising Shakespeare 'as a writer who comes closer [than the French models] to the essence of Greek tragedy while disregarding its form, whose English temperament is more congenial to Germans, and who by being a natural genius is more apt to inspire similar geniuses in Germany'.[1]

With the emergence of such playwrights as Goethe and Schiller in the *Sturm und Drang* movement at the end of the eighteenth century, the effects of this prophesied influence are evident. It is worth noting that Shakespeare not only provided inspiration for many of these writers, but that their plays incorporated themes of social protest – a not irrelevant historical fact when we consider the political approach to Shakespeare of Bertolt Brecht. The *Stürmer und Dränger* owing to their disruption of 'regular' form and their rebellion against the conventions of society, were direct forerunners of Brecht's Epic theatre, 'although their wildly emotional titanism contradicts his cool rationality' (Bartram 1982: 14). Indeed, if Max Reinhardt's desire to escape the real political world, his passionate need to unify rather than divide, his love of acting and his regard for actors, find a ready focus in *A Midsummer Night's Dream*, then the work and achievement of Bertolt Brecht finds its fullest expression in the dark political tragedies (or black Oedipal comedies) of *Coriolanus* and *Hamlet*. This chapter will examine the younger, and more politically aware, of these two directors and will demonstrate ultimately that it is in the shifting persona of Hamlet, Prince of Denmark (Courtier, *Soldier,* Scholar) that the character of Brecht is best understood.

Brecht began directing in Berlin just at that time, shortly after the end of the 1914-18 war, when Reinhardt's productions were beginning to falter; to fail principally in catching the mood of political crisis and growing desperation. Reinhardt, as his early rift with co-director Vallentin showed, was not primarily a socialist, or even a politically minded director; for Brecht on the other hand, political considerations soon proved to be his central guiding mission in the theatre. In important respects the politically controversial director, Leopold Jessner, 'an estimable vandal' (schätzenswerter vandale) as Brecht called him, was a more immediate and potent influence. Also, being (like Craig) more abrasive than Reinhardt, Brecht's relationship with actors, especially as a young director, showed signs of strain. In his first production, of Arnolt Bronnen's *Vatermord* (Parricide), Brecht tried to prick the inflations of expressionism repeatedly bringing the actors back to a precise meaning of their lines. Despite the fact that several members of the cast (of the Junge Bühne) were older, well-established actors Brecht lost no time in challenging them:

> And in came this thin, rather undersized Augsburger and told them in dry, clearly articulated syllables that all their work was so much crap. There were fearful explosions. (Willett 1967: 143)

The young director's sarcastic comments led to several resignations and eventually another director Berthold Viertel took over. However, as both playwright and director in many of his later productions Brecht soon came to be in a position of formidable power; he could write new lines ('my lines') for an actor of whom he approved or remove them from one that gained his disfavour. Despite his revolutionary new ideas, Brecht in many ways fits into a pattern we have already observed. In an article on Gordon Craig published in 1955, Peter Brook wrote of how Brecht 'dragoons his actors eliminating every vestige of their own personalities'.[2] Brook saw this control 'in direct line from Craig'; but, also clearly, Brecht was reflecting an older German tradition stemming from the Meininger and even before that. Yet whereas Duke Georg had shown extreme deference to the words of the playwright, Brecht would insist, Hamlet-like, that the play must serve the political interests and purpose of its director.

In the early 1920s Brecht found himself writing and directing in the harsh, post-war Germany of depression, poverty and political extremism. In such an atmosphere it was impossible, Brecht felt, to remain neutral. While Reinhardt could escape (to Salzburg in Austria), Brecht reacted sharply against both what he saw as expressionist self indulgence on the one hand, and the escapism of merely spectacular theatre on the other. Under the compelling force of expressionist thinking naturalism in the theatre had been driven into full retreat; the trend was towards a theatre of non-illusion. Expressionism at first had spawned exciting new techniques such as the cinematic style of production, the quick changes, the clipped talk; but in time it had ceased to be a positive force for change: 'writers often used this freedom in order to pursue high-flying utopian or apocalyptic ideas ... Soon the new forms became blown out; incoherence and exaggeration started to rank as virtues' (Willett 1967: 107).

The desire to challenge boldly the audience in the face of impending political catastrophe in the real world led Brecht (following the Russian director, Meyerhold, and the German, Leopold Jessner) to develop forms of theatre which would shake the spectator in a new way. Meyerhold had set a radical pattern in the Soviet Union, and Jessner's *Hamlet* (1926) in Berlin caused fury by its subversive tones. In Jessner's production the character of Hamlet seemed less important than the political situation, that 'something is rotten in the state of Denmark'. Here was clearly reflected Germany's growing political crisis in which espionage, violence between Left and Right and political assassination were the order of the day. ('Kidnapping, murder, threats/Extortion, blackmail, massacre:/ "Hands Up!" "Your money or your life"' (*Arturo Ui;*1b)). Prussian militarism was suggested in the uniforms of the court where the actor playing Claudius resembled Kaiser Wilhelm II: something clearly was rotten in the state of the Weimar Republic.

Thus Brecht's eclecticism is evident. He was not shy in borrowing from numerous sources: among them contemporary cabaret, eighteenth-century German, as well as Elizabethan writers such as Shakespeare. The artist, he complained, is continuously hindered by an evident reticence in taking over unbiasedly the experimental results of another artist and improving on them. Forgery in art is considered a disgrace. 'Shakespeare?' Brecht retorted when challenged, 'He was a thief too ...' During the 1920s, with his collaborators, he developed a new kind of didactic play, 'Lehrstück' (Learning play). As well as the use of music and of the chorus to supplement and vivify the action on stage, it also used placards and projected titles to comment on the story. The purpose of these experiments was as much to raise the political awareness of the performers as it was to entertain or instruct an audience ('it was so to speak art for the producer, not art for the consumer'). But he realized that the two constituent elements of drama and theatre, entertainment and instruction, were in contradiction:

> The instructional elements of a Piscator production or of a production like my *Threepenny Opera* were, so to speak, installed; they did not result organically from the whole, they stood in opposition to the whole; they interrupted the flow of the play and its events, they thwarted sympathetic understanding, they were cold showers for those who wanted to sympathize. (Trans. Carl Mueller; Corrigan 1963: 100)

By about the age of thirty Brecht's transformation as a Marxist was complete. Thus, in 1932, when he directed *Die Mutter* (The Mother), the style was designed to induce in the spectator a critical attitude, raising political consciousness. Marx had warned about religion being the opium of the people. In this production sensing the parallels between religion and escapist theatre, Brecht was careful to keep 'well clear of the general drug traffic conducted by the bourgeois show business'. Given the seriousness of the political crisis and Brecht's determination to make the audience 'cast its vote', it is not surprising that the director should have been attracted not by the apparent escapism of the *Dream* but by the harsh political realities that lie behind such plays as *Measure for Measure*, or the tragedies of *Macbeth*, *Coriolanus* and *Hamlet*.

In fact, after his appointment to the innovative Munich theatre, Die Kammerspiele, the first production planned was to have been *Macbeth*. Whether or not Brecht was daunted by the prospect of a major Shakespearean production is unclear. Having failed with his first attempt at parricide, *Vatermord*, perhaps he found old father Shakespeare too intimidating a prospect. He might not have agreed with Mary McCarthy that 'General Macbeth' is the only Shakespeare hero who corresponds to a bourgeois type – although he might have agreed with Terry Eagleton that in Coriolanus we find 'Shakespeare's most developed study of a bourgeois individualist' (1986: 73). Crucially he may have felt that he would have a freer hand with a less established work. Whatever the reason, Brecht chose to direct, and, with Lion Feuchtwanger, to re-write Marlowe's *Edward II* (1924). By the time they had finished only about one sixth of the original lines remained. In his approach to this play Brecht was influenced by the determination of Jessner and others to make classical works relevant to the problems of society, even if this meant jettisoning reverential attitudes to writers such as Shakespeare. Although *Edward II* is not Shakespearean, in this context it is worth consideration for a number of reasons. Brecht obviously viewed Marlowe's play as representative of a wider Elizabethan drama of which Shakespeare was merely a part; its importance in establishing his approach to Shakespearean production generally is suggested by comments he made many years later: 'We wished to make possible a production which would break with the Shakespearean tradition common to German theatres: that lumpy monumental style which the Spiessbürger so love' (Willett 1967: 143).

Epic Theatre

The word 'philistines' – used in some translations for 'Spiessbürger' – suggests Brecht's combative, at times bellicose, tone; he had little patience with those who did not see the world divided into various camps. Increasingly during the late 1920s class war was central to his view of the world and of the theatre. *Edward II* is also important because it is in this production that, according to his own account, the seeds of Brecht's Epic theatre were planted. Brecht began to flesh out the term Epic for the first time in 1926. A new kind of clarity was sought in which the various elements of the story could be spelt out clearly to the audience. In the nineteenth-century German playwright, Georg Büchner (1813-37), and in the Elizabethans, he found the example of a loose sequence of scenes of great chronological and geographical scope. No doubt Shakespeare inspired Georg Büchner, but 'without [Georg] Büchner,' wrote George Steiner, 'there might have been no Brecht' (1961: 272). Impressed by Büchner's *Woyzeck* produced at Frankfurt in 1919, he had noted 'the short scenes, the terse dialogue, the folk songs and the sinister poetic atmosphere which they punctuate': all these pointed to a new loose method of telling a story which Brecht found to be used also by the great Elizabethans. Just as Jessner stressed the core idea underlying the play, so for Brecht *Die Fabel* (the story) was to be all important. But he argued:

> As we cannot invite the public to fling itself into the story as if it were a river, and let itself be swept vaguely to and fro, the individual events have to be knotted together in such a way that the knots are easily seen. The events must not succeed one another indistinguishably but must give us a chance to interpose our judgement. (Willett 1967: 153)

There was little attempt in the *Edward II* production at realistic setting: settings (by Brecht's school-friend Caspar Neher) were suggested through the use of significant objects: a room was a room, and a king's chair was a chair but the room and the chair were kept in the style of the old German masters. In the lengthy battle scene the exhaustion of the soldiers was indicated by – plainly an unrealistic but striking effect – covering the soldiers' faces with chalk. By such techniques the emerging, revolutionary new Epic theatre sought to make a point abundantly clear: in this case the fear and exhaustion of the soldiers

in battle. External gesture ('gestus'), by which characters clearly
defined their roles in society, thus, was more important than the
representation of inner psychological truth. By contrast in
traditional 'dramatic' or Aristotelian theatre the aim was to draw
the audience into some kind emotional identification with the
main characters and, as Brecht saw it, to a surrender of
objectivity and judgement. In Epic theatre the audience would
be forced to hold apart, to see the harsh realities with a new
'cold' clarity – thereby achieving *Verfremdung* (a term first used
in 1936) which means alienation, separation or 'making strange'.
This would be substituted for *pity* and *terror*, the twin-yoked
classical cause of Aristotle's catharsis.

Although it is quite possible to understand or utilize the
concept of 'alienation' or 'separation' without questioning its
origin, it is not unreasonable to ask why Brecht should have
been so concerned with this attempt to distance both actor and
audience from underlying emotions. 'Distance, dear God
distance!' wrote Ruth Berlau, one of Brecht's mistresses, 'Not
only as a director does he require distance, *but also in his private
life*' (Fuegi 1994: 303). Interestingly one finds in Brecht's formative years a perhaps significant pattern. In childhood Brecht
suffered ill-health which may have given him a certain affinity
with his frequently sick mother. The enforced separation
between mother and son caused by these periods of sickness,
Ronald Hayman suggests, may have had serious consequences
for the small child. As his mother's health deteriorated, her ab-
sences and indispositions may have inflicted psychological
damage on the already nervous boy. In the summer of 1908, for
example, he missed six weeks of school having contracted a
facial twitch. He was sent to recover in Bad Dürrheim, though
his mother's illness was already straining his father's financial
resources (Hayman 1983: 8). The periods of absence, during
which he was sent away, or while his mother was in hospital,
may have led to Bertolt developing strategies for coping with
the extreme emotional pain of separation. Thus the psychological basis of Brecht's 'alienation' – with coolly removing
oneself from external involvement, with distancing oneself
from pain – may indeed have its source in his childhood

experiences of 'being apart'. While removing oneself enabled one to get a grip on life, allowed 'reason to rule', it left at times an unnatural emotional vacuum. In November 1927 Brecht wrote that the essential point of the Epic theatre is perhaps that it appeals less to the feelings than to the spectator's reason. Instead of sharing an experience the spectator must come to grips with things. At the same time, he believed, it would be quite wrong to deny emotion to this kind of theatre. In his essay, 'Alienation Effects in Chinese Acting', Brecht noted: 'That does not mean that the Chinese theatre rejects all representation of feelings. The performer portrays incidents of utmost passion, but without his delivery becoming heated ... The coldness comes from the actor's holding himself remote from the character portrayed' (Willett 1974: 93).

It is remarkable how often in developing his theory of the theatre Brecht uses the image of the small child. In his poetry the word 'Bébé' – referring to himself – is a recurring one. Modern psychoanalysis speaks of the child's terror in the face of its mother's threatened desertion and, thus, it is not altogether naive to suggest that Brecht's, at times obsessive, rejection of 'terror and pity' has something to do with his own early plight. Writing in notes to one of the first plays of his maturity *Die Mutter* (The Mother, 1932), Brecht refers to it as anti-metaphysical, materialistic, anti-Aristotelian drama. This, he explains, makes nothing like such a free use as does the Aristotelian of the passive empathy of the spectator; it also relates differently to certain psychological effects, such as catharsis. 'Just as *it refrains from handing its hero over to the world as if it were his inescapable fate*, so it would not dream of handing the spectator over to an inspiring theatrical experience.' In Brecht's *Galileo*, The Inquisitor (the inflicter of pain?) lectures Virginia (Galileo's daughter) on the new and old conceptions of the universe:

> Nice and roomy, but not large enough for innovators. Apparently they feel that it is unimaginably far-flung and that the [mother?] earth's distance from the sun [German 'Sonne'/'Sohn' (Son)] – *quite a respectable distance, we always found it* – is so minute compared with its distance from the fixed stars on the outermost sphere that our calculations can

simply ignore it. So who can say that the innovators themselves aren't living on a very grand scale? (*Virginia laughs. So
does the Inquisitor* (trans. Willett 1980: 62-3))

Perhaps in all this some caution is required. It is, as Galileo
himself would say: 'A hypothesis ... nothing contradicts it'
(trans. Brenton 1980: 11).

Due to its varied meanings and associations some critics
have questioned the use of the term Epic to describe Brecht's
kind of writing and production. Eric Bentley prefers 'Narrative
Realism',[3] and for Raymond Williams the alternative term
'open' theatre is in some ways preferable to Epic. Essentially,
what Brecht created, after long experiment, was a dramatic
form in which men were shown in the process of producing
themselves and their situations. 'This is, at root, a dialectical
form, drawing directly on a Marxist theory of history in which,
within given limits, man makes himself' (1968: 279).

Apart from its unemotional – or, at least, 'cold and
passionate' – nature, Epic theatre involved a new economic and
social subject matter. And complementing these a new attitude
to playing was demanded from actors: this was 'playing from
memory', acting as it were in quotation marks and from fore-
knowledge without ever pretending, as in naturalistic drama,
that cast and director are unaware of what is to happen. Just as
in Joycean terms the artist stands aloof, like the God of the
creation, coldly separate from what he has created, so in the
new Epic theatre not only the audience but the actors
themselves were encouraged to stand, as it were 'apart,
indifferent, paring [their] finger-nails';[4] but at the same time the
actors were not uncommitted – coolly, ironically perhaps, they
would lead the audience to a new way of seeing the truth. For
its own part the audience in seeing the situations on stage
depicted in a new way *then* (based on their new understanding)
might become emotionally involved: they might, for example,
grow angry at some injustice which before that had not been
clear to them ('the anger that is a practical expression of sympathy with the underdog'). Thus a new art or critical capacity
would be required from the audience: Brecht referred to this as
'The Art of Being a Spectator' ('the setting forth of actions so

as to call for a critical approach, so that they would not be taken for granted by the spectator and would arouse him to think'). In his essay 'On the Experimental Theatre', Brecht explains (Corrigan 1963: 106-7):

> The principle consists in introducing in place of sympathetic understanding what we call *alienation*.
> What is alienation?
> To alienate an event or a character is simply to take what to the event or character is obvious, known, evident, and produce surprise and curiosity out of it. (Brecht's emphasis)

After Brecht's death Helene Weigel recalled how the director would beg the actors: 'please be careful to remember every point where you in reading was [*sic*] astonished what you read ... on this same point ... this was Brecht's opinion ... the audience will be astonished, and don't throw this point away. Please don't make theories [?] ... show it.'[5]

Brecht takes the example of Shakespeare's *King Lear* in illustrating the dynamics of this new kind of theatre:

> We are not concerned with simply making the spectator immune to the wrath of Lear. It is only that the direct trans-plantation of this wrath must be stopped. An example: The wrath of Lear is shared in by his faithful servant Kent. Kent soundly thrashes a servant of the thankless daughters, who is instructed to disobey one of Lear's wishes. Shall the spectator of our time share Lear's wrath and approve of it, while in essence sympathizing with the thrashing of the servant, carried out on Lear's orders? *The question is this: how can this scene be played so that the spectator, on the contrary, flies into a passion because of Lear's wrath?* Only an emotion of this kind which can deny the spectator sympathetic understanding ... can be socially justified. (Corrigan 1963: 105-6)

The spectator, in other words, in this alienated view of the action is to be made to see Lear's essential cruelty in allowing Kent to beat up a servant who is, in Brecht's view, merely obeying orders. Whether such a sympathetic interpretation of Oswald in King Lear is justified we may consider later, but for the moment this statement provides a clear idea of how Brecht hoped to refashion old classical works and thus: 'Through alienation it became possible to produce entertainingly and instructively the worthwhile old plays without disturbing elements of over-actualization and museum-like treatment' (*Ibid.* 109).

Prominent among 'the worthwhile old plays' were Elizabethan works; and to some extent Brecht undoubtedly looked to Shakespeare as a model for the new episodic or Epic type of theatre in which he was interested. Brecht was impatient and dismissive of contemporary productions of Shakespeare which played up 'the dramatic' rather than the Epic nature of his plays. As his comments about *Edward II* show he was determined to introduce a new style of Shakespearean production which could not fail to challenge the spectator. Thus there was to be a new emphasis on telling the story with stark clarity – something which contemporary productions in the 1920s failed to do because 'it is a long time since our theatres played these scenes for the events contained in them; they are played only for the outbursts of temperament which the events allow'.

Not surprisingly Brecht was critical of the 'romantic' productions of Max Reinhardt. Indeed in the same season that he directed *Edward II* at the Munich avant-garde theatre, Die Kammerspiele, he was engaged (for a season) on an irregular basis as a dramaturg (assistant) in Reinhardt's complex of theatres in Berlin. Brecht was annoyed at being denied a Shakespearean production but his rebellious attitude did not endear him to the theatre managers: he seldom turned up and when he did his appearance probably didn't help – 'with his flapping leather jacket he looked like a cross between a lorry driver and a Jesuit seminarist.' Moreover his desire to pull the levers of power is conveyed graphically in this description by Carl Zuckmayer:

> Roughly speaking, what he wanted was to take over complete control: the season's programme must be regulated entirely according to his theories, and the stage be re-christened 'epic smoke-theatre', it being his view that people might actually be disposed to think if they were allowed to smoke at the same time. As this was refused him he confined himself to coming and drawing his pay. (Willett 1967: 145)

As a young man Brecht enjoyed depicting himself as a bohemian rebel, even as evil. His first play, *Baal*, was a kind of portrait of the artist as a young man. That this was all part of a rebellion against prevailing values, the values of his parents, is best illustrated in one occasion when Brecht lost his father's suitcase on a train. When his father remonstrated with him, Brecht, defiantly unrepentant, replied: 'First, you could have done the same thing yourself; second, I hope you never get it back; third, I hope the new owner of the things needs them more than you did, and fourth, you can easily get new things.' Brecht's father, comments Ronald Hayman, like his schoolteachers often inflamed his anti-conformism (1983: 33).

As his career gathered momentum during the late 1920s and early 1930s with a succession of successful plays and productions, this youthful powerless state gave way to a position of increasing authority in the German theatre and elsewhere. This was the fulfilment of an early urge to dominate and a sense that he knew best. As a boy 'his nature was always to boss others about, to impose his will on them'. In playing games, according to his brother Walter, 'we positioned the figures exactly according to Eugen's [Bertolt's] battle plans. He was the only one to control the game, whether as Napoleon or Frederick the Great. We were his generals and did what he told us' (Hayman 1983: 7-8). And this was a pattern – in which others followed the 'battle plans' drawn up by Bertolt – that repeated itself throughout his life. This was especially the case in the post-World War II generation of young intellectual directors amongst whom there were minds ready to be influenced. A German director, Jürgen Flimm, expressed with clarity how that influence was often felt: 'Brecht taught us that the producer [director] must take his [her] work very seriously – alter texts, comprehend them politically, take an extreme position; *he must appear in the production*' (Rouse 1989: 171).

In England the influence of the new thinking was evident in the work of Peter Brook during the early 1960s. Brook's staging of *King Lear* (1962) reflected the alienation techniques which Brecht urged in the quotation we have considered. In the later film version of Brook's *Lear* (1970), the knights return from hunting (I.iv) like a marauding army. The audience is drawn into feeling an unexpected regard for Goneril (Brecht's 'thankless' daughter) whose house has been invaded by this mob many of whom show little sense of domestic decorum. In this context Brecht's view that Oswald is the victim of one of Lear's henchmen seems quite credible. Those who saw the earlier stage version (described in a programme note as 'lucid and Brechtian') were aware that key lines and characters had been removed. Lines, for example such as Edmund's redeeming, 'Some good I mean to do,/ Despite of mine own nature' (V.iii.218-9) were deleted. Gloucester's blinding was made still more horrible by the removal of the good servant who protests at Cornwall's cruelty. Amidst the general acclaim, one French student expressed an underlying unease when he was heard to remark of Brook's production: '*Il a transformé Shakespeare en Brecht*' (Speaight 1973: 285).

While he was content to theorize about *King Lear* in 1939, Brecht had already written radio adaptations of both *Macbeth* (broadcast from Berlin; Oct.,1927) and *Hamlet* (broadcast from Berlin; Jan.,1931). Although Brecht began to adapt *Measure for Measure* for the Berlin Volksbühne in 1931, in its radically reshaped, anti-fascist form, it was not premièred until 1936 in Copenhagen. In fact the term 'première' for the new adaptation, *Round Heads and Pointed Heads,* is not quite correct – it was officially a rehearsal; but Brecht was later to say that this was the one truly Epic *performance* he had seen. The circumstances of the première were unusual because local pressure, as well as pressure from the Nazis, on the Danish authorities led to the play been banned in Copenhagen. Legally, however, the company was entitled to present a rehearsal but not a finished performance. Eric Bentley recalls how Brecht described this experience:

> How could we make a legally clear distinction between a rehearsal and a performance? 'Hm,' said one actor, 'in a performance you don't have a script in your hand: if you have a script in your hand, that makes it a rehearsal.' Actually, the actors had memorized their lines, but I sent them on stage that night with scripts in their hands. These

scripts got in the way of the action – constructively! Broke up the smooth lines. *Came between the lover and the shoulders he needed two hands to embrace. In other words brought about the Alienation Effect*, provided a more complex contour for the composition, added style. (1985: 64)

In subsequent evenings, this effect, however, was lost: 'Unfortunately, the actors learned to take the scripts in stride. Smoothed everything out. Returned to the performances they had been giving before the ban ... Such was my one evening of Epic Theatre!'

Brecht's *Coriolan*

In exile from (Nazi) Germany after 1933, until his return in the late forties, Brecht concentrated on writing rather than producing plays, although the première of his masterpiece, *Mother Courage*, was held in Zurich in 1941. In 1949 Eric Bentley, a pioneer translator, having returned from a visit to Germany, wrote: 'As far as I can discover, the one fresh style in German theatre today is that of Brecht. In other words, Brecht is important in German theatre now not simply because he is its only first-class playwright but also because his kind of theatre could be exactly the kind of corrective that is needed.' The corrective was needed to change the traditional baroque style of German theatre, represented in its final stage by Reinhardt – and then in a further unnatural chapter by the theatre of the Nazi period. Bentley concludes his essay on 'The Stagecraft of Brecht':

> It has even been suggested that Brecht will translate Shakespeare; perhaps he could not remake the German theatre, as he wishes to do, *without* translating Shakespeare, who is, after all, the leading German dramatist. Up to now Shakespeare has been the dramatist of German romanticism, which means that of late he has become a somewhat academic figure, a Walter Scott of the stage. Brecht would give us a very modern Shakespeare, doubtless; the hope would be that the modern style would contain more of the

original Elizabethan spirit than the romantic style did. (1953: 147,160; Bentley's emphasis)

The words, to a degree, were prophetic for much of Brecht's energies in the theatre between 1951 and 1953 was devoted to his most significant adaptation, that of Shakespeare's *Coriolanus* – and 'a large part of Brecht's initial *Coriolanus* adaptation was carried out through retranslation' (Rouse 1989: 173). Yet despite intensive research and preparation the production seemed ill-fated and was not performed until after the playwright's death. However the extraordinary political upheavals that coincided with the rehearsals for that production (together with Brecht's political view of the theatre) make a consideration of those and other contemporary events inevitable.

During the years of exile (1933-47) Brecht sought asylum in several countries but not in the Soviet Union, a fact that left him open to a snide comment similar to that once levelled at Bernard Shaw. Indeed Brecht's home was Germany, his spiritual home was Russia, but he lived (after July 1941) in the comfortable U.S.of A. Eventually the activities of H.U.A.C. – before which Brecht was called as an hostile witness in 1947 – made life far from comfortable. This, said Brecht, was history repeating itself: he had been thrown out of Europe by an *un-German* activities committee. After their hurried exit from 'the Land of the Free', Brecht and his wife, Helene Weigel, returned to the Soviet Sector of Berlin in 1948 at the height of the international crisis between East and West over the future of Berlin. The motives for his deciding to settle in this place at that sensitive time are disputed. Some see it as a gesture of support for the Communists and of his readiness to endorse very tough measures in the Communist struggle against the Capitalist states of the West. Others see it as a purely pragmatic move: as an artist he was being offered an experimental theatre and abundant funding, something he could not expect to be given in the West. But that Brecht was deeply suspicious of the East German authorities is confirmed by the care with which he ensured his own artistic independence. By 1950 he had acquired an Austrian passport (if we remember that Reinhardt 'escaped' to Salzburg in the 1920s from the political turmoil of Berlin, there is a certain irony in noting that Brecht negotiated this 'parachute' as part of a package in which he agreed to help revive the Salzburg festival). He placed the copyright for his work in the hands of a West German publisher (Peter Suhrkamp), retained a Swiss bank account, and even refused any binding contract – or salary – with his 'own' theatre company the 'Berliner Ensemble'. As Ronald Speirs noted (Bartram 1982: 176):

> There is an unpleasant discrepancy between the measures taken by Brecht to preserve a quite unusual degree of independence for himself in East Germany, and his irritation with other Germans, whose residence in the Soviet zone was *in*voluntary, for failing to share his view that 'ein befohlener Sozialismus besser ist als gar keiner' ('imposed socialism is better than none at all') (Speirs's emphasis)

There is ample evidence, in other words, that Brecht was happy to accord himself a highly privileged position denied to the ordinary citizens of the GDR. In 1954 after the riots of the previous year had left little doubt about popular dissatisfaction with the communist regime, Brecht opposed free elections on the grounds that the people were not politically mature enough to make the 'right' decision ('That will from them take / Their liberties, make them of no more voice / Than dogs that are as often beat for barking.' *Cor*.II.iii.214-6). No doubt he felt that to break open the locks of socialism would merely serve to bring in fascist or capitalist crows to peck the Marxist-Leninist eagles. He spurned their 'voices' in the full knowledge that he retained the vote himself. With his Austrian passport he could ensure a change of government (for himself) by leaving the country. As Günter Grass put it in his satirical *Plebeians* (Boss = Brecht):

> BOSS. And if it comes to nothing, I'll clear out.
> ERWIN. And if when Coriolanus first appears,
> The plebeians threaten: 'Then we'll emigrate,'
> Why couldn't Coriolanus mock the plebs
> By wishing them a rousing 'Bon Voyage'? (1966: 68)

Such facts might be considered irrelevant were it not for Brecht's deeply held – and frequently annunciated – views on the relationship between theatre and the politics of the real world.

It is here, too, that Brecht's interpretation of Shakespeare's *King Lear* is worth further consideration. In Brecht's alienated view of the action the audience's sympathy would be inverted or changed; in this instance towards a sense that Oswald had been wronged. Yet Shakespeare's insight into the workings of political power resists this interpretation. Despite the best efforts of Brook and others, Shakespeare's text seems to point to a more profound political truth; one which has survived the hazardous passage of the centuries remarkably well. By the time that Kent tackles Oswald (I.iv.84), Lear has surrendered his power and has only some minor vestiges of it left. The real power now lies with the two sisters (Goneril, Regan) and their husbands – unless one re-writes the play completely this is indisputable. Lear is both weak and vulnerable. As the Fool points out, Kent's defence of the old king is political folly:

> FOOL. (*to Kent*) Sirrah, you were best take my coxcomb.
> LEAR. Why, my boy?
> FOOL. Why? For taking one's part that's out of favour.
> (I.iv.96-8)

Oswald, in other words, in snubbing Lear does so from a position of strength knowing where the levers of real political power now lie. Lear may have been in his time a nasty, power-wielding tyrant but at this stage he had been reduced to an old man crawling unburthened toward death. Kicking a man, even an ex-tyrant, when he is down is not particularly brave. Although he mutters about '[taking it] again perforce' (I.v.39), increasingly Lear is anyone's political football: 'you base football player' (I.iv.84-5) Kent calls Oswald. The Fool (Shakespeare's, sometimes cruel, truth-teller) knows that Kent far from acting as the King's bully boy is taking a grave personal risk; as surely as he knows that his own life is in jeopardy every time he cracks a joke at Goneril's expense.

There is a significant connection between Brecht's own behaviour in East Germany and his vigorous defence of Oswald. Thus it is worth retracing the various steps that lead up to the incident(s) to which Brecht refers. Lear asks Oswald where Goneril is (I.iv.44) and Oswald brushes past Lear with the words 'So please you — (*Exit*)'. That is, so to speak, Insult Number One. Lear then sends a knight to 'call the clotpoll back'. The knight reports that Oswald has refused to come back saying in the roundest manner he would not. This is adding insult to injury because it shows how powerless Lear has become (Insult Number Two). Significantly, there is no suggestion in either of the two main texts of *Lear* that the old king is in a position to order Goneril's servant to return. Oswald, of course, does re-appear, but this is merely a way of rubbing the salt in the wound (You called, sir? I took my time in coming because really you are so inconsequential — Insult Number Three). Then comes the crunch:

> LEAR. O you, sir, you, come you hither, sir, who am I, sir?
> OSWALD. My lady's father. (I.iv.76-7)

This, in an even less coded form, is telling Lear how insignificant he has become — and, more importantly, where the true power lies. It is a deliberate insult (Number Four), this time delivered to Lear's face. If one were trying to defend Oswald one might describe him as a servant (an accomplice?) who believes in carrying out his mistress's instructions above and beyond the call of duty. Further, when Kent trips Oswald by the heels, he does not do so, as Brecht asserts, 'on Lear's orders'. Lear appears so pleasantly surprised that one of his servants has stood up for him that he rewards Kent from his purse. Put plainly, Oswald knows which side his bread is buttered on; Kent doesn't – or doesn't care because some other principle is involved. In fact Shakespeare frequently is concerned to explore this state of being 'out of favour'. Above all, he understands that those without power live a shadowy, twilight existence. In that shadow world their actions are easily construed as 'irrational' by a ruling discourse that perceives them as a threat. In age the characters of Lear and Hamlet differ by fifty years, or two generations. They differ too in that Lear, unlike Hamlet, has no compensating theatrical kingdom where with his professional actors he can make 'imaginary puissance'. But they have undeniably one quality in common: both live precariouly because each, in reality, is *not* king.

Such a clear political insight seems (at least temporarily) to have evaded Brecht who was prepared to lecture the common people of the GDR on their political immaturity. More interestingly Brecht seemed to know by some instinct which side *his* bread was buttered on. East side meant bread, butter *and* Jam. The proof of the pudding (drama), as Brecht was so fond of saying, is in the eating. Yet the fate of Brecht's own play, *The Life of Galileo,* itself reflected the truth with which Shakespeare is confronting the audience. One reason that the play was viewed with some suspicion by the East German authorities was because it referred to Galileo's conflict with 'the high-ups' (die Oberen) or 'die Obrigkeit', those in authority – without stipulating clearly (or clearly enough) that the authorities were fascist or capitalist (Bartram 1982: 185).

Why, then, try to rewrite a scene in a 'worthwhile old' play that still makes complete contemporary sense? There is something profoundly contemporaneous about Shakespeare's depiction of how power operates. As Jan Kott points out the most striking characteristic of Shakespearean tragedies is their historical universality. Shakespeare does not have to be modernized or brought up to date (1967: 162). It would not be difficult, of course, to expose areas of Shakespearean plotting that are hopelessly outdated, but Shakespeare's analysis of power remains chillingly relevant. Brecht's dictum that the text 'is only as sacred as it is true' might serve, but here there is not much devotion to truth. In Brecht's analysis of *Lear* we find not insight but rather the distortions of another kind of power. In Brechtian theatre what matters is *the power of the director* to do what he wishes with the text, whether or not it needs amending to make it relevant to a contemporary audience. Brecht confirms this impression when he writes:

> Today we see the theatre being given absolute priority over the actual plays. The theatre apparatus's priority is a priority of means of production. This apparatus resists all conversion to other purposes, by taking any play it encounters and immediately changing it so that it no longer represents a foreign body within the apparatus. The theatre can stage anything; it theatres it all down. (Williams 1968: 280)

It is in the nature of tyranny that the tyrant can proclaim edicts and pass laws even when people around him can see that he is bending the truth and is quite misguided. Lear in the opening scene of the play is an example. Later in the play, Kent is not so much the servant of an old tyranny, as Oswald is the servant of a new tyranny – just as Brecht himself was soon to be the servant or *accomplice* of a new (political) tyranny in the GDR. 'Brecht would not have wanted to calculate,' comments Ronald Hayman, 'how many of the charges he had laid against the Third Reich could equally well be laid against the GDR' (1983: 373). There was, indeed, to be no shortage of *fear and suspicion* in the GDR.

Shakespeare explores the dynamics of power once again in *Coriolanus*. Caius Marcius's attempt to remove the plebeians' political rights is suggestive of the potential tyrant in action. The tribunes, the representatives of the people, are on strong ground when they accuse Caius Marcius:

> We charge you that you have contrived to take
> From Rome all seasoned office, and to wind
> Yourself into a power tyrannical,
> For which you are a traitor to the people. (III.iii.66-9)

This conflict, then, between those without power and 'the high-ups' (die Oberen), was also central to Brecht's most serious attempt to modernize Shakespeare: the (abortive) 1953 *Coriolanus* or *Coriolan*. Goethe believed that *Coriolanus* was one of three tragedies (the others: *Hamlet*, *Macbeth*) which give Shakespeare a place among the world's greatest dramatists (Boyd 1932: 52). Despite this recommendation the play itself has never been a popular one. Günter Grass who would write a play about Brecht's (imagined) meeting with the workers during the 1953 uprising describes it as 'this forever green, hence sour apple', and admits that when he wrote his play he had never seen *Coriolanus* performed on stage (1966: xiv). Jan Kott noting that the play is 'indeed, harsh and austere' goes on to suggest that this 'does not sufficiently explain the dislike almost universally felt for so long with regard to one of Shakespeare's most profound works' (1967: 142). It seems that the play offends both sides of the central argument that dominates the action. It offends those with democratic leanings by suggesting that Caius Marcius is in the end indispensable; it offends enthusiasts for autocratic leadership by painting Caius so unsympathetically that one must be repelled by his arrogance. 'It is his brutal outrightness,' points out Günter Grass, 'that sets him between plebeian and patrician and prevents him from arousing the faintest sympathy or applause in either a proletarian or a conservative audience.' As an actor who has played the part of Caius Marcius, Ian McKellen commented: 'I do not see that there is any way of playing that first scene, without having the whole of a modern audience think – O my God, is he going to go on like this all evening?'[6]

Precisely because of its 'epic' qualities Brecht may have been strongly attracted to the play. Jan Kott points out:

> *Coriolanus* is a far more emphatic, direct and modern model of the theatre Brecht called epic than Shakespeare's Histories. Mother Courage feeds on war, unaware to the end that it is the war that feeds on her and will take from her everything she has got. (1967: 153)

In true Epic theatre the audience would not, of course, sympathize with the sufferings of Mother Courage. Yet this intention was often not perceived by those who saw the play. George Steiner wrote: 'We cannot detach ourselves from the play and merely pass cool judgement on her faults. We too are hitched to the wagon, and it is beneath our feet that the stage turns' (1961: 348-9). And this element of sympathy, Steiner goes on to argue, is because 'in the duel between artist and dialectician, he [Brecht] allows the artist a narrow but constant margin of victory'. And Eric Bentley comments: 'Epic theory cannot always be taken literally. It does not even square with Brecht's practice. He does not eliminate stage-illusion and suspense; he only reduces their importance. Sympathy and identification with the characters are not eliminated; they are counterpoised by deliberate distancing' (1967: 219).

But how much identification was Brecht, in fact, prepared to welcome? Professor Hans Mayer, a long time associate and friend of Brecht, attended the Zurich performance in 1941 and noted that, not for the first time, Brecht was frustrated by how an audience had misinterpreted the play. The spectator, as Brecht had learned previously – when his *Threepenny Opera* succeeded for what to him were the wrong reasons – is the one element the dramatist cannot control. Between the Zurich performance in 1941 and 1949, when *Mother Courage* was staged in Berlin after his return, Brecht struggled to create a truly alienated hero: one who would repel any sympathy that the audience might feel. The first scene was changed to build up in the audience a dislike of Courage because she was prepared to sacrifice her children. And Helene Weigel's performance as Courage was near to Brecht's ideal. After watching her in a 1956 London performance of the play Kenneth Tynan noted how 'her performance is casual and ascetic; we are to observe but *not to embrace her*' (*Observer* 2/9/56). Seven years before that Eric Bentley reported how 'to a perceptible degree Miss Weigel stands outside the role and in a sense does not even look like Mother Courage. She is cool, relaxed and ironical. Yet with great precision of movement she imitates exactly what Mother Courage was like'. (Yet Bentley in his *Brecht Memoir* recalls how during the final scene of this 1949 production both he and many of the audience were in tears). Bentley continues:

> At the very least, Helene Weigel's performance is a lesson in the craft of acting which the German theatre ... very much needs. One would like to see this actress in Shakespeare. She might cleanse and renew Shakespeare for the Germans, as Barrault has been cleansing and renewing him for the French. (1953: 158)

After his experience with such plays as *The Threepenny Opera* and *Mother Courage*, no doubt Brecht was drawn to *Coriolanus* not least because its hero defies any attempt to make him 'sympathetic'. And *Coriolanus* is not only a play with an alienated hero; it is also a play in which the hero's desire to destroy his own home (city) is thwarted by the intervention of the Mother figure – in this case, Volumnia. She it is who prevents the destruction of Rome by wielding emotional power over her son (Similarly, Gertrude in *Hamlet* plays a blocking or screening role (III.iv.3)). In Brecht's version the argument Volumnia uses is, in essence, that the role of the individual can no longer hold back the tide of 'social progress'. Yet even without this change the play, as Jan Kott reminds us, is profoundly modern: 'But the history that breaks Coriolanus is not royal history any more ... It is the history of class struggle ... History in *Coriolanus* has ceased to be demonic. It is only ironic and tragic. This is another reason why *Coriolanus* is a modern play' (1967: 147).

Due to lavish state funding Brecht, Weigel and others in the ensemble were able to plan the Shakespeare production with an enviable time scale. When one considers the combination of Brechtian innovation with the meticulous and painstaking preparation for *Coriolan* in the early 1950s, it is understandable why Peter Brook was later to describe the Berliner Ensemble as 'the best company in the world' (1988: 54). By contrast with some of his earlier adaptations of Shakespeare, Brecht's version kept close to the original. Only in one or two aspects was the play changed. In *Coriolan* he wanted the audience to side with the tribunes when they advise the people to fight for Rome. This is a just war which may help spread democracy. And it is the rise of democracy that has robbed Coriolan of grounds for believing himself to be indispensable. Unlike Shakespeare's Volumnia, Brecht's dissuades her son from attacking Rome by arguing that history is moving against him: in comparison with the many, the one no longer matters (Hayman 1983: 357). Much of the text (unusually) was respected and the play fine-toothcombed to establish the precise chain of events. In a tetra-logue (entitled 'Study of the First Scene of Shakespeare's *Coriolanus*') the relative merits of Brecht's proposed changes are weighed against the strength of Shakespeare's plot – and, as the following extract shows, Brecht's appreciation of that strength:

> P. The play makes their revolt come at an unfortunate moment. In the crisis following the enemy's approach the patricians can seize the reins once more.
> B. And the granting of People's Tribunes?
> P. Was not really necessary.
> R. Left alone, the Tribunes hope that the war, instead of leading to Marcius's promotion, will devour him, or make him fall out with the Senate.
> P. The end of the scene is a little unsatisfactory.
> B. In Shakespeare, you mean?
> R. Possibly.
> B. We'll note that sense of discomfort. But Shakespeare presumably thinks that war weakens the plebeians' position, and that seems to me splendidly realistic. Lovely stuff.
> R. The wealth of events in a single short scene. Compare today's plays, with their poverty of content!
> (Willett 1974: 254-5)

Brecht here is attempting to record his preliminary discussions with his assistants but as Günter Grass noted: 'In places the result has an involuntary humour, because – though cast in four parts – it is always Brecht, or someone very much like him, who is talking' (1966: xxxii). The most important actor, it seems, is the Hamlet director: Brecht.

In 1953 while rehearsals for this production were still underway, public discontent exploded in riots throughout East Germany; they were, however, particularly serious in the Soviet Sector of Berlin. The vehemence of this social upheaval seems to have surprised Brecht who was cushioned by his celebrity status from the harsh realities of life in the GDR. In fact between 1949 and 1953 Brecht seems to have expressed little interest in the welfare of the ordinary people. Brecht's plays would earn him the reputation of being a champion of the man in the street, sympathetic to his 'low' preoccupation with satisfying his appetites. It is surprising, then, as Ronald Speirs observes, that neither Brecht's public statements nor his private ones during his years in the GDR contain much evidence of concern for the problems of ordinary working people there (Bartram 1982: 177).

The main grievances of the rioters concerned increased work norms, lack of food and curtailment of political rights, including the refusal to hold free elections. The explosive mixture of food shortages, increased work load and a sense that those in authority were indifferent to the sufferings of ordinary people led to widespread civil unrest:

> Care for us? True, indeed! They ne'er cared for us yet: suffer us to famish, and their storehouses crammed with grain. (*Cor*.I.i.77-9)

Before we consider Brecht's response to these riots, it is worth recalling a key element in his theory of Epic theatre: that things are changing and that they are changeable. As Helene Weigel explained in a (previously cited) filmed interview:

> I think people are intelligent ... and looking at plays who [*sic*] are intelligent they understand them and understand too that it is not destiny, deity or kings that have the absolute power to change their life. Looking at small people like we do ... like we play them in our theatre. Maybe they learn a little bit to behave like thinking human beings.

One of Brecht's successors at the Berliner Ensemble, Carl Weber, explained the new approach to dramatic staging as:

> something that can be watched, can be judged and could be changed if the people on stage, in a given situation, would behave otherwise, for instance, as they behave in the play. And the audience should be able to make this judgement and to see the possibilities of a changement [*sic*] of the given situation (*Ibid.*).

Brecht's great anti-fascist play about the rise of Adolf Hitler was called *The Resistible Rise of Arturo Ui* (*Der aufhaltsame Aufstieg des Arturo Ui*). The word 'unaufhaltsame' (irresistible) exists in German; 'aufhaltsame' (resistible) does not. By coining a new word Brecht was showing that things can be changed; above all that oppression can be opposed: there is nothing inevitable in the progress of a totalitarian dictatorship (or, for that matter, in the creeping paralysis of a Stasi-dominated police state).

> Therefore learn how to see and not to gape.
> To act instead of talking all day long. (*Arturo Ui*. Epilogue)

This theory of Epic theatre accorded well with the opening scene of *Coriolanus* where the plebeians demand – and achieve – change. New political rights are granted in the form of the tribunes of the people.

Given the nature of the play being rehearsed, and also Brecht's frequently stated theories about theatre for change, the workers might well have expected more enthusiastic expressions of support from Brecht's Ensemble. The director was evasive and contented himself with studying this working class clash with authority. Günter Grass's play *The Plebeians Rehearse the Uprising* (*Die Plebejer proben den Aufstand*) explores these extraordinary events in which drama and real life seemed to meet in a head-on collision. It might have been easier for Brecht to adopt his not unusual evasive stance were it not for one obvious fact: the events in the play he was adapting mirrored uncannily the events on the streets outside.

When the riots first started, Brecht consulted with others in the Ensemble and then sent a cautious telegram of support to the government. This gave implicit support to intervention, if required, by Soviet tanks. Brecht, in fact, had little faith in the will of the people in such circumstances. He suspected, or at least gave the excuse, that fascist elements and Western provocateurs were responsible. Like Caius Marcius, Brecht preferred a kind of dictatorship (in this case Marxist 'of the proletariat' variety) to the will of the common people, who could not be trusted to make enlightened (i.e. Marxist- Leninist) decisions:

> Hang ye! Trust ye?
> With every minute you do change a mind,
> And call him noble that was now your hate,
> Him vile that was your garland. (*Cor.* I.i.179-82)

In refusing to countenance their demands Brecht was adamant. His loyalty lay first with the government and the 'storm troopers' of socialism. Despite the fact that his own plays *The Mother* and *The Days of the Commune* suggested the spontaneous revolutionary potential of workers such an 'unprincipled' uprising could never win his support:

> 'Sdeath,
> The rabble should have first unroofed the city
> Ere so prevailed with me! (*Cor.* I.i.215-7)

But for the workers of East Berlin, Brecht's refusal to support them must have seemed like betrayal ('He's vengeance proud and loves not the common people' (II.ii.5)). Many might have seen him as Jan Kott sees Caius Marcius: just an ambitious general, who hates the people and has gone over to the enemy camp when unable to achieve dictatorial power (1967: 164). In *Plebeians* Grass, with considerable irony, has his 'Volumnia' say to 'the Boss' (i.e. Brecht): 'Every mechanic, mason, carpenter/ Will call you traitor if you don't bestir yourself' (47).

However this comparison between the fictional general, Caius, and the factual director, Bertolt, can only be taken so far. One contrast above all others stands out. Seemingly there is nothing very complicated about Caius. In him a patrician arrogance is combined with unlimited amounts of personal courage and integrity of a fierce and uncompromising kind. 'Ruthlessly self-consistent and self-identical, Coriolanus is as superbly assured in his inward being *as Hamlet is shattered in his*' (Eagleton 1986: 73). As for any mystery in his private life, even the plebeians in the first scene know that he has a hang-up about his mother:

> 'He did it to please his mother, and to be partly proud.'
> (*Cor.*I.i.37)

With Caius, in other words, what you see is what you get; with Brecht that is rarely, if ever, the case. Even more than the mercurial Reinhardt, Brecht is a dialectical entity and the con-tradictions in his personality make him extremely difficult to fathom. Because Brecht did not believe in an inner reality, a higher reality, or a deeper reality, but simply in reality, he presented on stage the solid things of this world in all their solidity and with all the appreciation of their corporeality found in certain painters – 'Brueghel,' says Eric Bentley, 'is the painter from whom Brecht has learned most' (1953: 150). And like the figures in a painting, or the parts of a machine, Brecht believed human beings could be made and re-made at will. 'In a universe where people, including himself, were interchangeable with fictions, trying to find a real person with real opinions and real affections within his unending metamorphoses was an imposs-ible task' (Fuegi 1994: 357).

> We'll take a man to pieces like a machine.
> And how much will he lose? Not a bean. (Haym. 1983: 106)

Like the God Janus (like Hamlet himself), Brecht simultan-eously faces in opposite directions – the Brechtian smile is a warning: he is enjoying our confusion. On the one hand is the international socialist, the defender of Stalin's Moscow 'Show' trials, and the man who, implicitly at least, supports vigorous measures to suppress a popular uprising; above all the director who spurns the voices of the common man when they seek some sympathetic identification with him. Like Caius he imi-tates their 'voices' and like Caius he is vulnerable to a certain accusation:

> You speak o'th' people as if you were a god
> To punish, not a man of their infirmity. (*Cor.* III.i.85-6)

On the other hand is the sensitive artist, the humanitarian who deplores the sufferings of humanity and above all the director who, in his later years, it is claimed, adopted a con-sciously democratic form of theatre. As Edward Braun implies, in his maturity Brecht *affected* an open style: 'Now that he saw his method as finalized: as numerous accounts testify, each production continued to be a learning process, with Brecht seeming (*or affecting*) to know less about the script than anyone, and with suggestions welcome from any quarter artistic or otherwise' (1982: 178). One notes that the word 'production' is used here, not 'rehearsal'. Eric Bentley who watched Brecht direct Frau Therese Giehse as Courage in 1950 at the Kammer-spiele puts the word 'democracy' in a different context:

> A whole morning was spent on this: getting her up, sitting her down, changing the cues on which she does this or that. An American director would undoubtedly have consulted her along the way. *Brecht was the European dictator-direct in that he didn't consult actors.* Frau Giehse was of course free to tell him anything that was on her mind at lunch afterwards, *but he did not allow discussions during rehearsal.* (It was at lunch that I asked Frau Giehse if she always allowed her director to push her around as Brecht had done in preparing the end of the capitulation scene. 'Only if he's a genius,' she replied). If an actor wanted to try out an idea, he could say so *before* the rehearsal started, and Brecht would say: 'Don't explain, don't justify, but by all means show me. Show me right now'. And he was often happy to accept an idea that was entirely the actor's own. (1985: 69)

Along with his support for the GDR authorities during the 1953 disturbances, Brecht also offered some (no doubt unwelcome) advice to the regime: not only the people but the government, too, must learn from its mistakes. When the 'hard-line' Stalinist Kugar wrote of how disappointed the govern-ment was in the people, Brecht replied sarcastically that, in that case, perhaps a new people should be elected. But Brecht's ambivalence is a factor even in this apparently critical state-ment. It was, of course, calculated to irritate his Stalinist critics in the regime – and thus provide some token resistance – but it also incorporated Brecht's fundamental distaste for represent-ative democracy. Until the debris of the old ideologies, whether Nazi or Bourgeois, was cleared away, the people could not be trusted or given a vote: in other words a new people *was* needed to replace the 'uneducated' people of the GDR.

> What's the matter, you dissentious rogues,
> That, rubbing the poor itch of your opinion,
> Make yourselves scabs? (*Cor.*I.i.161-3)

A reviewer of the published Journals (1934-55) noted that Brecht obviously had a contempt for anyone who did not share his political point of view.[7]

Apart from these ideological reasons, Brecht had strong personal motives for not opposing too openly or vigorously the government of the GDR. His theatre and its future depended on his retaining the good-will of the government:

> PLASTERER. Go on! The government's building him a new theatre.
> ROAD WORKER. That's why he won't do anything for us.
> MASON. They're all the same. Bigshots! They're all the same. What are we waiting for? *He starts to leave.*
> (Grass 1966: 32)

This relationship was already under some strain because Brecht's Epic theatre did not please the GDR authorities; they preferred the Stanislavsky school of social realism. Apart from his comfortable lifestyle, crucially perhaps, the women in his life – his wife Helene Weigel and (chief) mistress Ruth Berlau – were more inclined to total support for the Stalinist regime. If Brecht was 99% Communist, 'the women in his life,' commented Eric Bentley, were '101%. It was Stalinist Communism I was talking about' (1985: 77).

The 'hardships' of Brecht's new lifestyle in the GDR are graphically conveyed in this quotation:

> When the curtain came down on this wondrous piece of modern theatre, Brecht had left, so I went to Weigel's dressing-room and later walked her home, 'home' at the time being the Hotel Adlon. Another Brechtian situation! The Adlon had been the Waldorf Astoria of Berlin. Now most of it was rubble but a surviving section housed the Brechts, and housed them in the Brechtian lifestyle: a big room for Weigel and Brecht here, and just down the hall, Ruth Berlau's smaller room. (Bentley 1985: 61)

Not long after the suppression of the workers' riots privately he triumphed in dispossessing Harich (an academic acquaintance) of his pretty wife, Isot Kilian, an actress of small parts for the Ensemble. 'Divorce her now,' was Brecht's advice. 'You can

marry her again in about two years' time.' That Brecht's autocratic control extended beyond the rehearsal chamber is indisputable. Weigel, meanwhile, went on behaving with enormous
tact and self-restraint, protecting the interests of her husband
and her company. When a visiting Pole, a potential assistant,
Konrad Swinarski started to flirt with Isot Kilian, Weigel took
him aside to explain that it upset Brecht if other men paid too
much attention to women he loved (Hayman 1983: 376). Apart
from Brecht's primitive need to dominate exclusively 'the
females of the herd', one notes here that Weigel's role is an
almost maternal one. Perhaps because of his own mother's
vacillating nature, Brecht early came to the conclusion that he
knew best and could control all femininity. As a young child
watching cows being milked he had insisted that the cowmaid's
technique was misdirected: 'Just pull the stopper out of the cow
and then the milk will come out by itself' (*Ibid.* 13).

For a man suffering now increasing ill-health, at the end of a
life full of dislocation and exile, such considerations (as comfort
and the approval of 'his' women) may have been enough to
silence any qualms of conscience. The *Journals* confirm that
Brecht was deeply disturbed by the workers' uprising of 17 June
1953 in which life was challenging his artistic integrity as never
before. After two months of apparently stunned silence he
finally wrote an entry on 20 August which began: 'June 17th has
alienated the whole of existence' (the editors take this to mean:
turned his world upside down). And of the workers he had
failed so miserably to support: 'Despite their pathetic helplessness and lack of direction ... this is the rising class...' [8] Certainly
one question received a decisive answer on that day in June
1953 (Galileo's): 'I see your people's divine patience, but where
is their divine anger?' (trans. Willett 1980: 68).

Even at the end of a life a man may be forced to tie up
emotionally the loose ends of his youth. The reasons for
Brecht's discomfiture may, in this case, have been particularly
deep-seated. For just as the events in the streets of Berlin
reflected the conflicts in the opening scene of *Coriolan*, so also
in the play's conclusion – when Caius turns away from the gates
of Rome – there was a perhaps even more crucial parallel but

one which was more psychological and personal than political. Ernst Schumacher, a Marxist and disciple of Brecht, may (perhaps unwittingly) have been hinting at this when he spoke at a 1988 conference on Shakespeare. He suggested that Brecht disliked the treatment of the people by Shakespeare, and the respect for Coriolanus, a very, very weak man. And so he changed the play to make the proletariat speak more simply and naturally, like Bolshevik communists. It was not very convincing. Much more convincing, Schumacher believed, is the change at the end of *Coriolanus*, where he is given the information that the people of Rome are against him (Elsom 1989: 144-5). It is Volumnia who convinces the 'very, very weak man' that he must not destroy his own home. And in Brecht's version the argument she uses is that the individual, whatever his personal feelings, cannot be allowed to stand in the way of the 'progressive' (i.e. communist) forces. The 'progressive' institution must triumph, if necessary, at the expense of the individual. When Peter Brook saw Brecht's *Coriolan*, adapted by the Berliner Ensemble in the mid-1960s, he wrote, 'In most respects, this version was a triumph'. Yet 'a tiny defect' (the latter of the two changes to which Schumacher refers) became for Brook, 'a deep, interesting flaw'. Further: 'Without the clash of the two protagonists in its most intense form, the story remains castrated. When we leave the theatre we carry a less insistent memory with us. The force of the scene between Coriolanus and his mother depends on just those elements that do not necessarily make complete sense' (1968: 91-3). Günter Grass could hear Helene Weigel pronouncing the adapted text and condemning her son:

> VOLUMNIA. Enough of childish mawkishness, know
> That you are marching on a very different Rome
> From the one you left. You are no longer
> Indispensable; you're nothing but
> A mortal peril for all. Wait not for the smoke
> Of submission! If you see smoke now
> It will arise from smithies forging
> Swords against you.

And Grass continues: 'Having written off her son, she brusquely leaves the stage with the other women. Even in Plutarch there is no such strait-laced coldness. Shakespeare follows him in allowing his hero to drink a last cup of kindness with the ladies' (1966: xxx).

It was a role for which Weigel was eminently suited. As director of the Berliner Ensemble, she revealed strong leadership qualities and formidable will power. Allied to this was Weigel's capacity for not only playing a maternal role in Brecht's life, frequently ensuring that he had some friendly breasts to lean on, but also on stage achieving, perhaps uniquely, the distance that Brecht was seeking for his 'mother'. And Caius Marcius's ultimate weakness in the face of Volumnia's persuasion finds now a new resonance. That Helene Weigel was influential with Brecht is undoubtedly true: although he tried with her to keep private and professional concerns apart, she it was, after the events of June 1953, who finally persuaded him to sign a very open-ended contract with the Berliner Ensemble (and thereby helped to ensure the future of this 'home'):

> You have won a happy victory to Rome;
> But for your son, believe it, O believe it,
> Most dangerously you have with him prevailed.
> (*Cor.* V.iii.187-9)

Brecht and Weigel's support for the regime was rewarded the following year when the Berliner Ensemble took up permanent quarters in the Theatre am Schiffbauerdamm (Again a touch of irony: this was the scene of Reinhardt's (1905) *Dream*). For her services to the state, in the same year, the government gave Weigel a prize and a cash sum of fifty thousand marks. 'It is probably true,' wrote Margaret Eddershaw, 'to say that without Weigel the Berliner Ensemble would not have happened.' (Bartram 1982: 138). Weigel who had dominated the stage with *The Mother*, Weigel who had alienated Mother Courage so brilliantly – so close to Brecht's dreams – had prevailed over Brecht's evasiveness and suspicion (i.e. she had encouraged him to side decisively with the government) and, in

so doing, had protected his 'home', this new 'Rome'
(Ensemble):

He did it to please his 'mother', and to be partly proud.

Inveigled or not ('Alone I did it. "Boy"!': V.vi.117), the whole
subject of the relationship between theatre and the real world
was increasingly to be an uncomfortable one. Before the
Coriolan rehearsals began in earnest Brecht suggested to Otto
Grotewohl (who had won favour by betraying his own SPD
party to the Communists) that had Grotewohl not been
Minister President he would have wanted to employ him as
chief Dramaturg at the Ensemble.

VANNI. I'm not sure you're good at distinguishing your
friends from your enemies, Mr. Galilei.
GALILEO. I can distinguish power from impotence. (*He
goes off brusquely*) (trans. Willett 1980: 88)

In years to come this naked pandering to authority proved
embarrassing. Eric Bentley recounts how in 1956 shortly before
Brecht's death he met the director (1985: 86-7). Brecht must
have sensed that Bentley wanted to discuss the Twentieth
Communist Party congress in Moscow at which Khrushchev
had recently 'told all' about Stalin. Brecht avoided the subject
for he was – like the new Soviet leader – ultimately open to an
obvious criticism: although he had (secretly) expressed reservations about Stalin, he had consistently co-operated with the
Soviet hegemony. Brecht in the period after the 1939-45 war
had effectively entered the service of the new Russian
imperialism – 'socialism' imposed on non-Russian territory by
the Red Army. Years before at the Fourteenth Communist
Party Congress, Khrushchev had played a supporting role in the
dictator's rise to power. The Congress was the first to reflect
Stalin's control of the Party organization, and one of his
opponents later called it 'a well rehearsed play, acted just as its
producer (Stalin) had planned over several years'. There is no
reason to suppose that Khrushchev, with only the humblest of
walk-on-parts, was dissatisfied with the play.⁹ Like Khrushchev,
during the Stalin years, Brecht had played a walk-on-part and

the subject in 1956 must have been a sensitive one. Having supped with the Devil (in various forms) all his life, Brecht was finally discovering that the spoon could never be long enough:

> Doesn't he make you think of Richard the Third?
> Has anybody ever heard
> Of blood so ghoulishly and lavishly shed
> Since wars were fought for roses white and red?
> (*Arturo Ui*. Act I)

While the harsh political truths of *Coriolanus* are undeniable, it was George Bernard Shaw who described the play as the greatest of Shakespeare's Comedies.[10] In that description there may be a clue to the Brechtian Oedipal enigma. Eric Bentley was perhaps close to the mark when he suggested that, in the last analysis, Brecht's view of the theatre is a comic one. (Hamlet, says Harold Bloom, is 'a nonstop joker' (1999: 390)). Writing of the sufferings of Galileo, Brecht noted the audience's sympathy for his sufferings: 'The spectator says that's extraordinary, hardly believable, its got to stop. The sufferings of this man appal me ... because they're unnecessary.' But Brecht adds: 'I laugh when they weep, I weep when they laugh.' If life is a comedy to one who thinks and a tragedy to one who feels, then as Bentley argues, Brecht's theory of theatre *is* a theory of comedy. Yet more than a long spoon one would need a very long lens of philosophical detachment to laugh at some of Brecht's chilling pronouncements. 'The more innocent they are,' he said to a friend concerning the victims of Stalin's Moscow Show trials, 'the more they deserved to die' (Bentley 1985: 78).

> The gods look down, and this unnatural scene
> They laugh at. (*Cor.* V.iii.185-6)

Just as in Yeatsian drama there is a moment ('Character isolated by a deed ...') which seems to define the hero so, in a sense, the workers' uprising of 17 June 1953 is surely the defining moment in Brecht's life. And, as Günter Grass showed with devastating effect, for once Brecht was caught completely in his own dialectic: there was such a glaring discrepancy between (theatrical) theory and (political) practice – Brecht's plebeians are victorious but Brecht had no intention of helping the construction workers of Stalin-Allee to their victory – that here no evasion, no witticism could serve to extricate him. And where now was 'the anger that is a practical expression of sympathy with the underdog'? In that moment Brecht's alienated chickens came home to roost.

It was right, of course, to argue that sympathy in the theatre is not enough; the old theatre could justifiably be challenged. At a time of crisis the theatre must become more in relation to the real world than – as a contemporary poet put it of one of Reinhardt's glossy productions – 'an act, an act' (Braun 1982: 106). There is something fine, idealistic (in the best sense of the word) about the refreshing challenge in Brecht's vision of the role of theatre for change, 'the awareness that life could and should be otherwise' (Ryan 1989: 48):

> How can the theatre be both entertaining and instructive at the same time? How can it be drawn away from this intellectual narcotics-traffic and be changed from a place of illusion to a place of practical experience? How can the shackled, ignorant, freedom- and knowledge-seeking human of our century, the tormented and heroic, abused and ingenious, the changeable and the world-changing human being of this frightful and important century achieve his own theatre which will help him to master not only himself but also the world? (Corrigan 1963: 109-10)

What invalidates this vision is the small print that requires change only according to the limited parameters prescribed by Brecht and Weigel. Eric Bentley was branded an Enemy by Weigel after he had implied that what was right about Brecht was Brecht and what was wrong about Brecht was his Marxism (Bentley 1985: 39,77,79).

What sets Brecht fundamentally at odds with Shakespeare is not only the narrowness of the ideological basis for change; it is also Brecht's belief that 'cool' understanding can replace sympathy. Unlike Brecht no matter how objective his analysis, Shakespeare never seems to lose heart. No matter how harsh the reality, insight and compassion are mixed inseparably:

> Vex not his ghost. O, let him pass. He hates him
> That would upon the rack of this tough world
> Stretch him out longer. (*Lear* V.iii.289-91)

'All Shakespeare's characters', wrote J.H.R. Lenz in his
'Anmerkungen übers Theater' (Observations on the Theatre,
1771), 'feel warm blood beating in their hearts.' The Circus
Animals (Mother Courage, Galileo and the other brilliant
dramatic creations of his plays) may be all on show but there is
something amiss in Brecht's foul rag and bone shop of a heart.[11]
('Like the painting of a sorrow, a face without a heart?' *Hamlet*
IV, vii. 108-9; *Cor* I. Iii.12; also Wilde's *Dorian Gray*.) He
assumed multiple characters, suggests John Fuegi, and saw his
own life in stage terms, looking for the dénouement or noting
as a difficulty approached: 'the fourth act curtain is about to go
up' (1994: 84). It is little wonder that his earliest (KPD) communist critics accused him of being out of touch with the real
world.

Brecht in the Image of Hamlet

In truth Brecht failed ultimately to match the real political
world with the world of the theatre. He certainly demonstrated
that one cannot be a substitute for the other. In this there may
be the recognition of an unpalatable truth, a truth that emerges
particularly from Brecht's experience with *Coriolanus*: politics
influences the theatre profoundly but the theatre's effect on the
politics of the real world (except as a useful image) is often
minimal. The director in the theatre may be a despot but in the
political theatre of the real world he is lucky to have a 'walk-on-
part'. The profound irony of Grass's *Plebeians* is that no
delegation of workers rushed to Brecht's theatre looking for the
great dramatist's support. In the play, 'Volumnia' says: 'All want
your help, the rebels want it and/ The state as well. Ah! What
power, coveted /By all, sits in this modest easy chair' (1966:
57). In reality, as Grass points out in his preface, Brecht was
little more than 'a kind of privileged court jester' (xxxiv). In
Hamlet, Prince of directors, one finds a remarkably similar
pattern. Like 'the Boss' politically powerless, he finds his

meaning, his definition ('a king of infinite space'; II.ii.257), in the theatre; he empowers himself in the theatrical sphere: the Wooden O, the stage, becomes his world. In The Mousetrap, Hamlet, without difficulty, directs a regicide in which a nephew, Lucianus, kills his uncle (III.ii.232-52); assassinating Uncle Claudius in the Court of Elsinore proves to be a much more demanding – and fatally delayed – challenge.

Illustration 4 | Portraits of Shakespeare and Brecht

'If Brecht is probably the most important playwright in the British theatre since the war, Shakespeare is certainly the most important playwright in the German theatre since the Renaissance.' Ronald Hayman, *The German Theatre* (1975: 7)

Shakespeare fascinated Brecht. Although the frequent references are not always complimentary, it is to him that the German director in his writings refers more than any other individual. It is not surprising that, for a director who delighted in being many-faced, in Brecht one recognizes elements of a legion of Shakespearean characters. Yet should one attempt to describe him in terms of any of these, Brecht is elusive and defies definition. Instead of one portrait we discover a gallery. Certainly Hazlitt was prescient when he wrote: 'It is *we* who are Hamlet.' 'As the Boss,' write Waidson and Holmes, 'Brecht has now been mythologized as a central figure in German drama of some importance, where he may play *a role more akin to Hamlet's than to Coriolanus*' (Hayman 1975: 53). The alienation effect is not, as Hanif Kureishi has suggested (echoing George Lukács), a load of pretentious humbug (*Drama* 1984/2: 5), but rather some testimony to the human capacity for facing almost unbearable emotional pain. In it, however faintly, one detects the cry of a small heart-broken child. ('Thou boy of tears' *Cor.*V.vi.104). 'It is difficult to believe,' argues John Fuegi in what is surely a moment of considerable insight, 'he [Brecht] was himself without pain and terror as he clung privately to others while publicly posing as tough and self sufficient' (1994: 529). In a poem entitled 'The Writer Feels Himself Betrayed by a Friend', Brecht wrote:

> What the child feels, when its mother goes away with a strange man .
> What the airplane feels, if it felt at all, when its pilot steers it drunkenly. (*Ibid.*)

There is a recurring need in Brecht's writing to re-find the lost mother figure. In the 'Indirect Impact of the Epic Theatre' Brecht describes how Helene Weigel played the Mother in Die Mutter:

> The mother has to discuss her revolutionary work with her son under the enemy's nose: she deceives the prison warder by displaying what seems to him the moving, harmless attitude of the average mother. She encourages his own harmless sympathy. *So this example of a quite new and active kind*

of mother-love is herself exploiting her knowledge of the old familiar out-
of-date kind. The actress showed that the Mother is quite
aware of the humour of the situation. (Willett 1993: 59)

In 1929, three years before writing this, Brecht had, in fact,
married the actress Helene Weigel. 'Midway between the world
of Oedipus and that of Marx,' as George Steiner puts it, stands
Brecht (1961: 349).

Like Polonius, in his youth Brecht may have suffered much
extremity for love, and his attitude to the play *Hamlet* is revealing of his confusion and of his underlying psychological
motivation. In his *Organum* resumé of the play he had added a
dozen or sixteen lines – and more. As a translator Eric Bentley
protested at Brecht's recreation of Shakespeare's play. 'I am not
happy about it,' Bentley wrote to his German friend, 'because it
introduces a principle not explained in the text: the idea that
you can *change* the play and make it definitely different from
Shakespeare's … I have no objection to such re-creations –
provided that the result is NOT called an interpretation of
Shakespeare. Interpretation and adaptation are in principle
different things.' (Bentley's emphasis). But Brecht was intent on
playing Hamlet to Shakespeare's play. He maintained that
'Hamlet turns around when he sees and envies Fortinbras'
(Bentley 1985: 100). This certainly is not the case. He returns
later and for other reasons; but the alteration may be significant
for there was always something suspect about Brecht's
'pacifism'. And, at least in some deep psychological sense,
Brecht, perhaps, has a point: it is, after all, to Fortinbras, the
military dictator, that Hamlet (Courtier, *soldier*, scholar) finally
gives his vote (V.ii.308). In so doing, it might be argued, he
becomes a willing accomplice in the establishment of a new
military dictatorship. In his sonnet (c.1940) 'On Shakespeare's
play *Hamlet*', Brecht imagined Fortinbras's role in ending
Hamlet's hesitation, prompting him 'to turn to (bloody) deeds
instead':

So we can nod when the last Act is done
And they pronounce that he was of the stuff

To prove most royally, had he been put on.
(Willett 1976: 311)

Brecht also says, with even more glaring inaccuracy, that
Hamlet slaughtered his mother. Brecht felt guilty about his own
mother's death; he had distanced his love, keeping silent and
refusing to express his feelings. 'But if we damn ourselves with
silence,' wrote Ronald Hayman, 'her death was a milestone on
his road to hell' (1983: 56). In 1939 Brecht was to damn the
Finns – who feared a Nazi invasion – for 'keeping silent in two
languages'. But what he wrote about *Hamlet* on the same occasion might well serve as his own epitaph:

> Hamlet is simply an idealist who collides with the real world
> and gets knocked off course, an idealist who becomes a
> cynic. The question is not whether to act or not to act, but
> whether to keep silent or not keep silent, *to be an accomplice or
> not to be. (Ibid.* 245)

[1] See Ladislaus Lob, 'German Drama Before Brecht: From Neo-
Classicism to Expressionism', in *Brecht in Perspective*, ed. Graham
Bartram and Anthony Waine (London, 1982), p.13.
[2] Peter Brook, 'The Influence of Gordon Craig in Theory and
Practice', *Drama*, No. 173 (Dec.1989): 40.
[3] Eric Bentley, *In Search of Theater* (New York, 1954), p.138.
[4] James Joyce, *A Portrait of the Artist as a Young Man* (London, 1988),
p.219.
[5] 'Brecht on Stage,' BBC2 (TV), 15/9/93.
[6] Ian McKellen, 'Crunching Butterflies for Breakfast,' *Drama*, No.155
(Spring 1985): 22.
[7] Douglas Sealy, 'Day by Day by Brecht,' *Irish Times*, 23/10/93.
[8] *Brecht's Journals (1934-55)* trans. Hugh Rorrison and ed. John Willett
(London, 1993), pp.454 and 531.
[10] See Introduction to Signet edition of *Coriolanus* ed. Reuben Brower
(New York, 1966), p.xxiv.

11 In old age, in his poem 'The Circus Animals' Desertion', Yeats
   admitted that: 'Players and painted stage took all my love, / And
   not those things that they were emblems of.'

4 | Tyrone Guthrie – The Firework Prince

'Some part of the advance in the director's status has …
been made over the dead body of the author.' (Tyrone
Guthrie, *A Life in the Theatre*, p.121)

'I've no interest whatever in [the director's] concept or
interpretation. I think it's almost a bogus career. When did
these people appear on the scene? One hundred years ago?
… I think we can dispose of them very easily again.' (Brian
Friel, *New York Times Magazine*, 29/9/91, p.55)

Scholars have long acknowledged the importance of the
iconoclastic director, Tyrone Guthrie, in the history of modern
Shakespearean production. In recounting *The Shakespeare
Revolution* (1977: 180), J.L. Styan tells us that 'Sir Tyrone
Guthrie's place in this story may not be underestimated', and
Norman Marshall in *The Producer and The Play* (1975: 185) con-
cedes that he 'has been the most powerful influence on Shakespearean production since Granville-Barker'. To attempt to tell
the story of the Shakespearean director in the middle years of
the twentieth century without reference to him would be,
indeed, like playing *Hamlet* without the prince. And in this case
that allusion may be of special relevance. In the 1960s Laurence
Kitchin went so far as to describe Guthrie as the greatest
director yet to emerge from the English Drama (1960: 92).
More recently, Samuel Leiter has argued that few individuals
have been so singularly responsible for the popular characterization of the last century as 'the age of the director' as has

William Tyrone Guthrie (1991: 77). Contemporary directors are equally fulsome in their praise. For Adrian Noble (artistic director of the Royal Shakespeare Company from 1990 to 2002), he is 'the person to whom most directors owe most, this century',[1] and Sir Peter Hall admits that he was 'a director whose technique I idolized'. In the foreword to Guthrie's autobiography, *A Life in the Theatre*, Hall writes:

> As the twentieth century draws to its close, the great originators among British Theatre directors begin to emerge clearly. The line marches from Poel to Granville-Barker; from Tyrone Guthrie to Joan Littlewood and Peter Brook. Among these, Guthrie was a towering figure in every sense, and this book explains why.

In playing Shakespeare, another director (one of Hall's great collaborators) has observed, the actor should be directed by Hamlet's advice to the players (III.ii.1-47). 'It can't,' urges John Barton, 'be quoted too often' (1989: 6). Yet not only that advice but the figure of Hamlet himself seems, at times, to haunt that colossus of the modern stage, Tyrone Guthrie. For despite the plaudits, the tributes to his stature, there is always in the mouth of the critic and the commentator a word of qualification, of warning and reservation. It is almost as though in the work of this director some perturbèd spirit was abroad which often appears to baffle both admirers and critics alike. Along with the prevailing airs from heaven, with him there were some, not infrequent, blasts from hell. In summing up his style and presence, words – some of which might equally fit Shakespeare's princely hero – occur with surprising frequency: 'mad' (Hall); 'dangerous' (Marshall); 'eccentric' (Styan); 'maverick' (Leiter); 'wayward' (Guinness); 'Quixotic' (Speaight); even 'dotty' (Tynan).[2] Yet to these the word 'genius' is often attached. In part this chapter will attempt to explain these conflicting judgments.

It will, in other words, not so much aim to outline the development of the open, or thrust, stage and the other great achievements which are often credited to this director; but it will attempt in some way to define the essence of the man behind the achievement, perhaps even, to 'pluck out the heart of [his] mystery' (III.ii.353-4). That, of course – as Guildenstern found to his cost – can be a dangerous enterprise but as Guthrie, himself, observed in a characteristic statement: 'Artistic or, for that matter, administrative achievements are only to be had by sticking your neck out as far as ever it will go.' In pursuing this somewhat different path of discovery both Guthrie's fraught sexuality and his ambivalent nationality will be seen to be of key interest. Above all, this chapter will attempt to answer one central question: Why was Tyrone Guthrie so fascinated by *Hamlet*?

In his biography of Guthrie, James Forsyth tells us that at university, 'Oedipus Biggs' was the director's 'pen name in very undergraduate bits of authorship' (1976: 38). With an impressively firm father and an 'overwhelmingly magnificent' mother, Guthrie, in Forsyth's view, had the required qualification for a profound Oedipus complex. Indeed Guthrie remained throughout his life preoccupied with the figure of Oedipus. He produced *Oedipus Rex* no fewer than five times during his career.[3] No other play appeared so often under his direction except *Hamlet* – a play, it is generally recognized with a strongly Oedipal theme. In his autobiography Guthrie reinforces this impression. In a chapter entitled 'The Director,' he writes:

> For *Hamlet*, or any of the masterpieces, or for any play which is not in an obviously familiar style and whose interpretation is not clearly charted and signposted, much more is required of a producer [i.e. director] … I know perfectly well that my comment upon *Oedipus Rex*, *Hamlet* or *All's Well That Ends Well* is not the final, any more than it is the first, interpretation of these works. (1987: 124)

All's Well That Ends Well (1959) would provide Guthrie with one of his greatest stage successes. But significantly it, like *King Oedipus* and *Hamlet,* has an insistent Freudian subtext: the Oedipal theme is fundamental. If the Oedipal obsession leads us to one obvious answer to the central question, then Guthrie's lifelong interest in the theatre, and in particular his interest in directing, leads to another (and, as will be argued, complementary) one. But is there a still wider context *of power and conquest* in which this question should be considered? – that, too, is an underlying challenge.

Illustration 5

Tyrone Guthrie (figure centre) stands temporarily dwarfed amidst construction of the Festival Theatre at Stratford, Ontario, in 1953. (Courtesy of the Tyrone Guthrie Centre, Annagh-ma-kerrig, Newbliss, County Monaghan.)

Guthrie's autobiography concludes with a chapter entitled 'Stratford, Ontario'. That place itself symbolized what many see as his greatest achievement: the development of the modern open or thrust stage (illus. 5). By the late 1950s when he was writing his life story the director had achieved his principal technical aim 'of getting out of the proscenium arch and back to something near the Elizabethan stage' (1987: 311). The evolution of that idea, which gained its momentum at Elsinore in 1937 with an unusual staging of *Hamlet*, has been fully explored elsewhere (Styan 1977); but if we wish to understand something more of the man himself it is worth travelling first beyond the scope of that book to the year nineteen sixty-three. It was in this year that the theatre which now bears his name was founded in Minneapolis, Minnesota.

Hamlet Director

Reflecting his own interest in the play, Guthrie chose *Hamlet* to celebrate the opening of the new theatre. Just as Hamlet instructs the players and then intervenes himself during the performance of 'The Mousetrap', so Guthrie at that hour of personal triumph seemed intent on being the princely director. As Alfred Rossi reports in *Minneapolis Rehearsals* (1970: 53), during one defining rehearsal of the final scene of the play he became involved vigorously in the action on the stage: he moved about as if he were a court member, shouting various comments to the combatants and to other court members. While the bouts were being played, you could see him, for instance, say something to a court lady and then give her a firm push in the direction of a guard six feet away – and she would run to the fellow and point at the action excitedly; or he might pound a nobleman on the back as a hit was made. 'His physical and vocal presence *among* the cast seemed to generate even more excitement in an inherently exciting scene' (Rossi's emphasis). On the first day of rehearsals the director was clearly determined to stamp his authority on the production. Even the principal actors were given detailed instructions with particular emphasis on phrasing, pauses for breath and cushioning of the 'r' sound in the middle of a word following a vowel as in 'buried' ('Speak the speech, I pray you, as I pronounced it to you – trippingly on the tongue.' III.ii.1). Usurping the role of playwright, for some court scenes Guthrie even wrote out (some in blank verse) numerous lines for fictional courtiers. For example (43):

> BARNARDO. Let's watch the play together.
> MACHLACHLAN. Mother says, These actors are the finest in the world.
> BARNARDO. Lord Hamlet thinks so too.
> MACHLACHLAN. He does?
> BARNARDO. One told me he had writ this play for them …
> BACKLIN. Give me a merry play with songs and dances.
> SLINGSBY. Agreed. I hate your melancholy plays.
> BACKLIN. And poetry – don't you *hate* it?
> SLINGSBY.Yes, I do.
> BACKLIN.Your Aeschylus, your Sophocles and stuff. Let them all burn, say I, they're garbage all. (Guthrie's emphasis)

This thumbing his nose at the fathers of poetic drama had, however, a sound practical basis: to provide a realistic background hum for court scenes.

Just as Hamlet instructs the First Player to add 'some dozen or sixteen lines' (II.ii.543) to *The Murder of Gonzago,* so Guthrie was anxious to place his individual mark on the text. Throughout his career such a concern with writing or re-writing texts had invited conflict with authors. Indeed, such a conflict is implicit in Hamlet's role; for Hamlet not only instructs and controls the actors, he also takes on something of the mantle of playwright ('my lines;' III.ii.4). As Guthrie puts it in the extract above:

> One [actor] told me he [Hamlet] had writ this play for them.

This question posed at the heart of *Hamlet* (Who is the true author of the stage production?) might well have played on Guthrie's mind when he invited playwright Brian Friel to observe his directing of the play at Minneapolis in 1963. Friel at that time was an aspiring young writer, some of whose short stories Guthrie had read and admired. Although a fuller significance of that invitation will become clear later, Guthrie may have been curious to see how Friel would react to this director-driven forum. For, as director in charge, Guthrie was undeniably in a commanding position to interpret the text for his own – in this case, Freudian – purposes.

Guthrie's interest in the Freudian interpretation of *Hamlet* went back at least to the 1930s when Ernest Jones's 'A Psycho-Analytic Study of Hamlet' (then revised as *Hamlet and Oedipus*) received widespread attention. Although these ideas had long circulated in psychoanalytic discussion (Freud, himself, had written notes on *Hamlet* in 1897),[4] they were fresh in theatrical circles. Laurence Olivier, in *Confessions of an Actor*, describes how before the Old Vic production of *Hamlet* (1936/37) Freudian ideas were given a new emphasis. 'Three of us,' wrote Olivier, 'Tony Guthrie, Peggy Ashcroft and I, went to see Professor Jones' (1989:109). The meeting was influential and the interpretation seemed to fit the play. Not only Guthrie's subsequent production but Olivier's later film version (1948) incorporated psychoanalytic interpretation of the text. Olivier, the actor and director, was not alone in being profoundly influenced by Guthrie's perspective on the play. But why was Guthrie so drawn to this – as many would see it – reductive interpretation? The answer, in line with an earlier (Oedipal) suggestion, lies in Guthrie's own troubled childhood years that seem to invite psychoanalytic investigation.

One passage, particularly, in *A Life in the Theatre* hints at the source of the difficulty and suggests that an incapacity to deal with emotion was rooted deeply in Guthrie's youthful experience:

> In my case, so extreme was this shyness that, when at a family Christmas gathering a well-meaning uncle asked me, right out in front of everybody, right there over the roast turkey, what I would like to do with my life, I blushed first as red as fire, then trembled and then started to weep, deeply embarrassing my parents, and indeed the whole tribe, by such an exhibition. I think the symptoms were the result of

self-conflict. I wanted enormously, indeed needed, to talk long and loud about myself, my prospects, hopes and fears. *But I dared not; I felt I must not.* (1987: 10)

The paradox of Guthrie is that while in rehearsal he carefully shied away from scenes of passion or sexuality, as his career gathered momentum he was increasingly drawn to plays in which these qualities were inherent. In these plays (e.g. *Hamlet, Oedipus Rex, All's Well*) passions ran strongly, sometimes openly, sometimes in subterranean channels. *But break, my heart, for I must hold my tongue.* (*Ham*.I.ii.159)

The need to come to terms with some underlying, and long unresolved, emotional complex would dog Guthrie's directing. Peter Hall sensed that Guthrie's tendency to provide distracting detail was often linked to the director's discomfort in dealing with passion or sexuality: 'At the worst he took refuge in flippancy ... He was a director whose technique I idolized, but whose work – because of its inhibitions – finally left me unsatisfied.' The play of *Hamlet* may have provided a particular focus in Guthrie's struggle to understand his own emotional entrapment:

> The poet is not Hamlet. Hamlet is what he might have been
> if he had not written the play of *Hamlet*.
> (*Hamlet and Oedipus* (1949:103))

With this tongue-twisting conundrum Ernest Jones (quoting Ella Sharpe) speculated about the emotional necessity that may have driven Shakespeare to write *Hamlet*. 'Any author,' agreed Guthrie in an article 'Why and How They Play Hamlet', 'must put into the creation of a very long, complex fictional character like Hamlet a great deal of himself ...' And for Guthrie, 'the character of Hamlet has an extraordinary validity and vitality'. Further, 'Hamlet is not only highly intelligent but also a resolute and capable man, rendered irresolute and incapable by self-conflict'. (Presumably Jones's conundrum suggests that Shakespeare by writing *Hamlet* avoided being similarly bogged down). 'This self-conflict,' continued Guthrie,

> is fascinatingly explained by Ernest Jones. His *Hamlet and Oedipus* brings psychoanalysis to bear ... and offers what is

to me by far the most interesting and convincing explanation of the crucial puzzle of the play – Hamlet's procrastination in the matter of vengeance. (*New York Times Magazine*, 14/8/60, p.40)

Given his fascination with the play – and this interpretation – it is tempting to apply Jones's formula to Guthrie himself – replacing the word 'written' with 'directed' (i.e. The director is not Hamlet … etc.). And, perhaps, the exercise is more than idle conjecture. Notice, for example, that Guthrie uses the same term – 'self-conflict' – about himself and about Hamlet. Peter Hall's quoted reservations about Guthrie's 'inhibitions' are typical of what was often observed by those who worked with him. '*Hamlet*,' says his biographer, 'was really the first stage classic he produced in depth, because in princeliness and sexuality there was much of Hamlet in him' (1976: 154). In conversation with Alfred Rossi, the following comments by Anthony Quayle tend to confirm that impression:

> QUAYLE. But it's true that Tony could never have directed, say, *Romeo and Juliet*. Any demonstration of love between a man and a woman, or a boy and a girl, this embarrassed him. He couldn't direct such a scene, and he'd just leave you alone to cope with it.
> ROSSI. Why?
> QUAYLE. I don't know. And who am I to pluck out the heart of his mystery? Perhaps his height had something to do with it. He was very tall – six foot six, I think. I once asked him if this had made him self-conscious when he was young, and I was surprised at the vehemence of his reply. 'I suffered agonies,' he said. 'It's as bad to be as tall as I am, as it is to be a dwarf. It was dreadful. Dreadful.' But I should think there were all sorts of inhibitions in him which made love scenes embarrassing to him. As a director he had a tremendous range: 'pastoral-comical-historical-tragical' – in all these fields he was a master. But straight-forward romantical floored him. And he'd be the first to admit it. It was the same with pretty women. They threw him off-balance, and he had a tendency to lash out against them. (1980: 27)

Guthrie had, as Peter Hall comments, 'a distrust of sex', and in the play of *Hamlet* Guthrie, perhaps, would see an image of his own predicament. Yet Guthrie was far from being a resolute and capable man, rendered irresolute and incapable by self-conflict. If he managed somehow to bypass these inhibitions, to sublimate these energies for artistic purposes, then his obsession with *Hamlet* may well have helped him to that end. 'It is probable that we owe our highest cultural successes,' suggests Sigmund Freud, 'to the contribution of energy made in this way to our mental functions' (1968: 86). Sir John Gielgud has commented on Guthrie's characteristic energy and brilliance, but this creative energy, whatever its source, was strangely bound and curtailed in certain directions.

Strangely, too, Guthrie brought intense, burning passion to his role as director. Peter Brook in *Threads of Time* (1998: 29), describes him as an Irish giant who had 'an extraordinary vitality', and whose 'excitement pulsed through every detail, bringing the player of even the tiniest role into a state of passionate involvement'. He admits that Guthrie was the only stage director that he admired 'almost to idolatry'. In an article, 'The Giant of Monaghan', Brian Friel, too, recalls the passionate ferocity that Guthrie at times channelled into rehearsals. Although Friel in this description does not identify the production, it was almost certainly that 1963 *Hamlet* in Minneapolis. The director at one point lost patience with the leading actor and this explosive outburst was the result:

> All very nice and charming what-would-mummy-say intonation! But for – sake you have a sword in your hand and murder in your heart! You're not a – Boy-Scout on – troop outing! You're simply — ing the whole thing up! (*Holiday* 35 (1964: 95))

The 'Freudian' resonance of Guthrie's outburst is striking. For Brian Friel who had travelled, at Guthrie's invitation, to observe the inauguration, these were crucial times in his own development as a writer. The months he spent observing Guthrie direct not only *Hamlet* but other plays such as *The Miser* and *Three Sisters* with such 'stars' as Hume Cronyn, Jessica

Tandy and George Grizzard would prove to be among the most important in his own life. Guthrie was at that time in a strong position to influence and oversee the burgeoning Friel talent. Naturally when dealing with 'a new or youthful playwright,' Guthrie would argue, a director 'will be apt to take … a rather more dominant line than would be seemly if the author were an established heavyweight' (1987: 122). If as a young man himself he had been overawed by the intimidating ancestral voices of Drama (Aeschylus, Sophocles, Shakespeare …), he sensed now, at the summit of his career, that he was in the driving seat – Guthrie Tyrannos, James Forysth calls him (1976: 280).

It is certainly some hint of Guthrie's influence on the young writer that shortly after his return from the United States Friel produced his first great international success, *Philadelphia, Here I Come!* (1964). Its Oedipal themes have a familiar ring. Its melancholy hero, Gar, mourns for his mother and resents the father figure that dominates him. Torn by self-conflict, he indulges (through the voice of Gar Private) in long, moody soliloquies of self-deprecation and despair. Seeing his home village, Ballybeg, as a 'quagmire' (a prison?) he plans to escape to the United States, a country that Master Boyle, his alcoholic old teacher, instructs him is 'a vast restless place that doesn't give a curse about the past' (1990: 44). For a playwright whose later drama has often been characterized as 'political', this was an early, intense psychological study. Recently Friel admitted the extent of his debt to Guthrie: '[*Philadelphia!*] would never have been written had I not been an apprentice there [Minneapolis] under the great Tyrone Guthrie. Indeed it was the first thing I wrote in a state of near giddiness when I came back to Ireland still on a Guthrie high.'[5]

Viewed then in terms of the director's power to influence and control, the invitation to Friel can be seen in a wider context. It may even provide us with a still more fundamental clue as to why Guthrie should have been fascinated by *Hamlet*. Both from Ireland, Friel and Guthrie were from different sides of the Irish cultural divide. The American context provided neutral ground – 'a vast restless place that doesn't give a curse about the past.' A place, one might suppose, where two Irishmen from radically different traditions of Irish life might comfortably find new common ground.

A Question of Nationality

Yet even the term 'Irishman' with respect to Guthrie is problematic.

> What Mr. Guthrie has done is to make subtle distinctions where Shakespeare made broad ones; one wonders whether the idea would have occurred to anyone but an Englishman

wrote Kenneth Tynan, in reviewing *All's Well That Ends Well* (1959). An Englishman? But, perhaps Tynan does not quite believe his own description for earlier in the same review he accuses Guthrie of an 'infuriating blend of insight and madness', and of having a 'zany *Doppelgänger*, darting about with his pockets full of fireworks' (1984: 259). More than just a touch of Captain Macmorris (*Henry V*) might be the subtext. Whatever about Tynan, Guthrie himself was quite capable of proclaiming his own nationality: 'It is a matter of some regret to me,' he writes in *A Life in the Theatre*, 'that, so far, I have made no great effort to join in the theatrical life of my own country' (258). Yet even in this comment there is some ambivalence. 'A matter of *some* regret.' (I'm Irish but …).

To understand the reservation, and also to understand something more of that key relationship between Guthrie and Friel, one must consider the director's background. With a Scottish father and an Irish mother, Guthrie's (maternal) ancestral home, Annagh-ma-kerrig, lies in County Monaghan. As one of the quirks of modern Irish government it is part of the Northern province of Ulster but not part of the political Ulster which is under British control. It is one of the few areas of the Republic where Orangemen, who believe in the Union with Britain, can be seen marching. As disputed territory it lies on one of the great fault lines of modern Irish history. Many of the plays of Brian Friel who now lives in County Donegal – another excluded area of Ulster – attempt to grapple with this painful, sometimes hellish, experience of being lost in loss itself. To suggest that anyone who has lived in such an area for long periods of his life could fail to have a profound sense of his own nationality is like suggesting that a person who lives on the San Andreas fault could be indifferent to earthquakes. To put it succinctly: Friel is a Catholic Irishman who was born in the Protestant-controlled North; Guthrie was a Protestant Irishman who was based for significant periods of his life in an ascendancy mansion in the Catholic-dominated South. More-over, County Monaghan lies not only just south of the British jurisdiction, but also far from the Dublin 'Pale' – what was once the heartland of colonial influence. If Guthrie was not entirely Irish he could at least lay claim to being a rebel Englishman, a not dishonourable status in Ireland, either North or South. No wonder these men from the border counties found a mutual sympathy and some common ground for their friendship in a timeless play that queries identity ('Who's there?' *Ham.* I.i.1), and in a vast restless place that 'doesn't give a curse about the past'.

Indeed this friendship, with its political and cultural over-tones, prompts us to consider another facet of Hamlet's world. It is worth remembering that as a director Hamlet's secret agenda is a political one: it is what drives him to stage 'The Mousetrap', a play to 'catch the conscience of the King' (II.ii.607). This might be read as part of an overall agenda of *power and conquest*. In other words, if it is true that Guthrie's fixation on the play may have been anchored partly in its Oedipal theme (*power* over the father, *conquest* of the mother), or, to put it in theatrical terms, with Hamlet as director (*power* over actors and playwright, *conquest* of the theatre), then might it not also be true that there was a more direct (and yet unconscious) political dimension to this preoccupation?

Central to the plot of *Hamlet* is the aggressive struggle of competing cultures and nationalities for land and influence. Given his own highly ambivalent situation – an Anglo-Irishman living in the nationalist stronghold of County Monaghan – Guthrie may have sensed an underlying significance, and perhaps unconsciously, cast himself as some Hamlet divided between his admiration for the enemy Fortinbras, the 'delicate and tender prince' (Signet ed. IV.iv.48), and his own multi-layered cultural identity:

> PAT. Will you shut up. As I was saying, he had every class of comfort until one day I discovered he was an Irishman.
> MEG. Aren't you after telling me he was an Englishman.
> PAT. He was an Anglo-Irishman.
> MEG. In the name of God, what's that?
> PAT. A Protestant with a horse.
> (Brendan Behan, *The Hostage*)

The lines from Behan's play while comical in themselves also betray the essential tragedy of a class cast by birth ('Since nature cannot choose his origin.' *Ham*.I.iv.26) in the role of oppressor. The horse is symbolic – suggestive of superiority, control and the not uncommon subjugation of a hostile population. In a passage quoted earlier, Guthrie describes his adolescent *Angst*, the emotional outpouring that so horrified his family. He describes not only embarrassing his parents, but also '*the whole tribe* by such an exhibition' (1987: 10). The patriarchal and colonialist 'stiff upper lip' fears such loss of emotional control, which it associates with the oppressed, the native (feminine) culture. But was this connection between *Hamlet* and the imperialist legacy of Ireland, past and present, ever clearly manifest in Guthrie's mind?

In 1938, for example, before rehearsals began for yet another production of *Hamlet*, Guthrie invited Alec Guinness, who was playing the title role, to Annagh-ma-kerrig. Guinness was honeymooning in Ireland and brought with him his new wife, Merula. The main quest was to allow both director and chief actor a chance to gather ideas for the new production in the remoteness of the Monaghan countryside. 'They both enjoyed themselves enormously,' notes James Forsyth. 'There was an unusual spark of response between these two men of alert intellect' (1976: 167). Despite that alertness it is not clear that either of them made any connection between *Hamlet*, the play in focus, and the torn and divided country in which they rehearsed. (Is the land that Fortinbras insists he must reclaim truly Norwegian land or is it Danish?). Undoubtedly Guinness sensed a conflict of cultures. In *Blessings in Disguise* (1986: 79) he writes: 'And yet, for all its Irishness, the house remained the house of a Scot. I never felt such awareness of Tony's Edinburgh forbears as I did there.' What is clear is that against a backdrop of impending disaster on the continent of Europe

Illustration 6

Hamlet (1938) directed by Tyrone Guthrie at the Old Vic. Hamlet (Alec Guinness) bows before a militaristic-looking old Hamlet. (Courtesy of the Hulton Picture Archive.)

that 1938 modern-dress *Hamlet* eventually did make some passing political statements. In one photographic record of the production (illus. 6), Old Hamlet is portrayed in Prussian helmet with Hamlet kneeling in dutiful, filial respect. There may be here a hint that Guthrie does not see Fortinbras's claim as an unfair one, or that he necessarily casts either Old or young Hamlet on the side of the angels. The shadow of Ireland's imperialist past appears even more clearly in a 1950 production of *Hamlet* directed by Guthrie at the Gate theatre in Dublin. There Hamlet was pursued by a gun-firing Rosencrantz and Guildenstern, and one reviewer (J.J.Hayes, *Christian Science Monitor* 22 July 1950) complained that although the setting was the Near East, 'the king's uniform was so like, in colour and design, that of a British field-marshal *that it was disconcerting.*'

Such moments are fragmentary ones. For as both Friel's *Philadelphia!* with its Oedipal undertow, and Olivier's Freudian film of *Hamlet* (Fortinbras was omitted) indicate, Guthrie's theatrical legacy – the influence he undoubtedly exerted – would be to privilege the psychological over the political. 'One could say,' wrote Forsyth (154), 'that, as Olivier made his entry into the Old Vic, Freud made his entry too and Tony Guthrie was responsible.' Although Alec Guinness asserts that in the 1938 *Hamlet*, 'there was no talk of such things [Ernest Jones *et al.*],' he recalls how Guthrie asked him to sum up in a word what *Hamlet* is about. 'Before I could give a floundering answer, he said with a frightening smile, "Mummy!"' (1986: 81-2). One review of the 1963 *Hamlet* noted its 'awesome sweep of tragedy, a vortex of it whirling in the exact centre of its spiralled layers of psychology'. Not altogether surprisingly, Fortinbras receives no mention, good or bad, by that reviewer (Rossi 1970: 85). But was this glaring failure to highlight the wider background issues of *Hamlet* – for example, Danish or Norwegian imperialistic designs – political naivety, or was it in some way linked with his own need to retain an ambivalent nationality, to be in a sense both colonizer and colonized? Of Guthrie, Anthony Quayle said:

> There were two sides in Tony which were at war with each other – very often the case in the most interesting people. One part of his blood was Irish – and very Irish too. The other part came from a line of eminent Scots churchmen – Dr. Thomas Guthrie was his great-grandfather – all fire and brimstone and austerity. So there was a chop on the waves. They weren't all going the same way. They tumbled and conflicted. (Rossi 1980: 29)

Plainly, there was a cultural edge to Guthrie's inner turmoil. Of his days at Wellington, the English Public school which he attended, Guthrie wrote: 'As I grew older, I reacted more and more against this conformity. I developed an exaggerated regard for "originality," an exaggerated dislike of English upper-middle-class routine … *Inwardly I rebelled and seethed with antagonism*' (1987: 9). Guthrie's rebellion against his British identity would express itself in multifarious ways. In one notorious production of *Henry VIII* in the late 1940s, Guthrie's irreverence for English institutions of church, state and crown found startling expression. The Bishop of Winchester was decidedly tipsy, and Cromwell was an agitated little man in a perpetual state of fluster and fuss. In the christening scene the Duchess of Norfolk, who was holding the child, let out a prodigious sneeze during Cranmer's speech prophesying a glorious future for the infant Elizabeth (Marshall 1975: 187). In the 1963 *Hamlet* at Minneapolis only budgetary considerations prevented Guthrie from portraying Gertrude sitting, in full riding gear, on a dummy horse having her portrait painted – a cheeky resemblance, no doubt, to a famous portrait of the young Queen Elizabeth II on horseback. Eventually, and despite his dislike of conformity, Guthrie would become *Sir* Tyrone, the impetus for the knighthood coming from the Canadian authorities who had been well served by the director.

Clearly Guthrie, the rebel, had much in common with his fellow countryman, Brian Friel. Both had an Irish identity: a sense, for example, of living in disputed, even lost, territory. On the other hand, Guthrie's roots were firmly embedded in the other (Northern Protestant) tribal tradition: Belfast, not Dublin, was Guthrie's spiritual home. As such in Friel's nationalist terms he must, in some sense, be part of the oppressing British presence in Ireland. In the Guthrie collection at Annagh-ma-kerrig there is a photograph of Guthrie at the opening of the tent theatre at Stratford, Ontario. Underneath the photograph (handwritten) is the inscription:

> Who were below him
> He used as creatures of another place
> And bowed his eminent top to their low ranks. (I.ii.41-3)

In the context of Stratford, Ontario these lines, from *All's Well That Ends Well*, are an amusing gloss on the international reputation of the director, his physical size, and his capacity for relating affably to actors and public alike; in the context of Newbliss, Co. Monaghan they bear an unfortunate tone of Sommerville-and-Ross condescension, even of colonial super-iority.

Culturally, then, as well as artistically, there were conflicting currents in this revealing friendship. One side of Guthrie could feel sympathy, even identification, with Friel. At the same time the relationship could be construed in terms of condescension or even antagonism; not just of father figure to son, of an older, more experienced man to a younger. It was more than that. For Friel was not just on the other side, different, in being a young nationalist, but also in being a playwright, a role – one of several in the theatre – to which Guthrie had aspired but in which he had failed. John Gielgud recalls that Guthrie 'always longed to be an actor' (Rossi 1980: 67), but as a young actor he had failed miserably – James Fagan, the Irish impresario, fired him after a short trial period. After mediocre results at Oxford, he achieved marginal success as a young writer but no dis-tinction. By the 1960s when he was doodling lines such as, 'Your Aeschylus, your Sophocles and stuff / Let them all burn, say I, they're garbage all', he knew that it was not as 'Oedipus Biggs' (the young writer) that he could ever challenge the fathers of dramatic literature. Yet from the 1930s, as the most brilliant young director of his generation, he had sensed his growing power, the pleasing sense of being – in this area, at least – Oedipus Rex ('You can't invent anything finer than

Kingship,' insisted Gordon Craig (1957: 45), *'the idea of the King'*. This aspiration to power is relevant to the preoccupation with *Hamlet*, a play that is centrally concerned with the challenge for political control. Hamlet's complaint that Claudius has:

> *popped* in between th'election and [his] hopes, (V.ii.66)

says something about the resentment of the powerless young against the powerful old, about the conflict, in the last analysis, between the sons and the fathers. We are constantly reminded in the play that one category replaces another in an endless succession of challenges: 'But you must know your father lost a father; / That father lost, lost his' (I.ii.89-90). At the end of the play it is the young Fortinbras who takes power from the 'uncle-father' (II.ii.377) Claudius.

By the time Friel came to observe him at Minneapolis in 1963, Guthrie had developed an aggressive stance in viewing the director as fundamental to the production process:

> And now, what does the director do? He bears to the preparation of a play much the same relation as an orchestral conductor to the rehearsal of a symphony. But the symphony is performed by the conductor with each member of the orchestra playing under his leadership. He does not play the leading part. He does more. *He interprets, shapes, guides, inspires the entire performance.* (1987: 122)

The final sentence might well describe Hamlet's orchestration of 'The Mousetrap', which flows naturally from his instructions to the First Player (II.ii), and from his advice to the players (III.ii). Paradoxically, Hamlet's advice to the players falls between the territory of the playwright and the director. Objectively, the words are Shakespeare's but, within the context of the play, the scene suggests the interaction between cast and director – Hamlet clearly setting his personal seal on the production:

> *He interprets, shapes, guides, inspires the entire performance.*

Hamlet, 'the master of the ceremonies,' as Dover Wilson calls him, 'wants full justice done to his essay in the art of drama' (1951: 154-5).

Years later, in the 1990s, Friel would articulate his distaste
for this aggressive take-over by the director,[6] a take-over expressed in the boldest terms for the modern (British and
American) theatre by Tyrone Guthrie. 'Some part of the advance in the director's status,' Guthrie would declare, 'has ...
been made over the dead body of the author' (1987: 121). It
was a philosophy he would take into every area of his directing.
Even when an author was still alive, the director did not believe
in seeking explanation or elucidation of a play. Describing his
frenetic style of interpreting, one critic refers to 'an orgy of
invention' (Marshall 1975: 187). For some, however, this was
less an orgy and more an invasion, with a host of other
directors like-minded in plundering and settling. For Friel the
occupying directorial forces should be sent well and truly
packing: 'I think we can dispose of them very easily again.'[7] Just
as Friel's home city, Derry (or Londonderry, as Guthrie might
have referred to it) and Guthrie's ancestral home, Annagh-ma-
kerrig, are situated on the most sensitive fault lines of modern
Irish history, so the friendship between Friel, the writer, and
Guthrie, the director, was formed around an area of contemporary theatrical controversy. Perhaps, in the soil of that No
Man's Land a time bomb was set ticking ...

Remarkably, given this colonialist minefield on his Irish
doorstep, Guthrie never conceived of his greatest obsession,
Hamlet, in broadly political terms. Yet *Hamlet* is (like *King
Oedipus*) a deeply political play. It concerns, as noted earlier, the
search for power, for land, and the problems arising from
conquest: 'Never alone/ Did the King sigh, but with a general
groan' (III.iii.22-3), gives a profound sense of the king's central
place in society; it echoes Sophocles, who makes it plain (for
example) that Oedipus's tragic mistake brings with it a general
malaise in nature as well as in society at large. In *Hamlet*
Claudius's opening speech confronts the political crisis in Denmark which has been caused, in part at least, by the conquest of
land from the Norwegians by Old Hamlet:

> Now follows that you know young Fortinbras,
> Holding a weak supposal of our worth,
> Or thinking by our late dear brother's death

Our state to be disjoint and out of frame,
Co-leaguèd with the dream of his advantage,
He hath not failed to pester us with message
Importing *the surrender of those lands*
Lost by his father, with all bonds of law,
To our most valiant brother. (I.ii.17-25)

Fortinbras's conveniently timed arrival in Act V has an unmistakable, if thinly veiled, purpose: 'To recover ... by strong hand / And terms compulsative those foresaid lands / So by his father lost' (I.i.101-3). Under the 'terms compulsative', he will be able to claim (with Hamlet's support!) the very throne of Denmark itself; but this is all connected in the fabric of the play with that early attempt (I.ii.) of the Danish court to forestall Fortinbras's attack. Doubtless even at that point Hamlet warms to the fiery young foreigner, and sensing what a pestering nuisance he is proving to Claudius, sees him as a potential ally. However the king's diplomatic holding measure in the opening court scene provides but temporary relief. By Act V it becomes clear that the 'little patch of ground', the Polish territory over which Hamlet soliloquizes, has provided only the briefest of diversions before the real conquest closer to home can begin.

Beyond the Pale

Ultimately what makes Guthrie's failure to foreground the political so striking is that the individual and the societal are commonly fused or connected in Shakespeare's perception of reality. (Take for example Cordelia's passion in *King Lear*: 'It seemed she was a queen / Over her passion, who most rebel-like/Sought to be king o'er her.' (IV.iii)). It is this fusion that may provide a further crucial insight into why Guthrie was so endlessly fixated on *Hamlet*. The interconnection appears in such lines as ' Never alone/ Did the king *sigh*', or '*popped* in between th'election and my hopes'. Still more clearly it is seen in Hamlet's depiction of the flawed state of Denmark, which becomes in turn an image of that fatal flaw in individual character:

So oft it chances in particular men
That for some vicious mole of nature in them,
As in their birth, wherein they are not guilty,
(Since nature cannot choose his origin)
By the o'ergrowth of some complexion,
Oft breaking down *the pales and forts of reason* ...
(Signet ed. I.iv.23-28)

This is part of the speech to which Olivier gives pride of place as a prologue to his film version of *Hamlet*; still, there is more here than what psychiatrist Anthony Clare calls 'a passage rich in topical psychological insights' (*Sunday Times* 28 March 1999). For an Elizabethan audience the word 'pales' might well have conjured up an image of that fortified area around Dublin ('the Pale') which kept at bay the wild, uncontrollable and – in English perceptions – un*reason*able Irish.

At the time of *Hamlet*'s composition (c.1600), Shakespeare had cause to ponder the maddening unpredictability of the troublesome Irish. The turbulent and irrational character of Captain Macmorris in *Henry V* (1599) seemed to reflect fellow poet Edmund Spenser's judgment that 'no laws, no penalties' could 'restrain' the Irish.[8] Yet in the same play Shakespeare had rashly predicted the triumphant return from Ireland of 'the General' (Essex). Shakespeare even makes an implicit comparison between the glorious Harry in France and 'the General' in Ireland (V.o.30). In fact, the Earl of Essex returned in September 1599 in disgrace, having failed to quell the Irish rebels, and to restore Elizabeth's 'sovereignty of reason'. To the queen, Essex, on his sudden return from Ireland, appeared as dangerously rebellious and even – especially after he had forced his way unannounced and uninvited into her bedchamber – *deranged*.[9] With those embarrassing contemporary references from *Henry V* still ringing in his ears, Shakespeare might well have viewed the neighbouring Catholic island as a place where English pales and forts (and English minds) were threatened by Irish intransigence and 'madness'.

Thus not a little strangely, (or, perhaps, not so strangely if we remember that Shakepeare's father was a Catholic),[10] it is Shakespeare's hero, Hamlet himself, whose pales and forts of reason seem most under duress. The presence of the ghost, confirmed as a reality by the sceptical gaze of Horatio, constantly disturbs and unsettles Hamlet. Horatio from Wittenberg – in Elizabethan times a decidedly Protestant location – even warns his friend that following the spirit of his father may deprive him of his 'sovereignty of reason' and draw him 'into madness'. 'Be *ruled*,' Horatio urges him, 'you shall not go' (I.iv.73-4, 81). The play makes it clear that Hamlet ignores that advice:

> There are more things in heaven and earth, Horatio,
> Than are thought of in [y]our philosophy. (I.v.168-9)

If the ghost beneath the stage is 'honest', as Hamlet seems to believe, then it must come from a Catholic purgatory, not a Protestant hell.

Puzzlingly, for much of the play Hamlet remains uncertain of this truth. He is convinced, and yet ... 'prompted to my revenge by both heaven *and hell*' (II.ii.587). His indecision – in any place apart from the theatre – strongly suggests this lack of conviction and certainty. Despite the obvious reductionism of the description, Hamlet's story *is* the story of a man who could not *make up* his mind. There is some corner of the Prince's mind that is for ever Ireland: some part, in other words, that is rebellious to the sovereign, *unruly* – 'beyond the pale'. He hesitates, in this ageless story, dangerously torn between conflicting faiths and loyalties. 'Hamlet,' says Mel Gibson who played the title role in Zeffirelli's (1990) film version, ' is a minefield of contradictions ... you never know when he is going to explode ... the man is a livin' bomb' (Boose 1997: 90). The fabric of *Hamlet* is woven from ancient, diverse and conflicting cultural strands 'in these islands'. Thus the fascination of Tyrone Guthrie with *Hamlet* gains an added political relevance. For that firework Shakespearean director, Tyrone Guthrie, lived in the ambivalent, disputed territory of Monaghan, on the borderline between Protestant British and Catholic Irish dominions, where ('lost in loss itself') his own divided loyalties must have constantly sought resolution: 'There were two sides in Tony [Guthrie] which were at war with each other ... *one part of his blood was Irish – and very Irish too.*'

'Ponder *Hamlet,*' Guthrie told a radio interviewer in Minneapolis, 'and you'll find much that is applicable to your own lives.' In his greatest tragedy, Shakespeare presents not only an image of a society threatened from without and divided within, but also simultaneously of an individual in deep crisis: 'So oft it chances in *particular men.'* Yet it is in the theatre that Hamlet struggles to bring these disparate ideas into a triumphant apotheosis. In the first play scene (the 'heroic' Pyrrhus and his merciless slaughter of old father Priam, the heartrending tears of the motherly Hecuba: II.ii.445-530), Hamlet tests his own Oedipal conscience; in the second more famous play-within-a-play (III.ii), he tests 'the conscience of the king'. As Olivier puts it, Hamlet has a 'weakness for dramatics' (1989: 109). 'Weakness', ironically, is the *mot juste.* Hamlet is a man with a theatrical solution to troubles both personal and political. If he aspires, in his *dis*united kingdom, to be a prince of power, a conqueror, it is in the theatre that he can begin to overcome his sense of helplessness. Driven by a culturally fortified agenda of power and conquest, he is constantly tempted by his daemon to invade the territory of both actors ('Speak the speech...'), and

Illustration 7 | Tyrone Guthrie as Hamlet

From the cover of Guthrie's autobiography, *A Life in the Theatre*
'A fellow of infinite jest, of most excellent fancy.' (V.i.180-1)

of playwright ('Some dozen or sixteen lines ... *my lines...*'). As such Hamlet provides an almost perfect image of the auteur director. No wonder that Tyrone Guthrie – so dynamic in inspiring 'the age of the director' – was fascinated by him.

[1] Adrian Noble interviewed by Ralph Berry (ed.) in *On Directing Shakespeare* (London, 1989), p.162.

[2] Peter Hall in foreword to Guthrie, *A Life in the Theatre* (London, 1960; repr. 1987). Norman Marshall, *The Producer and the Play*, 2nd edition (London, 1975), p.185. J.L.Styan, *The Shakespeare Revolution* (Cambridge, 1977), p.180. Samuel Leiter, *From Belasco to Brook: Representative Directors of the English-Speaking Stage* (New York and London, 1991), p.79. Alec Guinness, Cover of Guthrie, *A Life in the Theatre*. Robert Speaight, *Shakespeare on the Stage* (London, 1973), p.235. Kenneth Tynan, *A View of the English Stage* (London, 1975; repr. 1984), p.260.

[3] See James Forsyth, *Tyrone Guthrie: a Biography* (London, 1976), p.38. *Oedipus* productions: 1947 (Tel Aviv); 1948 (Helsinki); 1954 (Stratford, Ont.); 1955 (Stratford, Ont.); 1956 (Edinburgh). *Hamlet* productions: 1936/7 (Old Vic); 1938 (Old Vic); 1944 (London); 1950 (Dublin); 1963 (Minneapolis).

[4] See letter 71, 15 Oct. 1897, in *The Standard Edition of the Complete Works of Sigmund Freud*, Vol 1, edited by James Strachey (London, 1966), pp.265-6.

[5] Letter from Brian Friel to Joe Dowling (artistic director) and the cast of the Guthrie Theatre 1997 production of *Philadelphia!* cited in 'True Lives: Joe Dowling at the Guthrie', RTE (TV), 24/11/97.

[6] See Friel's comments in epigraph to this chapter. However, in a more recent letter (31 May 1993) to the present writer, Brian Friel has written of these remarks: 'I did say a few acerbic – maybe intemperate – things about directors ... but my comments haven't endeared me to directors in these islands.' With regard to the names Derry/Londonderry, those of Protestant background usually refer to the city as *London*derry. Friel's outburst of resentment against directors was made in 1991, when he was 62.

By a strange coincidence, this was also Guthrie's age in early 1963, when Friel visited Minneapolis.

[7] Friel interview by Mel Gussow, *New York Times Magazine*, 29 September 1991.

[8] Macmorris during an argument with the Welsh officer, Fluellen, threatens to cut off Fluellen's head (the seat of reason?). Another of Shakespeare's plays that concerns the 'Irish question' is *Richard II*. Returning from Ireland, Richard discovers that he has lost control of his kingdom. As the queen in her garden mourns her husband's loss of fortune, two minor characters, one a gardener, debate the state of the nation:

> Why should we, *in the compass of a pale,*
> Keep law and form and due proportion,
> Showing, as in a model, *the whole land,*
> Is full of weeds … (*Richard II* (III.iv.40-4))

[9] See David Starkey, *Elizabeth*, (London: Chatto and Windus, 2000), 323; also, the fourth (final) part of the TV series on which this book is based.

[10] See, for example, Dr. Eamon Duffy's article, 'Catholic in the Closet?' *Irish Times,* 8 December 1999.

The idea that Shakepeare's loyalties may have been divided is not, of course, a new one. In *England Under the Stuarts* (1904: 88-90), G. M. Trevelyan writes of Guy Fawkes as 'the professional soldier … brought back from Flanders out of the ranks of the English Catholic legion'. Further: 'This man, who had learned the sieger's art in mines and countermines where Dutch and Spaniard wrought *like moles after each other's lives,* could show his friends how to drive a tunnel safely through the earth, from the cellar of the building which they had hired as the basis of operations, to the foundation wall of the Parliament House.' Trevelyan goes on to speculate how Shakespeare's path might well have crossed that of the Gun Powder Plot conspirators. He notes how Shakespeare (whose own property was 'adjoining the very house of con-

spiracy') 'might well have had speech with these new neighbours'.
Trevelyan quotes *Hamlet*:

> For every man hath business and desire,
> Such as it is.

Trevelyan does not give the reference but the lines significantly
come from the scene where Hamlet first hears the Ghost of Old
Hamlet. In the same scene (I.v.138), Hamlet proclaims 'it is an
honest ghost', yet later will cast doubt on its reliability by referring
to it in terms usually suggestive of devilish connections:

> Well said, *old mole!* Canst work in the earth so fast?
> A worthy pioneer! (I.v.162-3)

Finally it should be noted that Hamlet refers to the individual
troubled by 'some *vicious mole* of nature ... oft breaking down *the
pales and forts of reason*'.

5 | The French Princes

> 'We want a king ... to rule us and to lead us out to war and to fight our battles' (I Samuel 8:19)

In 1948 at the Edinburgh Festival, while Tyrone Guthrie was commanding real soldiers from the local military barracks in pursuit of a theatrical dream (the open stage), another great director – but of continental origin – was preparing his own production of *Hamlet*. When, before his performance of Hamlet at that Edinburgh Festival, Jean-Louis Barrault spoke on 'Shakespeare and the French', he reminded his audience of a long tradition dating back to the eighteenth century. In fact, the first complete edition of Shakespeare in French was produced as early as 1776-82. About that time (the perhaps suitably named) Jean Francis Ducis became an adapter of Shakespeare's major tragedies for the French stage (Carlson 1966: 51). In the more recent past, Barrault pointed out, an impressive list of directors have staged Shakespeare including André Antoine who produced practically every play including *Titus Andronicus*. 'Shakespeare,' said Barrault in his lecture on Shakespeare and the French, 'is for us a vital need' (1961: 100). And the 'us' or 'we', in Barrault's case had a distinctly regal resonance.

Indeed the images of aspiring king and fantasy soldier have proved intrinsic to the concept of the Hamlet director outlined in the previous pages of this study. In the theatre, at least, Hamlet as director proves to be 'more like a general than a sad, screwed-up type guy'.[1] Yet the full development of that concept in the French theatre was slower and essentially different. For traditionally in the French theatre the playwright has been king. Not until the 1950s, when the influence of Bertolt Brecht was felt through Roger Planchon's *langage scènique*, was the autocracy of the playwrights truly challenged. 'Today,' writes David Bradby in the late 1980s, 'the major names in the French theatre are no longer those of the new dramatists, nor of the star actors but those of directors: Barrault, Planchon, Mnouchkine, Vitez, Chéreau, Vincent, Lassalle, Lavaudant.'[2] This chapter will probe how that transformation from the ascendancy of the playwright to the ascendancy of the director took place, and how a more aggressive and theatrically powerful director came to be accepted in the French theatre.

The difficulty of combining two essentially different forms of authority in the theatre is apparent in the case of the first of the directors mentioned by Bradby: Jean-Louis Barrault. Throughout his career, Barrault attempted to balance the conflicting prerogatives of director and playwright. Before considering Barrault's predicament in greater detail, it is important to consider briefly, in the wider historical context, the question of authority (and, more specifically, the question of Shakespeare's authority) in the French theatre.

Certainly the Napoleonic spirit and the historical impulses towards imperialistic control are nothing new in the French theatre. 'And what the French said and did in drama,' wrote Eric Bentley of the period 1650-1850, 'laid down the rules for the rest of the world' (1991: 20). Indeed these mechanisms have been built into the language of the theatre itself. The term *régisseur* (stage manager/director) – a word which the French have exported to the German and Russian theatres – in its Latin (Roman imperialistic) origins carries with it the implication of power, of regal and autocratic control. 'The Rexists' was the name given to the fascist party set up in Belgium in 1935, the year after a notorious production of *Coriolanus* in Paris encouraged a right-wing coup attempt, and helped to destablize the French government. It is, perhaps, a reflection of the sometimes puzzling French vacillation between autocracy and democracy that while in Russia and Germany *régisseur* came to denote the all-powerful director, the French have evolved a more neutral (playwright friendly?) term: *metteur en scène*. *Animateur* is a (now dated) term reserved for that elite who both direct and who have developed a formulated aesthetic approach to the theatre.

The True Creator of the Dramatic Work?

The modern crisis at the heart of French theatre was clearly foreseen by Jean Vilar in 1946 when he wrote:

> Two conflicting methods confront each other, and will oppose each other just as resolutely *in the decades to come* so that one can summarize thus: Which one, the author or the producer [director], is today, the true creator of the dramatic work? (1975: 36-7)

For Vilar, as we shall see later in this chapter, the answer was unequivocally in the author's – and, specifically, Shakespeare's – favour. In Barrault's case the answer is less clear. Barrault was always torn between two imperatives. It was, perhaps, for that reason that Hamlet proved for him to be a figure of such fascination.

'The Shakespearean hero,' said Jean-Louis Barrault, 'is the great human contribution to modern civilization', and this hero, 'whom I like to call the hero of superior doubt ... is best represented in its purest and most chaste state by Hamlet' (1961: 98-9). When, with his wife Madeleine Renaud, Barrault founded the Renaud-Barrault company in October 1946, the opening production at the Théâtre Marigny in Paris was of Gide's translation of *Hamlet*. It was a play that clearly fascinated him and to which he returned again and again. Samuel Leiter suggests that Barrault found the title role a never-ending source of revelation and made it the principal one in his repertory (1991: 190). In the year following Barrault's performance at the Edinburgh Festival, Eric Bentley saw the production in Paris:

> The most successful demonstration of the art of Barrault is his production of *Hamlet*. Except for Gielgud's, it is the best *Hamlet* I have seen; and in many matters of production (as

distinct from the performance of the main role) it is superior
to the particular Gielgud production that I saw. (1953: 52-3)

Illustration 8 | Jean-Louis Barrault as Hamlet

**'You shall see anon how the murderer gets the love of Gonzago's
wife.' (III.ii.251-2)**

As with other French directors there is a certain difficulty in separating the different roles of Barrault. 'Barrault,' noted Eric Bentley, 'is a very special sort of actor. Some critics scarcely consider him an actor at all. One commonly hears that he is "really" a director; but in its limiting sense, this allegation is unfair; Barrault is perhaps the most remarkable actor I have seen in Paris.' Barrault, however, was clearly not happy when not in charge: 'he was an *animateur* before he was an actor'; he needed to direct the play himself if his performance were to move comfortably inside it (Speaight 1973: 258). It is a comment on Barrault's approach to the totality of theatrical experience that he saw no difficulty in combining a multiplicity of roles. He strongly believed in the Craigian idea of a super theatre-artist that could write, act and direct, as well as contribute to the design of a production. At the Edinburgh Festival in 1948 Barrault was not only director and Prince Hamlet but also lecturer as well. Some timid (or democratically minded?) souls might think that any *one* of these might be sufficient for an evening's work.

To understand Barrault's approach to *Hamlet*, and to other Shakespearean plays, one must look again at the wider context in which this director appears; in particular we must examine Barrault's concept of 'total theatre', and how this affected his view of producing the classics, including Shakespeare.

> Pitoëff died in 1939, Lugné-Poe in 1940, Copeau and Dullin in 1949, Jouvet in 1951, Baty in 1952. But new directors, always more or less connected with Copeau, have ensured their succession. The most eminent among them today are Jean-Louis Barrault and Jean Vilar. (1961: 255-6)

Thus Jacques Guicharnaud summarized the passing of the French 'crown' from the old to the new (post-war) generation of directors. 'Barrault,' he continued, 'rapidly reflected all the most active influences: that of Dullin and Copeau, Gordon Craig, and most particularly the mime Decroux and Antonin Artaud.' Particularly significant in the context of Shakespeare is Artaud who firmly rejected Western theatre's 'enslavement to the text'. In Artaud's vision of theatre gestures would have the

same weight as words, and attitudes a deep symbolic signif-
ication.[3] The challenge was to create a 'metaphysics of speech,
gesture and expression' in order to banish from the stage
psychology and 'human interest'. The manifestation of dynamic,
external forces would make the whole of nature re-enter and
revivify the theatre: 'space thundering with images and cram-
med with sounds speaks too.' The aim was to bring about the
total involvement of the spectators in the spectacle: the two
closed worlds of stage and auditorium should go; the dramatic
action should take place in the midst of the spectators and flow
all around them (Knowles 1967: 42-3).

Where then does the playwright fit into this picture? This is
a most pertinent question in relation to the French theatre
where – as Norman Marshall puts it – 'the power and prestige
of the playwright has always been much greater than in other
countries' (1975: 81). 'Here in Germany,' declared Peter Stein,
'the author does not want to come into the theatre, because he
knows he has no business being there' (1987: 7). Such a statement would hardly be made by a French director. Among the
four associated directors of the Cartel (Dullin, Jouvet, Pitoëff
and Baty) who so dominated French theatre during the late
1920s and 30s, only Baty (trained by Reinhardt) was accused by
critics of challenging the autocracy of the playwrights – of
seeking, in some measure, to subjugate the author to the
director. In his work with the playwright Claudel, for example,
Barrault trod a fine line between respect for the playwright and
the need for adventurous staging in the manner of a Craig or an
Artaud. 'To read, to hear Barrault,' comments Jacques
Guicharnaud, 'one might think that *Claudel played the part of the
Father whose word was embodied by the Son, Barrault.*' Such was the
close co-operation between dramatist and director that Claudel
wanted Barrault to keep him informed as to the slightest details
of the spectacle; he wanted to participate in their preparation,
and he actually set up the staging of *The Oresteia* on paper. Their
collaboration was enhanced by the fact that both playwright
and director shared a common view of 'total theatre' (Whitton
1987: 149). In theatre as envisaged by both Claudel and
Barrault, language – the Word – was lyrically expressed,

according to a calculation of rhythms and intensities and even pitch, which was close to the operatic recitative. One of the recurring tensions of such theatre thus became the constant relation between the body – whose pulsations are perceptible in gestures and language – and the supernatural: between the breath of man's lungs and the breath of the Creator. 'And the Gesture in this kind of dramatic liturgy is of major importance. It is indissolubly itself and the meaning it symbolizes, like the gestures of a priest during Mass' (Guicharnaud 86-7).

Such a view of theatre was to be deeply influential in Barrault's productions of Shakespeare. Impressions of Barrault's *Hamlet*, *Henry VI*, or *Antony and Cleopatra* become more meaningful if we remember that Barrault's contribution – an extension of the theories of Artaud and Claudel – was 'an attempt to establish a vocabulary and grammar of theatrical symbols', based on the actor's vocal intonation and rhythms, and on the gestures and relative positions of the body. In some ways this represented a Western equivalent of Oriental theatre. Barrault thus tried to express the very mystery of Life, beyond 'the psychologism' still accounted dear by many actors. *A carefully calculated symbolic performance and the technical means offered by the modern stage combined to make up 'total theatre'* (*Ibid.* 256). As Eric Bentley puts it:

> Barrault, like Chaplin, acts with his body – with all of his body, limbs and torso. And of course with his face too – which means that the element of mind comes in (through the eyes and the features) as it could scarcely help doing. But the mind – the 'soul', as teachers of acting often prefer to call it – was already present in the theatre, to the extent that our theatre had any life at all. What Barrault has done is to give back to this soul its earthly covering, its body. And, after all, theatre is a highly physical art. It presents itself to the eyes. (1953: 52)

There is a clear example of this 'total' approach to theatre in Barrault's staging of André Gide's translation of *Antony and Cleopatra* (1945). Into this play the director introduced three mimed scenes, making of the carousel at sea a silent ballet. This worked up to a striking crescendo of movement; of the battle

of the galleys, a mime executed by three figures at the prow of a
ship, and three 'dancers' – Barrault, Decroux, and Jacques
Charron. The latter suggested the unhurried movements of the
galleys by their slow-motion twists and turns and the sound of
waves against the ships' sides by their glissades. The land battle
became a sort of Pyrrhic dance by two soldiers using stylized
cuts and thrusts and circling movements (Knowles 44).

   The relationship between this physicality and the text clearly
is seen in Eric Bentley's description of Barrault's *Hamlet* in
Paris:

> Barrault is the only actor I have known who, when he reads
> *Hamlet*, can believe his own eyes and ears, and consequently
> can stand by Shakespeare, however extravagant, irrelevantly
> funny, or obscene the poet may seem to be. For it is the
> extravance of Shakespeare that the Anglo-American colony
> should protest against, not that of Barrault, *who in this
> production is a loyal servant of his master*. Barrault is also the only
> Hamlet I have seen who really kills Polonius. The others just
> stick their sword into a curtain and resume their
> conversation with Gertrude. Barrault drives in his sword
> with sufficient force to penetrate curtain, clothes, and flesh,
> withdraws it, and wipes the blood off; at the end of the
> scene, as Shakespeare suggests, he lugs the guts into another
> room, and proceeds to make jokes about the murder, not in
> the high-comedy style that Olivier uses for all the witty lines
> in the play, but savagely. Barrault's relations with Rosen-
> crantz and Guildenstern – he tweaks the nose of one, slaps
> the cheek of the other – bring these often musty scenes to
> life. His direction of the play scene – but the list of admirable
> particulars is endless. (1953:54)

Robert Speaight praised Barrault's 'quite exceptional intelligence' and his 'genius ... for mime', but suggested that his
movement as Hamlet was not always helpful to the words; at
times it made them redundant. Barrault 'wisely ... modified his
plasticity' when he brought the production to Edinburgh (1973:
259). In New York some critics were clearly unimpressed by
Barrault's portrayal of Hamlet, a view anticipated in Eric
Bentley's observation that it was unpopular in 'the Anglo-

American colony'. Others were impressed by a portrayal that was both acrobatic and vigorous – played with savage energy and irony, unpredictable in the extreme. He introduced new stage business such as toying with his bare bodkin in the 'To be or not to be' scene as though it were a street tough's stiletto. The ghost scenes were accentuated by an accompaniment of a high-pitched whistle and ominous drumbeats (since some of these were included in Olivier's film version one wonders who was influencing whom).[4] Always profoundly physical, Barrault touched the First Player's face to verify the reality of his tears and grasped Horatio after seeing the ghost to assure himself of his friend's bodily presence.

In his search for 'total theatre' Barrault was to come close to Artaud's *athlète affectif*: one who could focus in bodily expression the full theatre creation. Artaud indeed had once paid the actor-director an unique compliment by saying of *Autour d'une Mère* (1935), 'that is true theatre and that is what Jean-Louis Barrault has created' (1958: 216). Mime, dance and other expressive means were all part of a total picture that Barrault was keen to explain, often at great length. 'He had consorted with Artaud,' observed David Bradby, 'from whom he acquired a taste for metaphysical speculation about the philosophy of performance' (1991: 166).

The Hero of Superior Doubt

Behind the sheer fire and physicality of his portrayal of Hamlet lay a deeply thought out conception of the part. 'The theatre is only useful to society,' he said, 'if it cleanses men, adjusts and restores them, and it can only reach that aim by being, above all, the art of justice.' In this search the hero is central ('He is chaste, pure, admirable, fascinating; his name is Richard II, Henry VI or Hamlet.') Shakespeare communicates to us the experiences of this hero, and with him we see that 'paradise has once again been lost and with it faith'. For Barrault, speaking in 1948, Shakespeare is profoundly contemporary: 'It is because at this moment ... and not in fifty years' time when things will be different, *Shakespeare is more modern than Molière.*'[5]

In the painful years of confusion and reconstruction after the Second World War, the director sees Hamlet as particularly relevant. Shakespeare's age, he argues, is like ours, an age most aptly described by Hamlet's phrase 'the time is out of joint', and further:

> It is an ambiguous world very much like the one we are living in now, and the Shakespearean hero generally finds himself caught between light and darkness, between the real and the unreal, between being and not being, in a most ambiguous and dangerous, albeit superior position which if one becomes conscious of it, makes action impossible … Thus conscience does make cowards of us all … And … enterprises lose the name of action. [*sic*]

Barrault argues that properly 'a tragedy can only end, not by the death of the hero but by the complete solution of the problems dealt with; a play is a complex of parts and not one single part; a tragedy can only end with the appearance of *the one who administers justice*, and not simply through the death of a victim'. For Barrault this 'same aura of justice' surrounds Fortinbras when he arrives on stage at the end of *Hamlet*, 'bringing to a world of death and suicide a breath of new life and a positive solution to what looked like an insoluble problem'.

On occasions, even in the 1940s, Barrault could sound remarkably like Jan Kott ('Shakespeare is more modern than Molière') but here we note the difference. What Kott sees in Fortinbras is in contrast to the French director. His senses well honed (under 'Nazi terror and Soviet repression') to recognize the totalitarian coup, Kott asks the pertinent questions: 'Who is this young Norwegian prince? We do not know. Shakespeare does not tell us. What does he represent? Blind fate, the absurdity of the world, or the victory of justice?' Barrault is content with the third of these options but Kott is not convinced:

> Shakespeare has only told us his name. But the name is significant: Fortinbras – 'forte braccio'. Fortinbras, the man of the strong arm. A young and strong fellow. He comes and says: 'Take away these corpses. Hamlet was a good boy, but

he is dead. Now I shall be your king. I have just remembered that I happen to have certain rights to this crown.' Then he smiles and is very pleased with himself. (1967: 59)

And how remarkably well – in the late 1940s – this description fits that Young Pretender to the French 'throne', Barrault himself. With the corpses of Copeau and the Cartel shortly to leave the stage, the young prince is set to claim his crown. 'Man is double' (*l'homme est double*), believed Barrault, and in the theatre the 'control' side of the actor must balance out the emotional, anarchic side (Dieckman 1975: 95-7).

In *Hamlet* those rebel princes, Fortinbras and Hamlet, can be seen as two sides of a coin. Fortinbras's military prowess contrasts with Hamlet's inability to fulfil his father's stern imperatives. Only in the theatre does Hamlet have an eye like Mars to threaten and command. Thus, not surprisingly, it is with the power-grasping, muscular Fortinbras – and not with the powerless (as he is usually perceived), indecisive Hamlet – that Barrault finally identifies. 'Every year,' he was to write in *Souvenirs pour Demain* (1972: 194), 'towards the end of January, in midwinter, you have one or two days of false spring. The air is pale and green, and the sun is all white, like a mirage of the first leaf. When I hear this brief explosion in the air and in nature, I now say, "There are the trumpets of Fortinbras" ('Voici les trompettes de Fortinbras').' This rhapsody on the young imperialist prince may sound strange to modern ears grown cynical about 'liberating' generals. Fortinbras's rule is likely, one suspects, to prove as far reaching in the political sphere as Barrault's in the theatrical. The scholarly Horatio compares Fortinbras to a predator: a shark – bigger, it seems, in appetite than intellect (I.i.97-9). 'Total theatre,' observed Gary Taylor in *Reinventing Shakespeare*, 'not for the first time bore an uncomfortable resemblance to its contemporary totalitarianism' (1990: 271).

It is the far-reaching nature of Barrault's power that makes the modern observer uneasy. Not content with playing the title role, directing – wholeheartedly aspiring to Craig's super-artist – he wishes to exert an astonishing level of control over his actors. Blocking by Barrault is mechanical and accepted without discussion. This, he believes, allows the actors time to concentrate on their characters without having 'to ponder the whys and wherefores of their movements ... he constantly adjusts and readjusts positions and gestures, and is apt to demonstrate what he wants without the slightest reservation' (Leiter 1991: 206). In Barrault's own words, a good director:

> works on stage at the side of the actors and shares equally in their efforts in order to help them to discover. He stands in front of them, nose to nose, in order to hypnotize them. He takes them by the arm, as if he were suddenly leading a blind man. He hides behind them, his mouth against their ear, as if he were their guardian angel – *or some demon, after all!* (Dieckman 194)

One observer, Jack Brooking, watched Barrault direct at the Odeon theatre in the early 1960s. He noted how precisely Barrault demanded from his actors complete obedience: 'When Barrault directs he is constantly on the move, explaining, demonstrating, mimicking. As he demonstrates, one witnesses a finely wrought performance. He does not work step by step with his actors, but rather shows them the full complication of the finished product' (1964: 7). Brooking noted that Barrault never draws ideas *from* an actor; he always gives *to* an actor. It is difficult to believe that this leaves much room for the actor's initiative or development. Yet Brooking reassures us that 'the actor is quite free to bring to the character and the moment as much as he wishes, as long as it fits into the rather precise framework established by the director'. Another observer who worked with Barrault noted how he appeared to lose his temper more often than he, in fact, did; yet Samuel Leiter still refers to Barrault's control as 'benevolent despotism'. In all of this Craig's disdain for the freedom of the stage actor is evident. For Barrault the director is king and the actors are merely subjects who are there to obey. Samuel Leiter's apparent defence of these methods is not entirely convincing:

> Naturally, actors must respect a director who acts out their roles for them or they will feel creatively frustrated. In Barrault's case, the director is himself so masterful an actor

that few who wish to work with him will dispute his methodology. (1991: 207)

What Leiter does not concede is that even actors with a deep respect for Barrault's talent might feel 'creatively frustrated'. Neither is it particularly reassuring to be told by Suzanne Dieckman (192) that '[Barrault] speaks of his relationship with actors in terms, once again, of love: "It seems to me that I help them to give birth ... I wed them" (*Il me semble que je les aide à accoucher ... Je les épouse)*', nor by Samuel Leiter that: 'the Renaud-Barrault company, after years of intimate work together under Barrault's inspiriting leadership, became very much like a large, happy family' (208).

This paternalistic vision fits in well with Barrault's concept of 'justice' in Shakespeare. And 'justice' clearly means something akin to what Plato calls 'justice' in *The Republic* – that is a concept which demands that each person should 'mind their own business, do their respective work'.[6] For Plato the rulers must rule, the soldiers fight, the shopkeepers trade and so on. For Barrault likewise, the dramatist and the director, at the summit of the pyramid, command the power held in a Platonic Republic by the philosopher kings, 'where the desires of the less respectable majority are controlled by the desires and wisdom of the superior minority'. This corresponds to what Copeau describes as a great moral and intellectual superiority on the part of the director. 'There is the sense of the perfect balancer,' as Gordon Craig put it, '... the king' (1957: 45). While in Barrault's theatre the philosopher kings are the playwright and the director, the actors to fulfil this concept of 'justice', once the instructions have been conveyed to them from above, must act as the king (or kings) sees fit. 'I run the risk,' says Barrault, 'of seeing that human being overwhelmed by his feelings, no longer having sufficient control *to obey me in what I have decided to have him do*' (Dieckman 95). Yet even Plato warns of the danger of the individual who tries to do every job, who attempts to take over every role ('I think you'll agree that this sort of mutual interchange and interference spells destruction to our state').

What fascinates Barrault in Shakespeare is the manner in which the playwright's power can turn a chaotic universe into one with a semblance of order. In *Hamlet* this is precisely what appeals to the director. Trumpets (or bugles) blaring, Fortinbras – almost in the clichéd manner of the U.S. cavalry – arrives to restore order where chaos has so clearly broken out. Order, of course, of a kind is restored at the conclusion of *Hamlet*. But is it Spring or merely a new, and possibly harsher, Winter? Fortinbras, that man of action, is not hamstrung in Hamlet fashion.

> That is the problem:
> How so ever thou pursuest this act
> Taint not thy mind,*   [*I.v.84-5]
> Taint not thy mind!
> The moment the consequences of an action are in doubt, the
> moment one asks oneself whether the action one is about to
> perform is not only useful but just, everything collapses.
> (Barrault 1961: 97)

The irony of Fortinbras is that he restores 'justice' (in Barrault's sense) without ever troubling his mind too much about the rights and wrongs of anything. The trouble with the Shakespearean hero is that 'whenever confronted with action he doubts its necessity, for in ages of conflict a morality of action is an encouragement to mediocrity, cupidity and injustice'. And for Barrault – that total man of action – it is clear which of the two princes provides the clearer image of authority. The king must rule. 'Are you the king or aren't you?' was how Jezebel put it to King Ahab when his conscience troubled him about taking over Naboth's vineyard (I Kings 21: 7). In this sense Jacques Copeau is – to use Jan Kott's image[7] – a Jaques who becomes a dithering Hamlet; for Copeau could never come to terms with his role in the theatre. Significantly in none of the plays of Shakespeare that Copeau turned to (*Twelfth Night, As You Like It, The Winter's Tale*) does a king *ascend* to power. They each suggest strongly the failings of authority and the necessity of some kind of renunciation, of salvation through exile. Copeau's inability to live within the power structures of the theatre fits in with this pattern. Barrault, on the other hand, that 'brilliant *homme de théâtre*', as Olivier described him, has made that accommodation more easily. His Shakespearean heroes (Richard II, Henry VI, Hamlet) may fail the Craigian test of kingly authority but they point the way clearly to that 'total' control which is needed for 'justice' to be established in the kingdom of the theatre. And Fortinbras – the strong-armed Fortinbras – shows Barrault the way. When Hamlet is dead, Fortinbras will rule. The king is dead – long live the King!

If Barrault in his loyalties was always torn between playwright and director, two French directors with diametrically opposed views, Jean Vilar and Roger Planchon, help to clarify the debate at the heart of this chapter. Vilar, as suggested earlier, held to a view traditional in the French theatre: that the playwright stands pre-eminent. For Roger Planchon, who took his cue from Brecht, the picture was different.

In his search towards a democratic basis for the theatre, Vilar was deeply suspicious of the new emphasis on the power of the director. In Vilar's view, regard for the author should be combined with respect for the rights of the actor. After the war when he was appointed as director of the state-sponsored Théâtre National Populaire in 1951, Vilar used his position to further his vision of the theatre. The scope of this chapter does not allow a full examination of Vilar's work; but apart from the trend of decentralization and popularization that he inspired, Vilar was also instrumental in asserting a view of the director's role which emphatically contradicted contemporary trends. In particular, it provided an alternative to the 'total' theatre of Barrault. Vilar's ideas for a democratic theatre are worth quoting:

> The first thing we have to get rid of today is precisely this notion of 'the art of direction' seen as an end in itself by such spokesmen as Gordon Craig. For my part, I never set anything definitely or precisely before the first rehearsals. I have no papers, no notes, no written plans. Nothing in my hands, nothing up my sleeve: *Everything in the minds and bodies of others*. Facing me, the actor ... To compel an actor to integrate voice and body into a predetermined harmony or

plastic composition smacks of animal-training. An actor is more than an intelligent animal or robot.[8] (Vilar's emphasis)

Vilar is acutely aware of the dangers of the too-powerful director, 'the gentle patient autocrat who is … in danger of falsifying the meaning of the play … of giving birth to a play the author never intended or wrote'. And for Vilar the classics and Elizabethan theatres were 'above all playwrights' theatres. And what playwrights!' Shakespeare, in Vilar's view, gives the director all the help he needs in interpretation. To give a scene of Shakespeare its full meaning, through the play of the actor's mind and body, for example, is a task demanding the use of all the director's artistic faculties, but it is never more than a work of interpretation. The text is there, rich in stage directions embodied in the lines themselves (locale, reactions, attitudes, setting, costume, etc.). One needs, Vilar argues, only have the sense to follow them:

> Whatever is *created*, beyond these directions, is 'direction', and should be despised and rejected. I take the example of Shakespeare because each of his works affords the over-imaginative director all the illusions and temptations of 'creation'. It is not for the director, using his imagination, to decide the interpretation of any of Shakespeare's characters; that's intolerable. The character himself, stripped and laid bare, must be left 'open' to the imagination of the public. (Vilar's emphasis)

Vilar evidently stands against the kind of director who exploits the play for his own purposes. For the director to be co-creator with the playwright is both unnecessary and wrong.

Therein lies a crucial irony. For it is Shakespeare's creation, Hamlet himself, who provides a compelling image of a certain kind of modern director, who with his own agenda in mind, does see himself as co-creator. With his group of professional actors, Hamlet's first directorial thoughts are to create an effect – his agenda demands it – not to be 'true to the author'. Adding 'a speech of some dozen or sixteen lines' (II.ii.543) to create a Mousetrap is firm evidence of that. Hamlet wants his audience *now* to take sides, to cast its vote. Brecht provides a provocative modern example of this phenomenon. For him the text is not only ever-changing but, as we saw in Chapter 3, is always subservient to theatre which 'theatres it all down'. And for Brecht the need to become king in the theatre surpasses other considerations. 'It was about that time,' Eric Bentley reports in his *Brecht Memoir* (1985: 65), '… that Brecht told me he had at last and definitely inherited the crown. When I asked what crown that was he explained that the German theatre always had a king … *now it was himself.*' Significantly the predecessors that Brecht named (Hauptmann; Kaiser) were both writers – not directors.

Given his interest in a theatre both democratic and popular, it is not surprising that Vilar was the first director in France to stage Brecht; but it is symptomatic of the gap that existed between their differing views of 'democracy', and their contrasting conceptions of theatre, that Vilar failed to understand him. It was Roger Planchon who came closer to the German master; and Planchon's ideas of democracy were not those of Western democrats.

'I am very much a figure at the crossroads,' Roger Planchon told Michael Kustow in a (1972) interview, 'I know deeply what if feels like to be outside culture.' Planchon's background is important in understanding his work as a director:

> When I began to do plays, I always had this wish, and still have it deeply, to bring things away from literature and connect them with real life, the everyday life of the next-door neighbour, the butcher, the grocer on the corner. Because that's what my parents were like, and I've never gone back on that idea. (1972: 43)

'For me,' says Planchon elsewhere, 'a situation in the theatre is true insofar as it has its roots buried deep in everyday life.' It is from such basic impulses that the inspiration for Planchon's work in the theatre has grown, and Planchon is attracted to Shakespeare because life with all its ferocity and beauty is reflected in his plays. In those plays, long before Shakespeare conceived of the rebellious, moody, but theatrically dynamic Prince of Denmark, the dramatist had created a series of prototypes. If Jaques in *As You Like It*, the melancholy dreamer, provides one forerunner, then both Hotspur and Prince Hal in *Henry IV Parts One* and *Two* are characters that provide key elements for the later complementary figures of Fortinbras and Hamlet (*2H* II.iii.31 '*the (mark and) glass*'). It is to the rebellious and militaristic princes, Hotspur and Harry, that Planchon is attracted. Jacques Copeau, sometimes judged to be the father of modern French theatre, proposed ideas of refinement and spirituality – certainly of a sacred regard for the playwright's text. If his 'visions and revisions' suggest, what Peter Brook calls The Holy Theatre, then Planchon's experience suggests The Rough Theatre. Or, perhaps, one should say Rough Sport. 'I came into the theatre,' says Roger Planchon, 'like poor people become boxers to escape from their background' (Kustow 1972: 43). This key idea of empowerment though the theatre underpins Planchon's whole outlook; similarly it forms a crucial part of Hamlet's strategy. Hamlet's sense of theatrical em-powerment is reflected in his delight after the success of 'The Mousetrap' that ensnares King Mouse Claudius. Indeed the idea of 'the play-within-the-play' allied to the theme of Father-Son conflict, is foreshadowed in *Henry IV*.

It is worth briefly exploring Planchon's predicament, as for him it is clearly revealed, in *Henry IV Parts One* and *Two*. In *2 Henry IV* the dying king confesses to Prince Hal that his power was achieved without much regard to scruple ('God knows my son/ By what by-paths and indirect crooked ways/ I met this crown.'; IV.iii.313-5). Shakespeare is describing a world where – like Planchon's – the Queensberry rules are not much in evidence. Hastings, Mowbray and the Archbishop learn to their cost that in this arena there is no such thing as a Gentleman's Agreement. 'Is this proceeding just and honourable?' asks Mowbray, with some naïvety, after the conspirators have been tricked into dispersing their army. To which he receives the curt reply: 'Is your assembly so?'(*2H4* IV.i.335). Soon the rebels – despite the Archbishop's plea 'Will you thus break your faith?' – are despatched for execution. This is cruel theatre, cruel sport of which there are many striking images in the play.

> PRINCE HARRY. He that rides at high speed, and with his
>   pistol kills a sparrow flying.
> SIR JOHN. You have hit it.
> PRINCE HARRY. So did he never the sparrow.
> (*1H4* II.v.348-51)

Because both rider and target are in constant motion the chances of sporting success are greatly reduced. It suggests a world of chance where not only are there no rules but no constant points of reference: a world in which snatching or grasping is the norm. 'For nothing can seem foul to those that win', and 'The times are wild; contention like a horse ...' ('Let order die!').[9] Even the modern term 'professional foul' seems too ordered, too predictable for such a world: a world of tricks and stratagems. It's cruel sport about who can outwit whom and the image of the cuckoo – a recurring one in *Henry IV* – seems particularly apt ('That ungentle gull, the cuckoo's bird ... did oppress our nest'; *1 H4* V.i.60). 'Virtue is of so little regard in these costermongers' times,' proclaims Sir John Falstaff in *2 Henry IV*, ' that true valour is turned bearhead' (1.ii.169). Brecht might well have identified with those sentiments, but then, as Terry Eagleton jokingly suggested, Shakespeare seems to have read Marx (and others) a long time before Brecht (1986: ix).

Such observations are not an interesting but irrelevant detour but rather central to an understanding of Planchon's approach to directing Shakespeare. When he produced *Henry IV* (in the Théâtre de la Cité) at Villeurbanne, a working-class suburb of Lyon, in 1957, he was set to shake the traditional interpretations and shock normal expectations. 'Prince Hal is not among Shakespeare's more attractive characters,' wrote Robert Speaight, 'call him an unhappy hypocrite, and you have said the worst of him. When Planchon allowed Hotspur to be stabbed in the back while the Prince was engaging him in front, he was falsifying both the character and the scene' (1973: 260). Yet Planchon's interpretation was consistent with the world view outlined above, and in *Henry IV*, the director says, Shakespeare's vision most closely corresponds to his own:

Henry IV is the kind of early work I admire the most. Of course, I like the 'cruel' Artaudian Elizabethan theatre, but in *Henry IV* there's a mixture, a kind of balancing point, and the play steps out into a sort of immense clarity, white light. For me it's one of the greatest plays in the world: it inspires me personally more than *The Tempest* or *Lear* or *Macbeth*. In *Lear* you find problems of metaphysics, death, tragedy – none of that in *Henry IV*. Romantic people like *The Tempest*: I, who am not in the slightest romantic, place a thousand times more value on something worn smooth, rubbed flat like *Henry IV* – because *I can find everything in this play*. Above all, you feel that it's impossible to step out of life, to switch channels. (Kustow 1972: 50)

The Shakespeare 'channel' is most worthwhile because it so clearly reflects life in all its tough, joyful reality:

Henry IV presents a tough, joyful world, hard yet full of gaiety. And there are little notes on life all over the place, little characters in corners, everything, everyone has its savour – the serving-boys at Eastcheap, the travellers who are robbed on the highway, everyone has his little quirk or quiddity – remember the Welshman who thinks he possesses magic powers … All this has a tremendous charm for me. And the discussions between the rebels, their arguments, that's just how it happens in life, just how plots and rebellions take place, when people's emotions are just as important as the serious problem they're discussing. There's such youthfulness in *Henry IV* that's what makes it great. Later Shakespeare grew much darker. (*Ibid.*)

The cruelty and barbarity of this world never blinds Shakespeare to its beauty. What Planchon admires so much in Shakespearean drama is that there is always a kind of call, life goes on, a new baby is born. There is no need to change this channel to find the good news: 'I'm always very struck by the T.V. news: they announce a great man's death and then they move on to the Sports news and the sweepstake results.'

Evidently this is a world in which Planchon feels at home. He can identify easily with Prince Hal's disreputable activities, for his own youth had something of the same sordid quality: 'You can imagine the kind of thing – stealing a little on the side, a bit of prostitution, horsing about, playing around.' In the 1958 revival the Prince was played by Planchon himself, and 'played as *one whose ambition is present from the beginning*, overlaid for a time with a youthful charm, but coming forth inexorably when opportunity allows' (Daoust 1981: 63). But like the ambitious Hal, eventually Planchon must distance himself from his former companions ('Most of these kids turned out very badly'). From all these cruel yet 'magnificent experiences' something has been learnt. As with the nimble-footed, madcap Prince of Wales, these events have been formative:

> The Prince but studies his companions,
> Like a strange tongue, wherein, to gain the language,
> … so, like gross terms,
> The Prince will in the perfectness of time
> Cast off his followers …
> Turning past evils to advantages. (*2 H4* IV.iii.68-78)

Like Hamlet, Hal is loved greatly of 'the general gender', and for the working class Planchon, it is Shakespeare's early, rough-hewn Prince who provides a most satisfying role model (*the glass of fashion and the mould of form*).

The Rough Theatre and the Brechtian Invasion

Not surprisingly, given these parallels, when in 1953 he opened his first (110 seat) pocket theatre at Lyon, it was to the Elizabethans and not to the rarefied world of the French classical theatre that Planchon turned. What interested him most was a theatre of texts, but different texts from those being performed. At the time he was much closer to the Elizabethans than to the French classics. However, at this stage, it was in Brecht rather than Shakespeare that he found inspiration. 'The day I read Brecht's adaptation of *Edward II*, I saw that his interest in Elizabethan theatre was parallel to mine.' He claims that 'as far as Brecht goes, I think I'm the director in France who has been most influenced by Brecht, by far the most influenced … but by the same token among all the Brechtians, *it's I who was the first to detach myself from Brecht*' (Kustow 1972: 48).

By the time, in the 1950s, that Planchon came to absorb
Brecht, the German director was drawing near to the end of his
life. Now plainly he was playing father figure, influencing – for
good or ill – a younger generation hungry for new ideas in the
tumultuous post-war era. Brecht, that many-sided character,
had played the belligerent general, or the rebellious son, often
enough, but in the shifting gallery of portraits by which he is
defined, there was another role for him to assume: the ageing,
reluctant and ultimately corrupted soldier, Falstaff. While
aspiring to the title of supreme Shakespearean director in the
late 1950s, Planchon had still to distance himself from the
senses-satiating, low-life-loving, Falstaffian figure of Brecht
('That villainous, abominable misleader of youth ... that old
white-bearded Satan': *I H4* II.v.468).

> Most people had swallowed Shakespeare first and then
> discovered Brecht: I did the reverse. First I achieved a great
> understanding of Brecht, and then, in order to get out of it, I
> turned to Shakespeare. (Kustow 49)

In the 1957 production Falstaff is a central character, just as
Brecht is an overwhelming influence. Falstaff became a key
image in the production, showing up both the feudal concept of
heroism on the one hand, and the hard materialism of the new
age on the other. The presence of Falstaff made it impossible
for Planchon to stage the battle scenes as glorious, or to present
the nobles as superior or honourable men (Daoust 1981: 62).
The idea of rebellion against the father is central to Planchon's
identification of the Falstaff figure, just as it is in his attitude to
Brecht himself. As he admits:

> And Falstaff, of course – for me he is the emblem of
> popular sanity, the epitome of impertinence. And I also find
> him enormously intelligent, an overwhelming combination
> of intelligence, malice, cunning ... the relationship with Hal,
> *the scene where he plays Hal's father, the whole idea of the play within
> the play.* (Kustow 49)

Apart from – like Falstaff – looking after the main chance
and playing at being king, Brecht is a father figure to the
youthful Planchon. In fact, as a young director, Planchon

travelled to meet Brecht and was deeply influenced by his conversation with the older dramatist. 'I spent five hours with him. He told me what he liked and what he didn't in our work, and we discussed it.' Undoubtedly it was Planchon's understanding of Brecht's thinking which helped to popularize the German director in France during the late 1950s. When Michael Kustow suggested that Planchon spoke 'as if Brecht were a great parental shadow across your work', and asked him 'How have you managed to get out from under this shadow now?', Planchon admits that it was not until his own adaptation of *Edward II* in 1961 that he felt a freedom from the 'Brechtian shadow'. Significantly, in relation to throwing off the mantle of the Brechtian father figure, Planchon rejoices in Prince Hal's rejection of his former associate: 'And I adore the brutal ending, so dry – Hal sweeping Falstaff away like rubbish, the hardness of life' (Kustow 49).

But if in Hamlet fashion the surrogate father is to be swept away, the mother is entertained with quite different sentiments. Planchon is quick to associate this vision of a theatre of 'real life' with his own mother's scorn for what seemed artificial in art. Planchon admits that his mother would mock at culture, laugh at it, not from inferiority, but from 'complete superiority'. His mother and people like her thought the arts were something completely artificial, nothing to do with real life. Planchon's sympathy for those 'outside culture', and his desire to bring them in is inextricably bound up with his feelings for his mother: 'People don't realize that for someone outside culture seeing a Shakespeare play can be humiliating – they can't understand, they say "It's not for me, what's going on?" When my mother makes fun, it's to defend herself against feeling guilty' (*Ibid.* 43). Perhaps this is why eventually he can reject, or at least moderate, the Brechtian influence while retaining the idea of popular theatre ('I've never gone back on that idea').

In his *Modern French Drama* (1991: 103), David Bradby contrasts the respective searches of Jean Vilar and Roger Planchon for *théâtre populaire*. 'The strength of Vilar,' he writes, 'was in his utopian vision of the theatre for all and the patient

intelligence which he brought to the realization of this vision.'
But after Vilar's departure from the Théâtre National Populaire,
those interested in political theatre began to ask whether its task
should be to unite its audience. Planchon as the successor to
Vilar in his championing of Popular Theatre was one of those
who saw the necessity of allowing the contradictions – of
dividing an audience. When, for example, Planchon differed
from the usual interpretation and depicted Hotspur's death as a
piece of trickery in which he is stabbed from behind ('For
nothing can seem foul to those that win'), no doubt implicit in
this was a harsh political message: when it comes to grasping
power, no quarter should be or will be given; and the audience
must be encouraged – as Brecht would put it – to cast its vote.
The contrast between Vilar's and Planchon's approach to the
text is one indication of the fundamental differences between
the two directors. As Bradby explains:

> [Vilar] did not attempt radical re-interpretations of the plays,
> but concentrated on making the text as clear and intelligible
> as possible. His faithfulness in *serving the text* is one of the
> recurring comments of all the critics (in sharp contrast to,
> say, Planchon, who is frequently accused of wilful distort-
> ion). (1991: 92)

If Vilar practised what he preached then, in fairness, this also
must be said of Planchon. The outlook of the director fundamentally affects how the performance will be played. How, for
example, should a director interpret the scene at the end of *2
Henry IV* when Prince Hal – even before the old king is
declared dead – takes the crown from beside his sleeping
father? In 1957 Planchon was bound to take a more cynical
view of this than Vilar who had developed an heroic style for
some of Shakespeare's history plays.

In his own arena, the theatre, Planchon himself has not been
shy about grasping power. An early reviewer commented on his
ability to impose a unity of style, investing both objects and
actors with a mysterious power that made them seem larger
than life.[10] Yvette Daoust writes: 'Planchon has a way of leading
an actor, through conversation, in time, to make the same

discoveries that he himself made in his preliminary work.'(21), and Gérard Guillaumat, one of the Villeurbanne actors, says: 'With Roger, at the start, you have a feeling of freedom. You have the impression that you could do anything. In the end it is not so. Gradually you feel caught in a rigorous *mise en scène*' (*Ibid*.). The influence of Brecht in the mid-1950s accentuated a tendency towards control that was already there; and Brecht was the inspiration for Planchon's development of the idea of 'scenic writing' (*langage scénique*):

> The lesson of Brecht is to have declared that a performance combines both dramatic writing and scenic writing; but the scenic writing – he was the first to say this and it seems to me to be very important – has an equal responsibility with the dramatic writing. In fact any movement on the stage, the choice of a colour, a set, a costume etc., involves a total responsibility … in the same way as writing taken on its own: I mean the writing of a novel or a play. (Cited in Bradby and Williams 1988: 55)

This clearly contradicts Copeau's notion that the director is in a descending line from the playwright;[11] even more it contradicts Vilar's emphasis on non-interference with the author's 'vision'. Following Brecht's dictum that action and situation are more important than character study, Planchon would ask of his characters 'not what they are, not even what they say, *but what they do*'.

In *Henry IV* (1957), for example, Robert Speaight noted that 'Henry's determination to join the Crusade, albeit abridged, was not easy to articulate while at the same time he was eating his dinner' (260). Since there is nothing in the text to suggest that Henry is eating his dinner when he speaks of the crusade this is creating a new 'scenic' dimension. It suggests strongly that the King's motives in organizing the crusade are far from pure and spiritual; on the contrary they are deeply materialistic. But is this entirely a distortion of Henry's character? For here is a king who can say to his son:

Therefore, my Harry,
Be it thy course to busy giddy minds
With foreign quarrels … (*2 H4* IV.iii.341-3)

Planchon concentrated on showing up the discontinuities in the characters' actions and emphasized contrasts between words and deeds. In another example the rebels decided on the partition of England while sharing out a meal around a table. No doubt this was an extension of elements in the text which support this view of human behaviour. (In converting *The Murder of Gonzago* Hamlet equally *magnifies* and is selective in his textual focus: '*one scene of it* comes near … my father's death'; *Ham.* III.ii.74-5). If it is true, as Terry Eagleton noted of *Henry IV*, that 'Falstaff appeals to the sensuous facts of the body to deflate ideological illusions', then this clearly matches the oral fixations of the German director which Planchon is reflecting – 'the self-pleasuring body which refuses to be inscribed by social imperatives' (Eagleton 1986:16). Such a Brechtian approach disturbed traditional views of the play and how it should be produced. It was also deeply thought provoking. As Bradby and Williams express it:

> The result of his production was to present a vast and detailed reflection on problems of power and its legitimacy, of order versus disorder and of ideas of national unity. As the Algerian war was building towards its crisis, these themes had an obvious relevance to contemporary France and one that was not missed by the spectators. (1988: 60)

Yet while Planchon warned his audience of the dangers of imperialism abroad, he seemed strangely blind to the dangers of a different kind of imperialistic practice – one which, arguably, he was following himself. The dictatorship of the proletariat might very easily translate to the dictatorship of the director, and Planchon, in claiming the prerogatives of an artistic prince, was never slow in asserting the director's right to rule.

In showing the relationship between individual and collective destinies, Planchon's *Henry IV* incorporated elements of Brechtian *gestus*, whereby each character clearly demonstrates his underlying attitudes and position in society. Even the costumes reflected the social status of the different characters. For the common people some rough materials were used with bland, dull colours; the soldiers with no rank wore impersonal costumes with suggestions of leather, metal and stiffness. The lords wore emblems of their riches; their costumes were colourful, obviously fashionable, and suggested warmth. The Prince was dressed with a refined simplicity; his friend Poins wore a shabby imitation of the Prince's clothes. The Prince's costume changed as he did – from something like blue jeans, to a double-breasted jacket, to a smoking jacket, and finally to the robe of state, made deliberately heavy-looking so that he looked almost crushed beneath its weight (Daoust 61). Thus the shift from footloose rebel to careworn ruler was suggested through the 'scenic writing'.

Planchon's enthusiasm for the cinema was reflected in the Brechtian technique of screening summaries of each scene before it took place. To allow speed of production and to give a true flavour of Shakespeare's rapid-fire, almost cinematic, narrative technique, huge medieval maps were used as backdrops. This reminded the audience of the struggle for power and territory that lies at the base of the plot. It also helped to clarify Shakespeare's play for a French audience many of whom were not sophisticated people. (Designer) Allio's sets, thus, like the textural adaptation were designed to help spectators disentangle a complex and unfamiliar plot. Speedy scene changes were made possible also by the use of models representing the various locations: London, the Gadshill road, the tavern, the royal palace. Other objects, placed conveniently to the left or right of the slightly raised played area, also served a symbolic function: a throne for the palace, stools and a barrel for the tavern.

In the 1960s Planchon distanced himself somewhat from the Brechtian influence so evident in *Henry IV*. Significantly, in that (1957) production Planchon called Part I 'Falstaff,' and Part II 'Henry V' – a recognition that in this production, at least, he had been partly overshadowed by the Falstaffian Brecht figure? In the presence of Falstaff, Poins and his other cynical, low-life companions, Prince Hal finds it impossible to inherit the riches of his own emotional life ('But I tell thee, my heart bleeds *inwardly* that my father is so sick': *2H4* II.ii.40-1). Later in his career that determination to re-find lost emotions would place Planchon apart from Brecht. Thus, of *Richard III* (1966):

> I cannot live without Shakespeare ... in his world I feel completely at ease ... I find in his plays the two things that excite me and that seem worthy subjects for the theatre: politics and love. In Shakespeare the social analysis never crushes the individual psychology of the characters while at the same time the characters do not mask the general view of the society that is being described. (Cited in Bradby and Williams 1988: 69)

Henry IV was one of several productions at Villeurbanne in the late 1950s that won Planchon the admiration not only of local audiences but, also, of the Paris critics. Despite recognition from the government, and the award of the title *centre dramatique national* to the successful Villeurbanne company, Planchon was wary of accepting further government-sponsored aid. Like Gordon Craig he favoured a 'Duce' within the theatre; but it was quite another thing to accept the dictates of a 'Duce' outside the theatre (Craig 1923: 17). Central to the director's power, in Planchon's view, was control of finance, which in turn deeply affects artistic decisions. In this consideration lay his reluctance to accept government schemes which would limit his own power. At the end of the 1960s, for example, he was offered the post of director of the Théâtre National Populaire in Paris, a not inconsiderable prize with its lure of a six million franc subsidy; but again sensing that this would limit his own freedom and influence, Planchon refused. In the end, apparently on the (inverted) principle that if Mahomet will not come to the mountain, the mountain had better go to Mahomet, the government caved in, and in 1973 the title Théâtre National Populaire was transferred from Paris to his own theatre at Villeurbanne. Significantly, however, Planchon retained his financial independence and the company continued to function legally as a *société anonyme* (a limited company). The waiting was over. 'Th' immediate heir',[12] the Prince, had finally ascended to the throne – and, reforming it altogether, on his own terms.

[1] J.D.Salinger's anti-hero, Holden Caulfield, makes this comment about Olivier's (film) portrayal of Hamlet. See *The Catcher in the Rye* (Harmondsworth, 1958), p.123.

[2] David Bradby, 'France' in the *The Cambridge Guide to Theatre*, ed. Martin Banham (Cambridge, 1988), p.367.

[3] See Antonin Artaud, *The Theatre and its Double*, trans. Mary Caroline Richards (New York, 1958), p.79.

[4] See Laurence Olivier, *Confessions of an Actor* (London, 1989), p.181: 'By this time [c.1951] I had become very friendly with our French colleagues, Madeleine Renaud and her brilliant *homme de théâtre*, Jean Louis Barrault, whom I first met during our Old Vic visit to Paris in 1945.'

[5] Jean-Louis Barrault, *The Theatre of Jean-Louis Barrault*, trans. Joseph Chiari (London, 1961), p.93. Other quotations from Barrault in this section, unless otherwise stated, are from the same source.

[6] See Plato, *The Republic*, trans. Desmond Lee (Harmondsworth, 1955), pp.202-6.

[7] Jan Kott, *Shakespeare Our Contemporary*, trans. Boleslaw Taborski (London, 1967), p.230.

[8] Jean Vilar, 'The Tradition of the Theatre', an unpublished translation by Christopher Kotschnig, reprinted as 'Theatre without Pretension' in *Directors on Directing* ed. Toby Cole and Helen Krich Chinoy (London, 1964), pp.267-70. Quotations from Vilar in this section, unless otherwise stated, are from this essay.

[9] Quotations in order: *1H4* V.i.8; *2H4* I.i.9; *2H4* I.i.154.

[10] Review by Jean Duvignaud quoted in David Bradby and David Williams, *Directors' Theatre* (London, 1988), p.54.

[11] Jacques Copeau, 'Dramatic Economy' in *Directors on Directing* ed. Cole and Chinoy, p.225.

[12] Compare 'th'immediate heir', *2 Henry 4* (V.ii.70), with 'the most immediate to our throne', *Hamlet* I.ii.109.

6 | A King of Infinite Space

> 'O God, I could be bounded in a nutshell and count myself a king of infinite space, were it not that I have bad dreams.' *Hamlet* II.ii.256-8

> 'As I write I do not feel a compulsion to tell the whole truth … Rather I side with Hamlet when he calls for a flute and cries out against the attempt to sound the mystery of a human being, as though one could know all its holes and stops.' Peter Brook, *Threads of Time* (1998: 1-2)

Over Peter Brook's centre at the Bouffes du Nord in Paris one word dominates: Theatre. Brook's *The Shifting Point* published in the late 1980s is sub-titled: *Forty Years of Theatrical Exploration 1946-1987*. Seen in terms of this theatrical search, Brook's career attains to a kind of unity that defies the image of a man constantly in a state of change. 'I want to change and develop,' the once aspiring young director is quoted as saying, 'and dread the thought of standing still' (Trewin 1971: 17). For Brook, even into his eighth decade, the restless search for perfection continues. As Michael Coveney puts it of *Qui est là*, a (1996) Paris production based on *Hamlet*: 'Brook is distilling everything down these days in search of the pure white light of theatrical expression.' John Peter's review of the same production is entitled: 'Any Answers?'[1] In fact, a profile of Brook in many ways focuses and encapsulates the flux of cultural forces that has provided the raw material of this study: Russian parents; British education; German heroes; lives (colonizes?) in France.

As the momentum of Brook's reputation grows with the years the commentator reaches for new superlatives: a Saint for a Secular Age; a King of Infinite Space; a Theatrical Deity. Brook has become – to put it in the slightly less flattering words of the critic of *Le Monde* – 'une vache sacrée'. Or something else – *shifting*.

Illustration 9

Peter Brook's Theatre at Les Bouffes du Nord in Paris.

'I want to be a vampire of the outside world,' the young director declared, 'and at intervals to give back the blood I have drawn out, in some creative form' (Trewin 17). 'Now could I drink hot blood,' says Hamlet, in the first flush of theatrical success:

> 'Tis now the very witching time of night,
> When churchyards yawn, and hell itself breathes out
> Contagion to this world. Now could I drink hot blood,
> And do such bitter business as the day
> Would quake to look on. (*Hamlet* III.ii.377-81)

'The youngest earthquake' – to move with Shakespeare's changing image – was how Sir Barry Jackson described the prodigy when he gave Brook, then aged 20, his first directorial responsibility at the Birmingham Repertory in 1945. Brook must sometimes, says his biographer, have felt the ground shaking beneath him.[2] Young Brook, like young Hamlet, was set to shake the world through theatre. In reviewing *Qui est là*, Michael Coveney suggests that Craig, Meyerhold, Stanislavsky, Brecht and Artaud are:

> The twentieth-century ghosts who haunt Brook's astonishing career in the same way as the supernatural goadings of a murdered father assail his son and heir. (*Observer* 14/1/96)

In this chapter we shall see that each one of these ghosts (and others) has played some role in the development of an elusive theatrical genius. Brook has chosen always to direct rather than act, but – if he were to play a role – one of his actors recalls him saying: 'Of course the only part I would be right for is Hamlet' (Trewin 35).

Although in his time a man may play many parts, Hamlet is a potent image linking Brook with others considered earlier in this study. Samuel Leiter, for example, compares Russian-born English Brook to German-born Russian Meyerhold: 'When Brook appeared the English theatre at last found its own Meyerhold.' For Leiter, Brook and Meyerhold are perhaps the twentieth century's two most outstanding examples of the director experimentalist, the artist-scientist who uses the theatre as a laboratory to see what chemical effect the combination of selected theatrical ingredients will have on the end result. Such men are for ever searching, asking questions, trying to discover that which is 'essentially undiscoverable – what is the theatre, what are its natural properties, and why does it exist?' (1991: 219). Both Meyerhold and Brook see in Hamlet an image of their own search. Meyerhold plans a book entitled, *Hamlet: The Story of a Director*, and envisages a theatre where only *Hamlet* (in different production styles) would be staged. When Brook first directed the play he took the production to Russia. The year was 1955 and Brook was aged 30 – a significant age (V.i.157). He, too, would play Hamlet at the Moscow Art Theatre.

When Brook approaches Shakespeare's text(s) in 1996 it is with nothing so pedestrian as a production of the play in mind. *Qui est là* becomes instead a reflection on the problems of theatre and the role of the director in particular. Structurally, *Qui est là* is a greatly shortened version of *Hamlet* interspersed with commentaries, spoken by actors, from the fatherly ghosts who have been Brook's inspiration. The setting for the production is simple: a square white platform and some plain wooden chairs. The actors wear casual, present-day clothes, supplemented with the odd cloak or cap. The beginning of the play is signalled only by a subtle alteration of the lighting. Enter Barnardo who looks at the audience and asks, Qui est là? An exploration has begun (Peters 4/2/96). The question that begins *Hamlet* 'Who's there?' is not only an existential challenge to every human being; for Brook it is a challenge to define his own role as director. Perhaps, somewhere, a King Mouse is stirring. To be King or not to be: to have power or not to have power – is that the question? '[Hamlet],' writes Jan Kott in *Shakespeare Our Contemporary*, 'considers all the pros and cons. He is a born conspirator.'

> 'To be' means for him to revenge his father and to assassinate the King; while 'not to be' means – to give up the fight. (1967: 51)

If there are, as is sometimes suggested, a lot of Kott marks on Brook's work, then the quotation may be particularly apt. Brook's great reflection on kingship, his 1962 *King Lear* either paralleled or reflected Kott's thinking closely; there seems to be some dispute about whether or not Brook, at that time, was greatly influenced by reading *Shakespeare Our Contemporary*.[3] 'Who is it that can tell me who I am?' (I.iv.212) is Lear's cry and Brook's production in Paris *Qui est là* leads to a similar question. Viewed not as a question but as a partial statement, *Qui est là* suggests: (He) who is there. And who that 'He' (who that King?) may be is the central, overriding question of this chapter. If the 'He' is Shakespeare, Hamlet's creator, then the challenge may be to wrest that creation from the creator – the ultimate challenge to the playwright father. An early critic commented on how Shakespeare appeared to be fighting a losing battle against his determined young director. Of *Qui est là*, John Peter writes: 'It is the way Brook and Carrière handle the language of *Hamlet* that makes the Shakespearean element the weakest in *Qui est là*.' Brook becomes Hamlet, *animateur extraordinaire*, rewriting the script for his own ends.

> For by the image of my cause I see
> The portraiture of his. (*Hamlet* V.ii.78-9)

This character has shaped the director's thoughts from the earliest days. At the age of 7, on Christmas day, using a toy theatre, the child prodigy had presented to his family a 4-hour version of *Hamlet*. His parents were enthusiastically supportive but baulked when Brook (who was acting all the parts himself) suggested that he repeat the experiment – using different settings. 'Frustrated,' says his biographer, 'the director went moodily to bed.' An early notebook is inscribed: '*Hamlet* by P. Brook and W. Shakespeare' (Trewin 89). The Oedipal challenge is undoubtedly one that has fascinated the director. His first production in the professional theatre, in 1945, was of Jean Cocteau's *The Infernal Machine* – 'an indifferent play,' J.C. Trewin calls it, 'on the Oedipus theme and the invariable working of destiny' (17). Nearly a quarter of a century later, seemingly at the summit of his career – in 1968, the year of *The Empty Space* – Brook directed Seneca's *Oedipus* at the Old Vic. ('Seneca can not be too heavy.'). That would be followed shortly by Brook's masterful *A Midsummer Night's Dream* (1970). It was to be his crowning achievement in the English theatre.

In Chapter One ('The Kings') of *Shakespeare Our Contemporary*, Jan Kott argues that *Hamlet* can only be understood in the light of Shakespeare's history plays (10-15). Kott imagines Shakespeare's kings as precariously situated, frightened creatures. There are, he suggests, a series of kings, every one of whom is an executioner, and a victim in turn. There are also (other) living frightened people. They can only gaze upon the grand staircase of history. But their own fate depends on who will reach the highest step, or leap into the abyss. That is why they are frightened. But Kott goes on to question this process further:

> What did in fact the Grand Mechanism mean for Shakespeare? A succession of kings climbing and pushing one another off the grand staircase of history, or a wave of hot blood rising up to one's head and blinding the eyes? (1967: 25)

Kott adamantly refuses to allow this process to remain a distant one. He sees the past in the future and the present. As Brook puts it in the foreword to the English translation of Kott's book: 'Kott is an Elizabethan … Shakespeare is a contemporary of Kott, Kott is a contemporary of Shakespeare.' In Kott's own words: 'Shakespeare not only dramatizes history; he dramatizes psychology, gives us large slices of it, and *in them we find ourselves*'(15). In *Qui est là* finding ourselves is part of Brook's search; and the 'us' or 'we,' in this case, may be more regal than general. To discover Hamlet (courtier, *soldier*, scholar) – and thereby Brook as Hamlet director – it may be, as Kott suggests, that Shakespeare's history plays are an essential interpretative tool. And it is in the French theatre that those history plays (for this director) take on a special significance.

'Fair Stood the Wind for France'

There has been no shortage in the French theatre of directors willing to stage Shakespeare's history plays. Vilar's democratically inspired *Richard II*, for example, was followed by Planchon's less heroic and more ruthless *Henry IV*. In the 1980s Ariane Mnouchkine revived both of these plays in striking new productions. Jean-Louis Barrault has confessed himself impressed by Henry VI (another 'hero of superior doubt'); Barrault, indeed, claimed a production of *Henry VI* as his finest. Planchon concluded a trilogy of Shakespearean productions with *Richard III*. One notable exception, one play for which directors have shown no enthusiasm, is (perhaps understandably) *Henry V*. There are times, as Jean-Louis Barrault has said, when Shakespeare's jingoism 'might irk a rather sensitive Frenchman' (1961: 95). The average French audience does not feel inclined to celebrate a comprehensive French defeat at the hands of a conquering English king. It might, indeed, take an Englishman to play old – or rather young – Harry in France. In 1972 Roger Planchon suggested that:

> About eight or nine years ago, in my opinion, a certain number of directors had attained a point of perfection in their productions. Strehler, Brook, people like that, were creating impeccable productions, and they felt the need to change things further. Most of these directors said: 'Let's chop up the text, let's write our own texts collectively...' (Kustow 51)

The fate of the text – and thus of the playwright – is indeed central to the story of Peter Brook and his approach to the French theatre at the end of the 1960s. By the close of the decade that firework prince, Tyrone Guthrie, was something of a spent force and Brook's dominance of the English scene was complete. It was time, perhaps, to look for foreign (vasty?) fields. 'Then in 1970,' Brook wrote in *The Shifting Point*, 'I moved to Paris' (105). In fact, the move had begun some time before ('It wasn't a sudden decision'). In Brook's need to expand horizons there is something of the adventurer, the imperialist, as well as the searcher for truth and communion (and all of these are in Hamlet). Which one of these, then, is the dominant impulse? – this must be a recurring question in any discussion of this director. To understand the attraction of the move to France and Brook's relationship with the French theatre, it is necessary to look beyond that date (1970) but also, in turn, to earlier events and influences in Brook's career.

In 1949, playing Samuel to the young David, Kenneth Tynan anointed Peter Brook as the future king. Very soon, Tynan prophesied, the young director prodigy would be at the height of his powers. Yet not all of Tynan's assessment is eulogistic. Brook is described as 'smug', and the English critic detected a 'sly throwaway sophistication' (1984: 84-6). Another critic writing of the young Brook suggested he might be a little too pleased with himself. During his productions Norman Marshall imagined young Master Brook skipping about in the wings saying 'Oh, what a Clever Boy Am I!' – a quality which Marshall admitted ceased after some years. Marshall gives some of the credit for that to Sir John Gielgud, 'and his dislike of producers [directors] who indulge in exhibitionist caperings' (1975: 198). In anointing Brook as king in place of the reigning Saul ('He has all Guthrie's genius for invention and adds to it a continental delicacy and finical flair: he selects far more critically than the older man'), Tynan, perhaps, did not guess that for this young prince ('One feels he has never travelled anywhere on foot or on buses, but is wrapped up in silk and carried') one (small) kingdom might not be enough. England might prove too narrow for his mind. In considering Brook it is ever a necessity to look beyond national boundaries, to France, to Europe and even beyond that. And in all of this the relationship of playwright to director is crucial.

In ' A Director's Theatre' written in the mid-1950s, Eric Bentley commented on the ascendancy of the director in the modern theatre (1969: 269): 'To speak of Shakespeare's *Hamlet* will soon be as unusual and eccentric as to speak of Schikaneder's *Magic Flute*. The playwright is just a librettist; the composer's name is Reinhardt, Meyerhold, Piscator, Baty, Logan, or Kazan.' While the continent of Europe, in Bentley's view, had a preponderance of directorial talent, England contained two rivals: 'the Russian-born Peter Brook and the Irishman Tyrone Guthrie.' Bentley praises Guthrie's technical excellence but – possibly mindful of Vilar's comment that an actor is more than an intelligent animal – dismisses Guthrie as 'the most expert sheepdog that ever came out of Ireland'. Unfortunately Bentley fails in his article to tell us into which canine category Brook falls (Tynan's review suggests helpfully that if you bit into Brook 'he would taste like fondant cream or preserved ginger'.) Bentley's linking the rise of the director with Europe is obviously significant. The continental influences were always more clearly recognized and welcomed by Brook than by Guthrie. Of Guthrie's closure of the Old Vic school in the early 1950s, Sir Peter Hall says 'he thought it was too arty, too *continental*'.[4]

In contrast to this from early in his career Brook's inspiration has come from the continent. 'Paris,' he writes in *Threads of Time*, 'naturally seemed the best place on earth; even its smells and its shadows had poetry – and it took me many years to understand what the director I most admired, Tyrone Guthrie, meant when he told me he disliked Paris and preferred the roughness of Belfast' (1998: 78). His first Shakespearean staging, of *Love's Labour's Lost* in 1946, was inspired by seeing a French production in Paris. In the early 1950s, Brook had conversations with Bertolt Brecht in Berlin. If Brecht was an early influence, Brook saw him 'in direct line from Craig' and was to draw parallels between the two men. In 1956 (shortly after his own 'Moscow *Hamlet*') Brook would visit Craig at his home in the south of France. In Paris the work of the exiled Irishman, Samuel Beckett was to have a huge impact on the young director; arguably it is Beckett rather than Kott who was the real inspiration behind *King Lear* in 1962. Certainly Roger Planchon was quick to identify Beckett as a negative influence in Brook's *Lear*: 'I think *Lear* is totally tragic and in that sense like Beckett, but there's also a tomorrow in the play, and this tomorrow is not like today, it will be something else' (Kustow 1972: 55).

Only after meeting the experimental Polish director, Grotowski, in the 1960s did Brook hear of Antonin Artaud – and then almost by accident began reading him. He dates this about the time he was working on the film of *Lord of the Flies* in New York (1964). The combining of elements of Artaud ('sudden shock') and Brecht ('cool analysis') was to be one of Brook's outstanding achievements in the theatre. As he writes in 'How Many Trees Make A Forest?'

> *Neither Brecht nor Artaud* stands for ultimate truth. Each represents a certain aspect of it, a certain tendency, and at our time perhaps their respective viewpoints are the most diametrically opposed. To try to discover where, how, and at what level this opposition ceases to be real is something I have found very interesting, particularly during the period in 1964 between the season of the 'Theatre of Cruelty' and the production of *Marat/Sade*. (Brook's emphasis; 1988: 42)

Yet for Brook diversity ('the shifting viewpoint') has always been strength. He concludes the same article: 'For Artaud, theatre is fire; for Brecht, theatre is clear vision; for Stanislavsky, theatre is humanity. Why must we choose among them?' Yet Artaud and Brecht, for all their differences, clearly had something in common: apart from belief in a strong director, they both rejected 'enslavement to the text', and emphasized 'theatre' above the work of the playwright. As we shall see this de-emphasizing of the text has been a major part of Brook's vision.

Given these strong continental influences, it is interesting to note that Brook begins *The Shifting Point* by marking out clearly a fundamental change in his own approach to directing; a shift that he contrasts with continental approaches in which the director imposes his will on a production. 'In France and Germany, this approach is much admired, and it is called his "reading" of the play. I have come to realize that this is a sad and *clumsy* use of directing: it is more honourable if one wants to dominate totally one's means of expression to use a pen as a servant, or a brush.' Significantly, however, he rejects another 'unsatisfactory alternative'. The unsatisfactory alternative is where the director makes himself the servant, becoming the co-ordinator of a group of actors, limiting himself to suggestions, criticisms and encouragement. Such directors are good men, Brook suggests, but like all well-meaning and tolerant liberals, their work can never go beyond a certain point. This change in approach was clearly evident in the early 1960s (Brook specifically mentions *Marat/Sade* in 1964), and marked a shift in emphasis:

> The rehearsal work should create a climate in which the actors feel free to produce everything they can bring to the play. That's why in *the early stages* of rehearsal everything is open and *I impose nothing at all*. In a sense this is diametrically opposed to the technique in which, the first day, the director gives a speech on what the play's about and the way he's going to approach it. I used to do that years ago and I eventually found out that that's a rotten way of *starting*. (1988: 3)

Brook instead relies on what he calls the 'formless hunch' which he brings to the production and the director 'is continually provoking the actor, stimulating him, asking questions and creating an atmosphere in which the actor can dig, probe and investigate'. But the essential difference between Brook and 'the well-meaning … liberal' is clearly marked:

> In these last stages, the director cuts away all that's extraneous, all that belongs just to the actor and not to the actor's intuitive connection with the play. The director, *because of his prior work, and because it is his role, and also because of his hunch*, is in a better position to say then what belongs to the play and what belongs to that superstructure of rubbish that everybody brings with him. (*Ibid.*)

The terms of Brook's engagement with actors and text is subtly expressed, but there can be no doubting the power and prestige invested here in the director. In the mid-1960s, with this concept of the director newly formulated, 'fair stood,' as his biographer puts it (quoting Drayton), 'the wind for France'. But to understand more fully Brook's royal road to supremacy means shifting our view, for a while, from the war-like Prince's progress in France. While keeping Kott's Grand Mechanism in mind, the shift involves turning to three plays – a tragedy, a romance and a comedy – with which Brook was preoccupied in the decade before his move to France. In following his climb up the 'grand staircase' these three productions – *Lear* (1962); *Tempest* (1968); *Dream* (1970) – are key steps.

Up the Grand Staircase

No doubt Brook sensed in the 1960s that the writing was on the wall for the director as autocrat. In *The Producer and the Play* (1957), Norman Marshall had argued that 'the era of the producer [director] is over'. There was no longer, he was sure, any figure to match the masterful originality of a Meyerhold, a Stanislavsky or a Copeau (1975: 279). In *King Lear*, a play with which Brook was preoccupied in the early 1960s, the image of 'the writing on the wall' may be relevant; for the story of Lear, in some important respects not found in earlier 'Leir' stories,[5] clearly parallels that of Nebuchadnezzar in the Book of Daniel. Certainly Shakespeare was familiar with the Daniel story, not only through knowledge of the Bible, but also because from early medieval times the story had been dramatized. In the Daniel story, King Nebuchadnezzar loses his power when he grows arrogant and abuses it. Eventually he regains his throne but only after he has been truly humbled, like Lear going mad and living amongst wild beasts. When, after Nebuchadnezzar's death, his son Belshazzar sees the Writing on the Wall, it is a terrible omen which heralds (as Daniel explains to him) the end of a dynasty (Daniel 5). Jonathan Miller notes the number of Biblical references in Shakespeare's play – Miller stresses the New Testament – and he goes on to assert that '*King Lear* is a Stuart, not a Druid, play about statecraft and its breakdown *when authority is removed*'. Further: '*King Lear* raises the … kind of questions that people must have asked themselves when the nature of sovereignty began to appear to be unstable' (1986: 131). To be king or not to be king – yes, that is the question.

The plot of *Lear*, with its reduction of the king to sub-human terms, 'a poor, bare, forked animal' (III.iv.101-2), might well be interpreted as a veiled warning to the Stuart kings of the growing demands of a new capitalist middle class for power; it might even be seen as a muted prophecy of a new kind of democratic power, a rejection of autocratic rule by a single individual or *tyrannos*. Sensing that the time for that modern *tyrannos* of the theatre, the director, was running out Brook's need was to stake out some new territory; in a changing world to outline a new role for the director – and it is as *director* that Brook has always operated. Closer to the Platonic ideal of minding one's own business than many French directors, he has never dabbled seriously in either acting or playwriting (in the formal sense). How then to retain or even enhance the power of the director in an era – the subversive 1960s – that clearly views such power with suspicion?

Part of the importance of Brook's *Lear* lay in the director's ability to make the audience see the story in a totally different light. 'Every *Lear* that follows Peter Brook's *Lear*,' wrote Martin Esslin, 'will contain its influence, or react against it.' (1987: 175). Jan Kott noted that 'there is in *King Lear* – and Mr. Brook was the first to discover it – a combination of madness, passion, pride, folly, imperiousness, anarchy, humanity and awe, which all have their exact place in time and history' (1967: 296). Jonathan Miller believed that audiences who had grown accustomed to the Druidical stereotype, which had perpetuated itself in a clone for the best part of a hundred years, were startled to hear the lines spoken by a cantankerous, bullet-headed warrior (1986: 78). With the manipulation of the text something strange is happening to Shakespeare. Shakespeare becomes more like Brecht ('*Il a transformé Shakespeare en Brecht*'), or Beckett according to the whim – or the vision – of the director. The playwright, indeed, has become librettist. 'When Peter Brook restaged *King Lear* or *A Midsummer Night's Dream*,' wrote Jonathan Miller in *Subsequent Performances*, 'the result was determined not only by his substantive theories about the meaning of text and about the motives of the characters but also by *his resolution to change the identity of plays in general*' (1986: 72). Brook, in other words, like Hamlet, seeks power through theatre, seeing the playwright as servant, not master.

What amounts to a power struggle between playwright and director retains its potency during the 1960s and is crucial to an understanding of why Brook chose to direct *The Tempest* in 1968. Why, asked Ralph Berry in an interview (1974) does the director choose 'one play at a given moment when presumably you feel that this is the moment, this is the right play for now?' To which Brook replied: 'That's a vast and in a way absolutely marvellous question, because through this question (I don't think there's any other) everything is brought into relief' (1989: 131). For Brook *The Tempest* has always been a challenging and important play. He had tried, somewhat unsuccessfully, to direct the play in 1957 and again in 1963. 'Brook does not like to repeat himself,' noted Robert Speaight, but this was one play that Brook was prepared to return to again and again. In Speaight's phrase he was 'searching' (1973: 253). 'Nothing in the play,' Brook wrote in *The Empty Space* (106), 'is what it seems, how it takes place on an island and not on an island.' Central to *The Tempest* is the regal, magical figure of Prospero with his ambivalent attitudes: to power on the one hand and his books on the other. Potentially in the power structures of the modern theatre, only two figures are capable of fulfilling Prospero's role: the playwright or the director (certainly not the actor: 'It is quite clear that an *ordinary* actor pretending to be a god is ridiculous. One sees that even in productions of *The Tempest* where a lot of girls try to be goddesses: *The Tempest* is usually a disaster.')

The conflict between author and director is made manifest in Brook's *The Tempest* (1968). For this unusual production Brook used an international company set up at the invitation of Jean-Louis Barrault as part of the *Théâtre des Nations* Festival events in Paris – a concept that would lead to the establishment in 1970 of the International Centre for Theatre Research (C.I.R.T.). In *The Tempest*, Brook experimented with his foreign actors to find 'a universal, synthetic theatre style'. Possibly taking their cue from Marowitz's collage *Hamlet* (1964) – which Brook's biographer summed up as a 'brief and pointless *Hamlet* variation, the lines in a scrambled shake-up and the Prince as a stricken clown' – the company treated Shakespeare's text as so many words and images which they felt free to 'alter, mutilate, rearrange, and cut at will ... A scrambled plot, newly devised character relationships, startling time shifts, choral chanting, words as sound effects rather than as symbols of meaning,

incantations, overt sexual imagery, acrobatics, disparate costumes, Grotowski face-masks, mingling with the audience – all
were features of this much criticized experiment' (Leiter 1991:
232). At the Round House, where Brook's production in
England was staged, the experimental replaced any orthodox
approach to the text. 'The plot,' wrote Margaret Croyden, 'is
shattered, condensed, *deverbalized*' (1969: 126). Caliban emerged
from between the legs of a giantess Sycorax standing at the top
of the scaffolding and evil was born. He raped Miranda and
became master of the island in a sexual orgy. 'So the plays
submerged ideas were dragged to the surface, improvised and
explored in terms of such clues as Shakespeare has provided,'
noted J.L.Styan. He added: 'The result was *mutilated Shakespeare
but original Brook*' (1977: 217). And the submerged ideas were
not just Shakespeare's. Rape was, apparently, a recurring theme
in Brook's mind in 1968. In *The Empty Space* (81), illustrating the
idea of alienation, he wrote:

> A girl, raped, walks on to a stage in tears – and if her acting
> touches us sufficiently, we automatically accept the implied
> conclusion that she is a victim and an unfortunate one. But
> suppose a clown were to follow her, mimicking her tears,
> and suppose by his talent he succeeds in making us laugh.
> His mockery destroys our first response. Then where do our
> sympathies go? The truth of her character, the validity of her
> position, are both put into question by the clown, and at the
> same time our own easy sentimentality is exposed.

This, it seems, is the new enlightenment *à la* Brecht and Brook.
'After us,' as W.B.Yeats said of Jarry's *Ubu*, 'the savage God.'
Yet rape and pillage have always been the stock-in-trade of the
imperialist adventurer.

   Who then is the true theatrical magician, the real Prospero,
who can conjure up all these marvels? Is it the playwright
working in his isolated cell ('mine own library with volumes
that/ I prize *above* my dukedom': I.ii.168-9), or the director
working with a group of actors? Not only with *Lear* and *The
Tempest* (1968) but, perhaps, even more so in the *Dream* (1970),
Brook was laying claim to be the true magician. 'The audience
was to look into the magic box,' wrote J.L.Styan of the *Dream's*

unusual box-shaped set, 'not only to see the magic but also to
be shown what was up the magician's sleeve … for a month
Brook had made the actors practise their tricks in improvisation
and rehearsal, and in this setting the audience willingly accepted
any invention of the company. The show was indeed
breathtaking. The purple flower became a twirling plate on a
juggler's wand, passed spinning from Puck to Oberon, a magic
image in itself' (1977: 225). Importantly, too, in the *Dream*
Brook moved further away from the text emphasizing now a
synthesis of bodily and verbal poetry. During the rehearsal
period Brook developed, with the cast, exercises in non-verbal
communication which were incorporated into the action of the
play. 'One would think that in all this the lines would be
drowned,' pondered J.L.Styan, '*true the text was often at variance
with the action.*' Yet, like Styan, many observers were enthusiastic
despite this. 'Never before,' noted Norman Marshall of the
verse speaking, 'can this play have given so much pleasure to
the ear. It was the ultimate magic of the production' (1975:
327). J.C.Trewin judged that Brook had 'polished the mirror' –
not demolished the play. A few critics remained stubbornly
unimpressed, thinking it a tiresomely self-indulgent display of
directorial gimmickry: a director-shaped commodity.

De-emphasizing the words ('the death of the word'), the
text, inevitably lessens the influence of the playwright and
increases the stature of the director working closely with his
actors. In 1968, the year of *The Tempest*, it is thus no surprise to
find Brook airing his criticisms of the role of the French
playwright. For in the 1960s in France the playwright – and not
the director – was still ultimate king:

> But this way of thinking hasn't reached the French theatre,
> where it is still the author who at the first rehearsal does a
> one-man show, reading out and performing all the parts.
> This is the most exaggerated form of a tradition that dies
> hard everywhere. The author has been forced to make a
> virtue of his specialness, and to turn his literariness *into a
> crutch for a self-importance that in his heart he knows is not justified by
> his work.* Maybe a need for privacy is a deep part of an
> author's make-up. It is possible that it is only with the door

closed, communing with himself, that he can wrestle into
form inner images and conflicts of which he would never
speak in public. We do not know how Aeschylus or
Shakespeare worked. All we know is that gradually the
relationship between the man who sits at home working it all
out on paper and the world of actors and stages is getting
more and more tenuous, more and more unsatisfactory.
(1968: 38-9)

What Brook does not mention is that some French
directors, not least Jacques Copeau, have also carried on this
one-man show, reading out and performing all the parts. Yet
this unofficial declaration of war against these rebel kings of the
French arena is not unexpected (some pages earlier in The
Deadly Theatre he reminds his readers of the list of the dead in
Henry V), for it is in France that the real cockpit of war lies and
where the battle between playwright and director is being
joined. This was the battle clearly foreseen by Jean Vilar in 1946
when he wrote of two conflicting methods which would
oppose each other just as resolutely in the decades to come:
'Which one, the author or the producer [director], is today, the
true creator of the dramatic work?' (1975: 36)

Rather scornfully, Brook continues: 'If the author were a
master and not a victim one could say that he had betrayed the
theatre.' And the director continues to soften up the enemy
target with a list of searing criticisms:

> When new plays set out to imitate reality we are more
> conscious of what is imitative than what is real: if they
> explore character, it is seldom that they go far beyond stereo-
> types; if it is argument they offer, it is seldom that argument
> is taken to arresting extremes; even if it is a quality of life
> that they wish to evoke, we are usually offered no more than
> the literary quality of the well-turned phrase; if it is social
> criticism they are after, it seldom touches the heart of any
> social target; if they wish for laughter, it is usually by well-
> worn means. (1968: 39)

But is this just an attack on the modern playwright who 'has
been forced to make a virtue of his specialness, and to turn his
literariness *into a crutch for a self-importance that in his heart he knows*

is not justified by his work', or does it extend to such figures as Shakespeare ('We do not know how Aeschylus or Shakespeare worked')? Part of the crime of the author, it seems, is to work in secret; that is, of course – unlike the actor – quite outside the control and influence of the director.

To answer that question, and also to explain more fully why Brook was soon to take his crusade to the continent, it is necessary to examine, in more detail, Brook's attitude to Shakespeare himself. There can be no doubt that for Brook Shakespeare is not only an inspiration ('experimental, popular, revolutionary'),[6] but also an overpowering, even an oppressive, figure. In *The Empty Space* (39) he writes: 'In the second half of the twentieth century in England ... we are faced with the infuriating fact that Shakespeare is still our model.' Yet Brook in his interview with Ralph Berry acknowledges Shakespeare's unique achievement: 'What passed through this man called Shakespeare and came into existence on sheets of paper, is something quite different from any other author's work. It's not Shakespeare's view of the world, it's something which actually resembles reality' (1989: 132). This de-egotizing or de-individualizing of Shakespeare is characteristic of Brook's approach. The sense that Shakespeare's achievement is unique may be important here. For in 1974 (the year of this interview) the director was preparing one of his first (and subsequently rare) productions of Shakespeare in France –*Timon of Athens*, a play about a world in transition. Brook in his interview with Berry is quick to regain something of the initiative from this overwhelming father figure of the English drama. 'And that is that this fabric reaches us today, not as a series of messages, which is what authorship almost always produces – it is a series of impulses that can produce many understandings.' Thus 'every interpretation of this material is a subjective act'. Now it is the interpreter (i.e. the director) who retains his individuality, not the playwright who becomes amorphous, de-individualized.

Perhaps in elucidating this relationship, it is worth citing Roger Planchon whose career, in some respects, has parallels with Brook. 'I think it's terrible to direct Shakespeare during the daytime,' said Planchon, 'and come home at night to scribble a page':

> It's like facing a firing squad. You see something perfect in the day, and at night you can't be satisfied with your own little droppings. So I write with a feeling of *powerlessness*, which is huge. (Kustow 1972: 51)

('What to an Imperial spirit must ever be a pang,' noted Winston Churchill in 1936, is *'powerlessness.'*)[7] There are indeed times when this sense of wanting to get 'out from under the parental shadow' is clearly evident in Brook's pronouncements. Thus in *The Shifting Point*: 'Yet we are all sick to death of Shakespeare. We've now seen all the unknown plays. We cannot live on revivals of the masterpieces' (1988: 55). And in an interview with Ralph Berry: 'However much I love Shakespeare, the moment I'm told that I'm *serving* Shakespeare, there's another instinct that says, "Fuck Shakespeare – why him more than anyone else?"' (1989: 142).

It may not, then, be altogether an exaggeration to say that much of Brook's career has been an attempt to come to terms with the overwhelming greatness of Shakespeare, his universality, his achievement – and, ultimately, has been an attempt to outgrow or outstrip this dominant figure. Thus the move to France may have an added significance. For the French have always had an ambivalent attitude to Shakespeare. Voltaire first welcomed him and then condemned him as a Barbarian; and this ambivalence, as Jean-Louis Barrault reminds us, has continued ever since (1961: 91). To the French Shakespeare has appeared often as a wild Heathcliff, a cuckoo's offspring; and Shakespeare is often side-lined because the French, in any case, have their own proud literary and dramatic heritage. 'For more than a century after the Restoration, Paris was the capital of a critical domain that thoroughly repudiated Shakespeare. So what draws contemporary Shakespearians to Paris, that city of displaced desire?' asks Gary Taylor in *Reinventing Shakespeare* (1990: 362). With the foundation of Le Centre International de Recherche Théâtrale (C.I.R.T.) in 1970, Brook too, in a sense, became a cuckoo in the French cultural nest. But better that than reign in England with William the Conqueror?[8]

> Two stars keep not their motion in one sphere
> Nor can one England *brook* a double reign.
> (*1Henry 4* V.iv.64-5)

'Brook', says one critic, 'is British theatre's *king across the water.*' An examination of Brook's work at the Bouffes du Nord as well as his extensive travels, suggest this journey, this distancing from Shakespeare toward universal forms of theatre and communication ('The complete truth is global; the theatre is the place where this great jigsaw can be played.' *New York Times* 20/1/1974). The improvisational work with actors of many nationalities which was characteristic of the C.I.R.T. group's experiments in Africa (1972) lessens further the importance of text.

In improvisational work the role of the director is still crucial, although Bradby and Williams assure us that Brook is 'the least intrusive of directors'. Yet in the same passage the writers comment: 'What of Brook's role in the work of the C.I.R.T.? A few influential voices have accused him of being manipulative in his approach, exploiting actors as objects in the enactment of his obsessive visions' (1988: 165). A frequent image used about Brook's work is that of the scientist and his laboratory experiment (both of his parents had scientific training). Who, then, are the guinea-pigs? Kenneth Tynan's description (1977: 20) of Brook's subtle psychological manipulation of actors gives us a clue: '[He] would talk an elderly actress into climbing a rickety staircase ... simply by letting it be known to other members of the company that he thought she was physically unable to do it, and that he would never dream of asking her ... and she virtually insisted on doing it.'

The sense that there is a deeply negative and pessimistic side to Brook's experiments since the early 1960s is reflected in criticism of the philosophy that underpins his work. Echoing Kenneth Tynan's attack on Brook's *Iks* (an improvisational drama based on Colin Turnbull's study of the tragic demise of a north Ugandan tribe, *The Mountain People*), for its 'pessimism and misanthropy', Bradby and Williams comment:

> An interpretation of Brook's world-view as one of facile nihilism is indeed understandable in the light of … Brook's thematic material since *King Lear*. He seems to have been fascinated by the belief that, in certain extreme situations, civilizing social restraints reveal themselves to be false and shallow, crumbling to unleash the human beast within. From *Lord of the Flies* ('a potted history of man') his sensory assault version of Weiss's *Marat/Sade* (during which the copulatory revolution of the lunatics continually threat-ened to spill over into the auditorium) to *The Mahabharata* ('the great poem of the world'), his anti-idealistic bent has chosen to portray, by the death throes of liberal altruism and humanism, the destruction of innocence by experience. (1988: 169)

In a mood of cool 'moral neutrality', increasingly the director's work at the Bouffes du Nord has taken on a quasi-scientific nature. Brook's turning to Turnbull's book as a source for improvisational work is typical of a move away from the texts of individual playwrights. A production in 1994, 'The Man Who', was developed in co-operation with researcher Oliver Sacks. Significantly, in an interview with John Cornwell (*Sunday Times* 13/2/94), Sacks says: '*It's Brook's play now* and I can take very little credit for its success' (illus. 10). 'Director Peter Brook,' suggests Gary Taylor, 'searches for a form of theatre that can dispense with authors and texts altogether' (1990: 309).

Despite the distancing from Shakespearean influence, Brook would stage several productions in the 1970s after his move to France. In a 1974 staging of *Timon of Athens* the director proceeded in the experimental manner of the 1968 *Tempest*. The performance was 'staged' in the orchestra area of the old theatre (the Bouffes du Nord was once a music hall) with the audience, seated on wooden benches, involved frequently in the action. Harsh white lighting was used throughout and audience and actors were clearly in a shared space. Although the text was barely cut, the work of the playwright was being manipulated in an 'idiosyncratic interpretation of the text', and the international

cast spoke Carrière's French translation 'in a welter of incom-
prehensible pronunciations' (Leiter 1991: 237). Four years later
Brook returned briefly to Shakespeare with two successful, but
very different productions: *Measure For Measure* (at the Bouffes
du Nord) and *Antony and Cleopatra* (at the RSC in Stratford). In
Measure For Measure Brook was stressing contemporary issues:
Isabella was played as a Joan of Arc-like feminist and the
Duke's homosexual attraction to Lucio was emphasized.
Carrière's translation was performed in a stripped-down workshop style, using no music and in a setting made up of little
more than several benches and some straw. As though to
emphasize his mastery of two kingdoms, running almost con-
currently with this was Brook's *Antony and Cleopatra* at Stratford
starring Glenda Jackson and Alan Howard. Confounding
expectations this was a much more traditional production. The
almost complete text was spoken in the classical manner.

Apart from these passing flurries of Shakespearean activity,
Brook's energies were directed elsewhere during the 1970s. In
fact a brief survey of the director's main productions during
that decade presents a certain pattern that reflects on his
attitude to Shakespeare. Improvisational work in the middle
years of the decade led to the controversial *Iks* (1975). In *Ubu
aux Bouffes* (1977) – a conflation of Jarry's *Ubu* plays – Brook
explored the destructive power of the dictator who crushes all
before him, a dictator whose world vision contains no possibility of transcendent understanding. It showed a world of utter
materialism and egotism – the world as stomach. Although *The
Conference of the Birds*, a twelfth century Sufi poem, was still being
performed in 1979, work on this had begun years before. In
1972 – no doubt inspired by Jacques Copeau who in 1924 led
his company into the French countryside in search of spiritual
regeneration – Brook and his company left Paris for rural
Africa. They toured extensively experimenting through improvisation with the twelfth-century poem by the Sufi writer, Farid
Uddin Attar. As though to counter the materialistic tendencies
in *Ubu*, *The Conference of the Birds* dealt with religious themes such
as the search for God and the rejection of worldly vanity. Here
was the search for a spiritual element, the thirst for a beyond, a

something more; above all the possibility of crossing barriers. Brook, rather strangely, describes the theme as 'that of a group of birds searching for a mythical king' (1998: 190). Was Copeau's dream of communion an inspirational factor in Brook's African adventure? Perhaps it is wrong to push the comparison too far. It may, for example, be significant that Brook so dislikes the play that for much of his life inspired and fascinated Copeau: *As You Like It.* In 'An Open Letter to William Shakespeare, or, As I Don't Like It' the tone is particularly negative (1988: 72-5).

The Making of a King

These three major productions – *Iks*, *Ubu* and *The Conference of the Birds* – all represented a celebration of different aspects of reality, and a move away from the Shakespearean threshold. Yet by the mid-1980s, in 'Butter and the Knife', Brook admits that he has still not matched Shakespeare's blend of universal (butter) and specific (knife):

> So one asks: How can one find this outside Shakespeare? Is it possible to have butter and knife by other means? (1988: 155-6)

Clearly dissatisfied, Brook concludes his article with the significant words: 'In *The Mahabharata* I will start the search again. Perhaps this time we will be able to bring all these elements together.' The words were something of a prophecy for it was finally in *The Mahabharata* (1985), an ancient Sanskrit heroic poem, that Brook was to discover a source of material great enough to challenge Shakespeare. The eighteen volumes and almost 100,000 verses make it eight times the length of the Odyssey and four times the length of the Bible (An Indian elephant to crush a British lion?). Brook himself says that the poem is 'richer in dramatic material than *Conference* and *more universal than Shakespeare's complete works*.'[9] Involving intensive research, extensive travel, detailed translation and the mobilization of famous actors from around the world (including the star of Grotowski's *The Constant Prince*, Ryszard Cieslak), this production must count surely as the summit of Brook's career. The performance has been seen as above all a hymn to Brook's skill as a director, as an intercultural catalyst. The following passage reflects this sense of having found a greater than Shakespeare: 'So, for example, the tragic figure of Dhritarashtra, an old king blind from birth who can only hear second-hand reports of the actions of others, comes to life in an astonishing performance by the facially ravaged Cieslak. He saws and spits his way through the text, disinterring echoes of Lear, Gloucester and Oedipus' (Bradby and Williams 1988: 176).

However, for some Indian critics, Brook's enterprise is less the greatest cultural event of the century, and more a chef's salad with a flavour of India, spiced with the maestro's own dressing of Shakespeareana. What is more, the great epic poem when wrenched from its cultural context becomes deeply flawed, even meaningless ('one cannot separate the culture from the text'). In the view of Gautam Dasgupta, the intercultural elements in Brook's production, most significantly the Shake-spearean ones (Dhritarashtra comes across as Lear; Krishna as Prospero; Kunti, Gandhari and Draupadi as Lear's daughters), may have served as easy referents to his western audience, but they fail to do justice to specific traits of these characters, traits that stem from a complex underpinning of Brahmanic and Vedic precepts (Williams 1991: 265). Simultaneously, it seems, Brook can transform Shakespeare by removing him from his cultural base, while introducing the Bard as a bastardized cuckoo chick into the Indian cultural nest. Rustom Bharucha noted how Duryodhana evoked Richard III in his Machiavellian strategies and self-destruction ('I want to be disconnected'). Further, 'the shockingly truncated' (Dasgupta), or 'the five minute encapsulation' (Bharucha) of the *Bhagavad Gita* removes one of the poems most profound elements – it is as if one were to stage the Bible without the least mention of the Sermon on the Mount. In its conclusion Brook's imposition of a frame-work of tragedy in the Shakespearean manner is alien: 'the tragic is irreversible. It has no place in the endless cycle of birth and rebirth, the crux of Hindu thought.' Once more Brook seems insensitive to the abuse and rape of women: 'Instead of heightening the outrage inflicted on her (Draupadi) Brook covers it up with facile theatricality' (*Ibid.* 244).

For both Rustom Bharucha and Gautam Dasgupta, Brook's pillaging of Indian material to 'sell' to the 'international market' is a form of cultural imperialism ('it none the less suggests the bad old days of the British Raj'). Rustom Bharucha is particularly scathing about Brook's appropriation of material for his own ends: 'Brook seems to use the characters to tell *his* story, so that they rarely ignite and acquire lives of their own' (Bharucha's emphasis). And sadly – particularly given the often idealistic terms in which this great intercultural enterprise is framed – amongst Indians who helped the director in his researches for the production, 'there is a sad consensus of having been used by Brook, of being "ripped off" as the Americans say'. The Boy (an echo of *Lord of the Flies*?), a character entirely of Brook's and Carrière's invention, asks the dying Krishna: 'Why all your tricks and your bad directions?' 'Imagine', Bharucha adds in parenthesis, 'a child saying that to a god!'

> What cannot be denied is that Brook controls his disparate materials with total authority. He puts his stamp on all of them, whether it is a mask or a prop or an instrument. His eclecticism is perfectly disciplined, there is never an element out of place. *He knows what he wants and he gets it.*[10] Once he places his mark on his materials, they no longer belong to their cultures. They become part of his world.

The poem, indeed, fulfils a number of Brook's fundamental objectives, and is the fulfilment of a search for a kind of personal liberation. Firstly, since the poem is universal, since it grows out of an anonymous culture, the individual ego of the writer or playwright is not a threatening factor (threatening to whom?). In the second place it provides a final escape from the Shakespearean 'parental shadow'. In *The Shifting Point*, Brook argues that:

> *The Mahabharata* cuts to shreds all the old, traditional Western concepts, which are based on an inessential, degenerate Christianity in which good and evil have assumed

very primitive forms. It brings back something immense, powerful and radiant – the idea of an incessant conflict within every person and every group, in every expression of the universe; a conflict beween a possibility which is called 'dharma', and the negation of that possibility. (1988: 163)

William Golding may have been in an Elizabethan tradition in believing that human beings make evil like bees make honey, but Brook has progressed to a 'dharma' which is beyond – and, in Brook's view, greater than – Shakespeare.

Yet at the heart of all this there is another issue still more significant: for the poem is often seen as a treatise of royal initiation, the making of the king, Yudishthira. This theme of the king and what it takes to become king is central. In the *Bhagavad Gita*, Arjuna, who is a key protagonist in Hindu mythology, agonizes that:

> I desire not victory, O Krishna, nor a
> kingdom, nor pleasures. Of what avail
> will a kingdom be to us, or enjoyments,
> or even life, O Govinda?[11]

Like Hamlet, Arjuna is brought to the point of confusion and despair by the knowledge that to become king he must fight, kill and overcome those with whom he is related in blood. He, too, is torn between mother and father, between love and power. Both Arjuna and Hamlet are tortured by inner conflicts, inducing in them a kind of paralysis. But, just as Hamlet finds a way out, achieving mastery in the theatre (a king of infinite space), the Hindu protagonist, Yudishthira, also moves beyond doubt to claim his throne. The significance of that for Brook is clear. As Michael Kustow expresses it:

> And if *The Mahabharata* is about the many-faceted making of a king, then Peter Brook's journey to *The Mahabharata* – which began more than ten years ago and is studded with apparent digressions and indirections – is about the forging of a theatre-maker, and the redefinition of what theatre is. And just as *The Mahabharata* is presided over by gods and superhuman presences – Brahma, Shiva, Vishnu /Krishna –

so Brook has been led by mentors – Shakespeare, Jerzy Grotowski, Antonin Artaud. (Williams 1991: 256)

In reaching out for an international perspective which transcends national boundaries, Brook has outgrown Shakespeare, and in the C.I.R.T. his own ambitions have received a manifest fulfilment:

> In terms of my own life and my own search, the work with the group has shown me that it is possible to make a theatre experience in a purer, simpler, more essential way. I have always searched to make this sort of experience, but the links between the performing group, *the content, myself as director* and the audience, have never been as organically related as they have been in the Centre. The work in the Centre is organically related to *me*, and is absolutely central to *my own* search. (Cited in Bradby and Williams 185)

This contrasts interestingly with what he wrote at the beginning of his career:

> The producer [director] is working with three elements: his text, his audience, and his medium, and of these only the first is constant. It is his primary duty to discover every intention of the author and to transmit these with every possible means at his disposal. (Cole and Chinoy 423)

In the more recent passage the work, even the individuality, of the author has disappeared, shredded into 'content' ('Kill the beast! Cut his throat! Spill his blood! Do him in!'); but the (He who *is* there) 'I', and '*me*' and '*my own*' and '*myself*' of the director is alive and well and living in Paris (and elsewhere).

To regain people's trust in the theatre, Brook suggested in *The Empty Space* (109) that, 'we must prove that there will be no trickery, nothing hidden. We must open our empty hands and show that really there is nothing up our sleeves' . Yet when Jean Vilar tells us that he has nothing up his sleeve, it is easier to believe him than to believe that magician, Peter Brook. 'It has always been better to experience the splendour that Brook can produce,' says his biographer with some insight, 'than to hear him explain why and how he has contrived it' (1971: 168). Still, according to a recent book by the director, There Are No

Secrets (1993). *No* secrets? But Brook knows that his news is
not true; neither he nor the world has grown honest ('As I write
I do not feel a compulsion to tell the whole truth ... Rather I
side with Hamlet ...' (1998: 1-2)). 'As fluid as his father's
ghost,' writes Terry Eagleton of Shakespeare's elusive Prince,
'and as fast talking as any Shakespearean clown, Hamlet riddles
and bamboozles his way out of being definitely known,
switching masks and sliding the signifier' (1986: 71). Does that
profile fit *this* shifting Hamlet? 'Hamlet,' says Harold Bloom in
Shakespeare: The Invention of the Human, 'has survived everything,
even Peter Brook' (1999: 391). It is a measure of Brook's
success in playing his most treasured role that Bloom, in a
chapter entitled 'Hamlet', can make that association.

> Nor do we find him forward to be sounded,
> But with a crafty madness keeps aloof
> When we would bring him on to some confession
> Of his true state. (*Hamlet* III.i.7-10)

Brook has spoken most critically of a theatre where the
images are of 'kings and queens and goddesses' (Berry 1989:
130). Yet in the theatre the regal images, not least with regard to
the director, persist. As King of Infinite Space, Brook now is
seen by some as a seeker after truth and a new communion; by
others as a master-manipulator of other human beings. For
some his experimentation, (*O, reform it altogether!*), is manna from
heaven; for others his imagination is more akin to Vulcan's
stithy. Is he driven by a spirit of health or by a goblin damned?
It may be because of what that modern prophet of the theatre,
Kenneth Tynan, once called his 'sly *throwaway* sophistication',
that we do not know the answer to that question.

> Another night at the circus
> They say it's the best in the world
> The magicians can fool you completely
> And the animals do what they're told.[12]

Illustration 10 | Brook as magician

Illustration 11

'Ay, every inch a king.' (IV.v.107) Actor Paul Scofield in William Shakespeare's *King Lear,* directed by Peter Brook (1962). (Courtesy of the Shakespeare Centre Library, Stratford-upon-Avon.)

[1] See Michael Coveney, 'Can't Make a Hamlet Without Breaking Heads,' *Observer*, 14 January 1996. Also: John Peter, 'Any Answers?', *Sunday Times*, 4 February 1996.

[2] J.C.Trewin, *Peter Brook: A Biography* (London, 1971), p.24.

[3] See, for example, Daniel Labeille, ' "The Formless Hunch": An Interview with Peter Brook,' *Modern Drama* 23 (Spring 1980): 221.

[4] Peter Hall, Introduction to Tyrone Guthrie, *A Life in the Theatre* (London, 1987).

[5] See introduction to *The History of King Lear* in Wells and Taylor, *William Shakespeare: The Complete Works* (Oxford, 1988), p.909.

[6] Comments made at Unesco's Shakespeare Quatercentenary celebration in Paris (1964), quoted in Trewin, *Peter Brook*, p.148.

[7] Winston S. Churchill, *Great Contemporaries* (London, 1937), p.28.

[8] A title that according to one possibly – I must admit *probably* – apochryphal tale, Shakespeare applied to himself. See *The Oxford Book of Literary Anecdotes,* ed. James Sutherland (Oxford, 1975), p.17. 'Forget Shakespeare. Forget that there ever was a man with that name. Forget that the plays have an author.' Cited in John Lahr's insightful review of Brook's most recent *Hamlet* (2000) at the Bouffes du Nord (*The New Yorker*, 18 Dec. 2000, p.100). It is perfectly proper, writes John Peter in a review of the same production, to call this … 'Brook's Hamlet.' ('Is brevity the soul of wit?' *Sun. Times,* 10/12/2000).

[9] See Jean-Claude Carrière, *The Mahabharata,* trans. Peter Brook (New York, 1985), p.161: 'Stamping elepants crushing chests; fathers can't recognize their sons.' See also David Bradby and David Williams, *Director's Theatre* (London, 1988), p.175.

[10] Rustom Barucha, 'A View from India', in *Peter Brook and 'The Mahabharata': Critical Perspectives*, ed. David Williams (London and New York, 1991), p.246. See also: Trewin, *Peter Brook*, p.12. Also: Patrice Pavis, *Theatre at the Crossroads of Culture*, trans. Loren Kruger (London, 1992), p.186, 'and thus to see inter-cultural transfer as a process whereby the target culture appropriates the source culture.'

[11] See Marishi Mahesh Yogi on the *Bhagavad-Gita: A new translation and commentary with Sanskrit text Ch. I-VI* (Harmondsworth, 1969), p.56.

[12] From the Vlasov/Sidorova song 'Circus', in David Downing, *Russian Revolution 1985: A Contemporary Fable* (Sevenoaks, Kent, 1983), p.89.

Conclusion

'What do you want to be when you grow up, Billy?'
'I hope to be an actor.'
'But, Billy, actors don't grow up. And you, Lancelot?'
'A drama critic.'
'Really? That's unusual. I hope you won't find it a bore after
a year or two. And you, Penelope, if you ever grow up?'
'I'm going to be a director, a director, a director.'
'You always were a chatterbox, Penelope. Not one of you
has said you want to be a playwright. How sad. All of you
wish to put the cart before the horse.' Alec Guinness, *My
Name Escapes Me: the Diary of a Retiring Actor* (1996: 11)

'So long as this world exists,' wrote Gordon Craig in *On the Art
of the Theatre* (1911), 'the calmest and the shrewdest personality
will always be king.'[1] The major directors represented in this
study share Craig's enthusiasm for kingship. Like him they
aspire to be in charge in the theatre, to be *tyrannos*, ruler – even
despot. They may not want to be (as one Hollywood film
director put it with embarrassing frankness at the 1998 Oscar
awards ceremony)[2] King of the World but they see their own
role as the decisive, driving force in production. Craig envisaged
a single, controlling voice in theatre to replace the babble of
conflicting voices. He likened the theatre to a ship where the
captain (director) 'is the king and a despotic ruler into the
bargain' (Cole and Chinoy 158). But as Captain Bligh, Craig
clearly fears a mutiny on his Bounty: 'For *compromise* and the

vicious doctrine of compromise with the enemy is preached by the officers of the theatrical navy' (Craig's emphasis). Craig identified the enemy within the theatre as the actors, stage managers and others who lacked a unifying authority. For him, initially at least, the playwright was not the problem. The term 'artist of the theatre' suggests a respect for creation, a shared artistic responsibility. Providing the author kept to his own territory (i.e. writing text, not stage directions), he was not perceived as a threat. However, as Chekhov clearly understood at the turn of the century, the new emerging type of director would soon demand even greater powers of control. To be truly in charge came to mean not only commanding actors, but, in essence, meant the power of re-writing (or 'rewrighting')[3] the play – of, in Hamlet's terms, converting *The Murder of Gonzago* into a Mousetrap for the king.

Replacing the father (even a dead one), replacing what Charles Marowitz calls 'the tyranny [of] the play', could never be an easy or straightforward task: text and stage are separate but they are also inextricably linked. Even Meyerhold, 'the great assassin of the art of the dramatist' found assassinating Shakespeare was a bridge too far, a challenge too great:

> And, like a neutral to his will and matter,
> Did nothing. (*Hamlet* II.ii.484-5)

Brecht, by converting *Coriolanus* into a Marxist tract, merely proved (as Peter Brook helps to point out) how well balanced, how psychologically sound, the original was. Brook, himself, unwittingly, would prove the same point in 1962 when he deleted many of Shakespeare's notes of compassion from *King Lear*. It seems ironic to contemplate a twentieth-century director removing (in effect) Oscar Schindler from the pages of a seventeenth-century text. Replacing the *tyrannos*, then, is a two-edged sword for the Hamlet director, as it is for the Hamlet himself.

When in *The Art of the Theatre* (1905), Craig wrote that, 'it is an offence to poach on what is the sole property of the playwright', and when he described how the director 'takes the copy of the play from the hands of the dramatist and *promises faithfully to interpret it as indicated in the text*,[4] he seemed to accept the ascendancy of the author. Yet, caught in the turbulent and rebellious mood of twentieth-century thought, neither Craig in his later practice, nor Meyerhold who was a fellow spirit, would accept for long such a conservative position. Future directors, following in their steps, such as Brecht, Guthrie and Brook, would see themselves *enlarging* rather than diminishing the director's power to change the text – even, Hamlet-like, incorporating new lines into the play. Above all, they would feel free to amend and interpret the text as they saw fit. Thus still more fundamentally in Planchon's theatre during the 1950s the 'scenic writing' (langage scènique) of the *metteur en scène* would be given equal weighting with that of the textual writing of the playwright. In France, where traditionally the playwright has been king, Patrice Pavis expresses that sea-change in French theatrical thought with an almost metaphysical flourish when he declares that:

> Text and stage are perceived at the same time and in the same place, making it impossible to declare that the one precedes the other. (1992: 29)

As Pavis waves a metaphysical wand over his crossroads, the sub-text is clear: more power to the director. In this theory the map (text) and journey (staging) come into existence at precisely the same moment – a rather strange theory, one might imagine, since it is difficult to know why anyone should embark on a journey with no prior notion of the destination. Even Hamlet is drawn to *The Murder of Gonzago* because 'one scene of it comes near the circumstance … of [his] father's death' (III.ii.74-5); the changes, the *orchestration,* he intends are wrought in the light of something already experienced.

As a rebel of French theatre, Roger Planchon was much inspired by German theatrical thinking, particularly the work and writings of Bertolt Brecht: a director (as Waidson and Holmes suggest) for whom the image of Hamlet seems particularly fitting. The Wittenberg-trained Hamlet figure, in fact, has a distinct relevance not only to Brecht but to Germany itself, and thus to the whole history of the director. In the theatre Hamlet may, in the manner of his father, have an eye like Mars to threaten and command (O, reform it altogether), but he also admires real conquerors. Although a man of 'conscience', Hamlet imagines himself as a real, not just a theatrical, *tyrannos* and is, perhaps understandably, incensed when someone else *pops* in between the election and his hopes. Like Auden's tyrant he is greatly interested in armies and fleets. Indeed Edward Gordon Craig who so identified himself with Hamlet would, like Jean-Louis Barrault, express his unreserved admiration for Fortinbras and his army; and Craig's interest in fleets was noted earlier. If *'Deutschland ist Hamlet'*, as the poet puts it, then Germany has also been the country where Fortinbras and his successors for many years held sway:

> I could see in Hamlet the history of the theatre. In Hamlet all that is living in the theatre is struggling with those dead customs that want to crush the theatre. (Senelick 1982: 69)

In Hamlet Craig sees the new struggling with the old, youth struggling with age – and sons struggling against fathers. Seen in these terms, Meyerhold's youthful rebellion against a stern Bismarckian father becomes in a later period of his life a struggle against the fathers of the Moscow Art Theatre; first against the Meininger-inspired Stanislavsky, and later Nemirovich-Danchenko. It was a struggle to replace their obsessive realism, (and their deference to the Playwright King) with his theatricalism. Indeed, the two main developing traditions of directing that were identified in the opening chapters – that of Stanislavsky (essentially, diffusion of power *from* the director) and that of Craig/Meyerhold (centring of power *in* the Hamlet director) – may well be seen in terms of a conflict between fathers and sons. It is a conflict that lies at the heart of the story of the director and his changing role.

Throughout this study the importance of certain images and certain identifications has been emphasized. The Shakespearean plays, the roles with which a particular artist identifies, tell us much about that director. Certainly a recurring pattern in this story is that of figures who have identified themselves with Hamlet, the director as they see him, blasting aside the corrupt or dated practices of the theatre. The death-obsessed, disease-imaged Hamlet himself is prompted to action, to his revenge, by both heaven *and hell* (II.ii.587). Like the plague, says Artaud, the theatre is the time of evil, the triumph of dark powers that are nourished by a power even more profound until extinction (1958: 30). Jean-Louis Barrault (to whom Artaud gave singular praise) describing his own hands-on style in rehearsal says: '... He [the director] hides behind them [the actors], his mouth against their ear, as if he were their guardian angel – *or some demon, after all!*' (Dieckmann 1975: 194). In the Hamlet director daemon is mixed with demon. And it is some aspect of the devil that makes this kind of director so challenging a figure. Was there not something of the cunning necromancer, asked Harold Clurman, the diabolic magician, in all of Meyerhold's productions? Of Meyerhold's experiments, John Gassner wrote: 'Without doubt this master of *la poésie de théâtre* entranced all who saw his productions, even if they could not be entirely certain he was not confounding art with artifice and making them connive in his misdemeanour.'[5] For Harold Bloom, Hamlet is a theatrical villain-hero. On the one hand 'a transcendental hero'; on the other 'a new kind of villain, direct precursor of Iago and Edmund, the villain-as-playwright, writing with the lives of others as much as with words' (1999: 406). As author of his own stage play, Steven Berkoff, with ease, places the Prince of Elsinore among Shakespeare's villains in his masterclass in evil. Perhaps he should know. He *is* Hamlet (1989).

Similar judgements have been made about Guthrie's antics. Kenneth Tynan accused Guthrie of an 'infuriating *blend* of insight and madness', and of having 'a zany *Doppelgänger*, darting about with his pockets full of fireworks' (1984: 260). The Hamlet director fantasizes about – and in Meyerhold's case realizes – a theatrical Charge of the Light Brigade seeking the bubble reputation even in the cannon's mouth. Ironically, German-born Meyerhold was most Hamlet when he came to direct *Hamlet* – that is, he faltered in the face of the father(land).

> He stayed too long in Wittenberg,
> In the lecture hall and the pubs.
> And therefore he lacks determination. (G.A.Craig 1981: 765)

Essentially, the Hamlet director is a rebel fighting against, it seems to him, huge and impossible odds. Above all he is a man with an (often frustrated) mission, a man, one might say, with a chip on his shoulder. 'As obsessed with treachery as Hamlet,' is Dennis Kennedy's judgement on that side of Craig (1993: 54). In Konstantin Treplev (*The Seagull*), Anton Chekhov created, complete with allusions to Hamlet, a satirical portrait of this figure. On a more serious note, Roger Planchon speaks, not only of his deep attachment to his mother, but also of his profound sense of inadequacy in the face of Shakespeare's achievement and of his struggle to remove himself from 'the Brechtian [parental] shadow'.

What was demonstrated in the chapter on Guthrie – another with whom the Hamlet identification is strong – is that a profound sense of inferiority is part of the Hamlet director's psyche: 'but no more like my father/ Than I too Hercules' (I.ii.152-3). In Guthrie's case his failure, first as an actor and then as a playwright, gave a special impetus and urgency to his challenge against the fathers of dramatic literature:

> Your Aeschylus, your Sophocles and stuff
> Let them all burn, say I, they're garbage all. (Rossi 1970: 43)

Edward Braun postulates a similar lack of confidence, in fact a deep sense of inferiority, as the motive behind some of Meyerhold's experiments (1982: 118). The Hamlet director is the Man who would be King but who, no matter how great his achievements within the bounds of the theatre, never feels confident in his cuckoo kingship: 'O God, I could be bounded in a nutshell and count myself a king of infinite space, were it not that I have bad dreams' (II.ii.256-8). In Brecht's case – the hostility to his overpowering father is well documented – the struggle becomes an obsessive preoccupation with being the dominant theatrical male. In his endless need to control an astonishing array of women for use both in writing and re-writing plays, as well as for personal sexual satisfaction, one sees a primitive pattern in which the dominant male animal of the herd monopolizes the females. Senelick's striking phrase 'amorous *Blitzkrieg*' can be applied as aptly to Brecht as to Craig. Guthrie's (and Hamlet's) plain hostility to pretty women is merely a neurotic variation on the same misogynistic theme. One of the strange discoveries of John Fuegi's detailed analysis (1994) of Brecht's career has been the emergence of women into positions of significance in the story of that writer-director.

Absence can be as significant as presence. Coleridge characterized Ophelia as representing Shakespeare's charm of creating female character through *absence* of characters, through 'outjuttings'. Certainly neither Ophelia nor Gertrude, in terms of dialogue, amount to very much, yet *Hamlet* without them would be as pointless as *Hamlet* without the Prince. 'If the female nothing,' writes Terry Eagleton, 'were simple absence, it would pose no problem; but there is no simple absence, since all absence is dependent for its perceptibility upon presence' (1986: 64). The role of women in the story of the Shakespearean director – their absence as much as their presence – is equally significant. Female directors are noticeably absent from this study, yet (as in *Hamlet*) women are an essential, if sometimes invisible, force or presence. Although it is not apparent at first actress Ellen Terry, for example, is a key figure in this saga. This is not only because of her relationship with Henry Irving and Herbert Beerbohm Tree, the forerunners of the modern director in Britain, but also through her children, Edy and Gordon Craig:

> Of course, I thought my children the most brilliant and beautiful children in the world, and, indeed, 'this side idolatry', they were exceptional, and they had an exceptional bringing up. (Terry 79-80)

The effect of this exceptional bringing up on Craig is clear enough and needs no further comment, but it is worth noting that it was Edy Craig who trained Margaret Webster in the techniques of the theatre (Leiter 1991: 109). That training, combined with a move to the New World where attitudes were less rigid, allowed Webster to become the most celebrated woman Shakespearean director of the middle years of this century – a figure in her own right. This was the case, certainly until the late 1950s and early 1960s brought women such as Joan Littlewood and Ariane Mnouchkine onto the scene. In Webster's attempts to create a listening directorship, reconciling diversity and unity, there are the elements of something new. This was partly, it is true, a reflection of the American experience (a mistrust of the King is buried deep in the American psyche), but also it is a reflection of her femininity. In the line Ellen Terry – Edy Craig – Margaret Webster one sees the beginning of a Mother – Daughter tradition in directing, complementing (and challenging) the usual Father – Son pattern.

In the 1990s a new generation of female directors has begun to reveal how women may be having a profound effect on the role of the director. One example illustrates this with clarity. Invited by German director Peter Stein to the Salzburg Theatre Festival in 1993, Deborah Warner agreed to direct one of Shakespeare's most masculine plays, *Coriolanus*, a play about war and politics – two subjects *supposedly* alien to women. The reaction of the German actors to Warner's non-intrusive style of directing caused dissent, as Peter Stein acknowledged. Some, perhaps reflecting a traditional German antipathy to allowing women any place of power in society, rejected her approach as inept. Others, however, such as Bruno Ganz (Caius Marcius), who described her as 'in-cr-ed-ibly brave', were enthusiastic. His recorded comments reward close scrutiny because they strongly suggest that Warner is attempting to break free of the traditional colonizing role of the director (*à la* Marowitz). In Chapter 1 we noted how Stanislavsky's intrusive finger became symbolic of both sexual and imperialist conquest. In the following description it is clear that Ganz's finger too has become a signifier, a characterization of the director's usual colonizing interference – but, interestingly it seems, Warner rejects that invasive approach:

> I think for a great deal of people … German actors are not used to the way she is working, because her respect for actors is so … much more than we are used … because

usually directors go deeply into actors' business to the point of … (*holding up his little finger*) this finger. They are used to get, I would say, much, much help from directors … we German actors. But she … *there, there is a kind of border … and she says that's your business, that's acting* and she wouldn't dare to interfere in things she believes that is acting [*sic*]. I liked it very much. It was new for me too, and somehow very hard. But I understood the idea and I liked it.[6]

Warner is not alone in questioning this role of director as power-broker. At the end of their respective careers, both Joan Littlewood and Ariane Mnouchkine – both directors who have 'not always resisted the temptation to be dictatorial' – have delivered scathing judgements on the role of (what in this study has been termed) the Hamlet director. 'It's called directing,' says Joan Littlewood in a TV interview (BBC 1; 19/4/94), '… even Peter Brook, they're all directors … but people [actors? audiences?] are too good for us to superimpose our little egos on them.' During an interview with Adrian Kiernander in 1993, Ariane Mnouchkine was even more outspoken:

K. And yet painters and composers have continued.
M. Ah yes, but they're real artists.
K. And the *metteur en scène* isn't?
M. No, he's not. An author will, if he's a great author. I think directing, the *mise en scène*, is an art, but it's a minor art, and I'm sure one day it just sort of … less and less and less am I interested by what is called *mise en scène*.
(Kiernander 1993: 143-4)

'Great plays,' Glenda Jackson told Charles Marowitz in conversation, 'are great plays because they survive the tampering of idiots over the centuries' (Marowitz.1986: 156). Gordon Craig may have been prescient, at least so far as his concept of the directorial despot is concerned, in believing that women would prove to be the ultimate challenge in the theatre. And the enigma of Craig, as indeed the enigma of Hamlet, is the love-hate relationship with the mother.

'The Drama,' said Ellen Terry, 'is the child of the theatre' (Clurman 1972: xii). In this present discussion that statement is a highly significant one and not just because it comes from the mother of that *enfant terrible* (the Father of all the Hamlet directors), Gordon Craig. The early directors thought of the text first (drama), and the performance (theatre) second. In Copeau's formulation the line is in a descending one from the dramatist down. Yet in the most primitive forms of theatre the playwright did not exist; the actor did. Theatre was essentially about a community defining itself. 'Words,' points out Harold Clurman, 'did not constitute the core of the rituals and tribal celebrations of primitive communities … Theatre precedes drama' (*Ibid.* xi). Guthrie reflects this notion when, in espousing the open stage, he argues that the purpose of theatrical performance is not to create the illusion that a palpable fiction is a fact, but rather to recreate in ritual terms an ordered and significant series of ideas. Secondly that it is essentially a sociable, communal affair (1965: 70). In 1963, at the Stratford, Ontario Festival, G. Wilson Knight reflected on the paradox of this movement in emphasis from the text to the performance, to the ritual of theatre:

> The long fight starting with Poël and carried on by Barker for respect to Shakespeare's text joined to a rejection of spectacle has culminated in the open stage of today whose chief danger is *the loss and dispersal of words* and whose chief virtue is once again spectacle; for its finest effects are *visual*, made by human figures, elaborate costumes and fine properties in magnificent interplay. (1964: 298)

For much of the twentieth century there has been just such a turning away from the words of the playwright (drama) toward 'Theatre'. Antonin Artaud declared that instead of continuing to rely upon texts considered definitive and sacred, it was essential to put an end to the subjugation of the theatre to the text, and to recover the notion of a kind of unique language half-way between gesture and thought (1958: 89). Patrice Pavis registers 'a clear change of perspective, a desire to get away from a logocentric notion of theatre, with the text as the central and stable element and *mise en scène* necessarily an incidental transcription, representation and explanation of the text' (1992: 32). THEATRE (not 'text') is the word that presents itself to the eye over Brook's centre at the Bouffes du Nord in Paris. Essentially the trend amounts to a repudiation of words – at least as conveyors of meaning. Gordon Craig noted that the word 'theatre' is derived from the Greek word 'to see' and means 'a place for seeing shows'. Craig adds: 'Not a word about its being a place for hearing 30,000 words babbled out in two hours.' Once in a German theatre Craig saw a notice that read: *Sprechen Verboten*. 'The first moment,' Craig remarks, 'I thought I was in heaven' (Marshall 1975: 42).

What Terry's statement suggests is a reversal of the once accepted hierarchy in which the playwright king hands down the script to lesser mortals. In Terry's phrasing, drama – and thus the playwright – becomes the child, not the father, of theatre. Thus drama, the written text, is placed in a subservient position. In essence the new theatrical order is now ruled over by an alliance between director and actor. In Oedipal terms it might even be seen as a mother-child (Terry – Craig) alliance or conspiracy set against the fathers of literature. Craig, the espouser of wordless theatre, the Son (with a partial mother's blessing) becomes the Father. But as in *Hamlet* the mother fixation is a mixed blessing. In his murderous impulses, Hamlet's agony is intensified by his insight that he cannot separate Gertrude and Claudius: 'My mother. Father and mother is man and wife, man and wife is one flesh, and so my mother' (IV.iii.53-4). Only when Gertrude is dead (and he himself is dying) can he finally despatch Claudius to death. The Reduced Shakespeare Company had a textual point to make when they depicted Claudius and Gertrude as two halves of one person. Yet the crossroads of Oedipus has three roads – one might say, Father, Mother and A.N.Other. At the point of connection the roads are inseparable. In Olivier's *Hamlet* film, after the prince's snide 'Farewell, dear mother', and Claudius's disgruntled 'Thy loving father, Hamlet', the camera moves swiftly to show a pair of clenching, murderous hands. But do the hands belong to Hamlet or Claudius? For a moment, at least, there is confusion. The enigma of Hamlet is that he both adores and hates his mother ('O most pernicious woman! (I.v.105) … but go not to mine uncle's bed' (III.iv.150)), just as he adores the (dead) father, and reviles the (living) 'uncle-father' who has 'popped in between th'election and [his] hopes' – and who now possesses the mother as well as the kingdom. Paradoxically, Claudius's line 'My crown, mine own ambition, and my queen' (III.iii.55), might just as well be Hamlet's, and Hamlet confusingly identifies himself with Claudius (In the Mousetrap it is the *nephew*, not the brother, of the rightful king who murders). Hamlet, as Craig puts it, is total contradiction.

Illustration 12

'Gordon Craig in Clever Contradictory Mood.' (Cartoon by Max Beerbohm)

In *Threads of Time*, Peter Brook quotes only twice from *Hamlet*. On the second page he identifies with Hamlet's desire for secrecy; but the other quotation is from Claudius ('My words fly up, my thoughts remain below.' III.iii.97). When he directed *Hamlet*, he says, this was the line that he found 'touched [him] most deeply' (1998: 81). O day and night, but this is wondrous strange. If Gordon Craig who began this study exemplifies perfectly this contradictory nature – 'Do I contradict myself?/Very well then I contradict myself,/ (I am large, I contain multitudes.)[7] – and is the prototypical Hamlet director, then Peter Brook who concludes it, is the culmination, refinement and fulfilment of Craig's ideal. This brief history, indeed, might be said to begin in 1897, when Craig plays Hamlet in Irving's costume, and concludes with Brook's *Memoir* and his production of *Qui est là* (1996) in Paris. In the mid-century the two men would meet and become friends, shortly after Brook's own 'Moscow *Hamlet*', in 1956.

In this relationship one can trace a clear line of development, a refining process. Craig's theatrical dictator is a no-nonsense, colonizing blood sucker; and Craig had Henry Irving as a role model. In fact, Bram Stoker, Irving's Acting Manager appears to have largely based Dracula on Irving.[8] If Hamlet in the warm after-glow of the Mousetrap can dream of drinking hot blood, then Brook can dream of drawing blood and giving it back in some creative form. But Brook, the vampire-chameleon, sensed that Craig's despotic ruler would not wear well in the latter part of the twentieth century. In *There Are No Secrets*, he writes: 'The period of the twenties and the thirties was for the European theatre a time of extraordinary animation and fertility … Certain styles of acting, certain relations with audiences, *certain hierarchies, such as the place of the director … became established. They were in tune with their times*' (1993: 91). Sensing the need for change, Brook resourcefully sought a new way to achieve an old objective. In *Threads of Time*, Brook describes a producer, Binkie Beaumont, who presented him with a model of a new, less obvious orchestrator of theatrical events:

Many people loved Binkie; many more hated him. He was a monopolist, *a subtly concealed dictator*, but his aim was not only power and riches; he also loved quality, and this is what brought us together. He wanted the theatre to be a place of style and beauty, and as this was what I wanted too, *there was nothing but agreement between us*. He became a good, even endearing friend as well as an object of almost irresistible fascination. I studied him like a teacher, as he was the first example I had met of a man totally equipped to achieve his ends. He knew his world and he knew his people, and he could play on this keyboard with exquisite finesse. He was gentle, charming, and seemed to be totally self-effacing ... *in his quest for absolute power* he could never be caught opposing anything head-on. (1998: 42)

But once achieved, how is this *absolute power* to be employed? That, too, is a central question of this study. In the same book, Brook provides little detailed description of any classical production, but one exception, in a passage of key significance, concerns an unusual production of *Oedipus* in Nigeria. As Brook watched the performance which began by entertaining its audience with a comical Oedipal figure, he observes:

> The performance seemed to have the same scoffing approach that has become so common in Western theatre today, where the modernizing and 'sending-up' of great works cheapen them, depriving us of a whole level of emotion that is richer and more precious than all the pleasure that debunking can bring. (1998: 185)

Brook's brave statement runs against the spirit of a theory-driven age more attuned to 'sending up' classical works than praising them. As such, for this writer at least, it is a welcome statement. And, perhaps, one detects in the passage quoted a note of contrition: for Brook and his radical cohorts have spent not a little time in such trivializations. Yet the power of the director, like the power of the king, is dwarfed by deeper truths. As Antigone, daughter of Oedipus, says to King Creon:

> You are merely a man, mortal,
> Like me, and laws that you enact
> Cannot overturn ancient moralities

> Or common human decency,
> They speak the language of eternity,
> Are not written down, and never change.
> They are for today, yesterday, and all time.
> No one understands where they came from,
> But everyone recognizes their force:
> And no man's arrogance or power
> Can make me disobey them. (*Antig.* trans. Taylor 1986: 151)

The verities of Sophocles's and Shakespeare's truth may not be eternal, but they have an astonishingly long shelf life. The 'trousers down' distortions and destructions – deconstructions, to put it postmodernly – often, as Brook suggests, leave us cold and deeply unsatisfied. In his description of the Nigerian *Oedipus,* Brook admits that his misgivings prove unfounded. He continues:

> But even as I voiced these reservations to myself, the laughter suddenly ceases. 'You have murdered your father!' Oedipus is stopped dead in his tracks; he and the audience are appalled at the same moment and to the same degree. The meaning of family, the sacred nature of family relations, is present to everyone – this likeable hero, who could have been part of any African family, has blundered into the most appalling crime of all.
>
> The most appalling? The silence seems to say that nothing could be worse, until even that silence grows more intense a few moments later as Oedipus and audience both learn that he has broken the most sacred of all taboos and has taken his mother to his bed. The gravity and the tension remain unchanged to the end of the performance, leaving the audience deeply shaken. (1998: 185-6)

As Hamlet contemplates the assassination of his step-father, he orders the players to perform a scene in which elderly Priam is murdered by young Pyrrhus. Hecuba's tears for her slaughtered husband move the First Player, just as they no doubt move Hamlet himself. This same Oedipal conflict – the crossroads between old father Shakespeare and the Hamlet director – is the key to this study.

The dilemma of the Hamlet director is whether or not he should replace the father. To be king or not to be: for him, that is the question. Chekhov's Hamlet director, Konstantin Treplev (Meyerhold's part in the 1898 *Seagull*), exposes the riddle when he says of the writer, father-figure, Trigorin: ' … entering like Hamlet: "Words, words, words"'. But Chekhov's play also anticipates what Brook calls 'the tragic rejection of the father figure that is so much part of our time' (1998: 14). It points, in other words, to an underlying truth: that the old hero, the figure in black, the Hamlet misogynist, is now a shrunken and failed entity, a dead bird. In the end the seagull may be, as Raymond Williams suggests, the suicidal Treplev.[9] But in that play it is the other seagull, the modern Ophelia, Nina, who provides a new direction, a hope and vision for the future. What's finer than kingship, she (like Antigone) seems to tell us, is fairness and the idea of justice.

Illustration 13

'Why look you, how unworthy a thing you make of me. You would play upon me: you would seem to know my stops …' Zinaida Raikh auditions for the role of Hamlet in Olesha's *A List of Benefits* directed by Meyerhold (1931)

Directors are not just creatures of power, they are also, paradoxically, artists. The rise of the director's craft and the hegemony of the director has been intimately connected with the rise of technology, and the endless possibilities this offers in terms of modern staging. Technology, in itself, tends to emphasize – perhaps exaggerate – how much our world is changing and has been changed. Margaret Webster had a point when she insisted that fundamentally Shakespeare's characters inhabit the *same* world as we do. To put it mildly this runs contrary to the *Zeitgeist*. To support her view of 'the universality of man, annihilating the gap of time as easily as the division of race', Webster would quote Shylock: 'We too have "organs, dimensions, senses; affections, passions". We are "subject to the same diseases, healed by the same means, warmed and cooled by the same winter and summer … If you prick us do we not bleed? If you tickle us do we not laugh? If you poison us do we not die? And if you wrong us, shall we not revenge?"'[10] It is not difficult to demonstrate that *technologically speaking* we are worlds apart from Shakespeare. It is less easy to demonstrate that people have been transformed either physically or spiritually, even that the fundamental questions of love and power have been resolved. 'And maybe, after all,' writes Fintan O'Toole, 'Shakespeare survives in the 1990s not just because his work fits some aspects of contemporary [postmodern] culture, but because it also resists other aspects of it' (*Irish Times* 21/2/96). Brecht proclaimed the end of jealousy and envy in a new Marxist world order: no one demonstrated the enduring nature of those deadly sins more tellingly than he did. No wonder the Bible was his favourite book! 'Then I looked at all the injustice that goes on in the world. The oppressed were weeping and no one would help them. No one would help them because their oppressors had power on their side' (Ecclesiastes 4: 1). Things are changing; things are changeable; but some things are more changeable than others.

What's finer than kingship is fairness and the idea of justice. In striving for that our age tends to see kings (and goddesses) as part of the problem rather than part of the solution: 'intolerable' is Brook's word. This is where the concept of the

Hamlet director now seems most dated and vulnerable. Yet few would deny that there is a key role in theatre for the enlightened 'ideally critical audience' (i.e. director) of which Jacques Copeau echoing Granville-Barker, spoke. There is undeniable sense in Craig's notion of the one who has an overall view of the production. Such a figure, however, should surely be a communicator rather than a despot or a colonist. Guthrie was right when he argued that part of the director's role is to protect the weak actors from the strong. 'My chief humour,' Bottom, the actor, tells Peter Quince, the poet-director, 'is for a tyrant' (*Dream* I.ii.24). In that, too, there is a warning.

[1] E. Gordon Craig, *On the Art of the Theatre* (London, 1957), p.45.

[2] James Cameron, director of the film 'Titanic'. Was actress Kate Winslett (ex-Ophelia) less than impressed?

[3] The neologism belongs to Amy S. Green. In *The Revisionist Stage: American Directors Reinvent the Classics* (Cambridge, 1994), she writes: 'Derived from "playwright," the new coinage distinguishes a director's revision from a new author's "rewriting" of an old play … Its spelling also underscores the idea that these directors *craft or shape old scripts into new theatrical events.*' (p.xi).

[4] E. Gordon Craig, *The Art of the Theatre* (1905), reprinted in Cole and Chinoy, p.151 and 149.

[5] Harold Clurman, *On Directing* (London, 1972), p.172. Also: John Gassner, *Directions in Modern Theatre and Drama* (New York, 1956), p.197.

[6] See 'Deborah Warner's *Coriolanus* at Salzburg,' The Late Show, BBC 2 (TV), 3/10/93. For discussion of Warner's 'open' style of directing, see also: Robert Smallwood, 'Director's Shakespeare', in *Shakespeare: An Illustrated Stage History*, ed. Jonathan Bate and Russell Jackson, (Oxford, 1996), pp.180-2.

[7] The line, in fact, is from Walt Whitman ('then and always his [Gordon's] particular hero' (Terry 326)), but Craig's pronouncements are frequently in a similar vein. See, for example: Gordon Craig, *The Theatre Advancing* (London, 1921), p. li.

[8] See Barbara Belford, *Bram Stoker: A Biography of the Author of 'Dracula'* (New York, 1996).

[9] Raymond Williams, *Drama From Ibsen to Brecht* (London, 1968), p.103.

[10] See Margaret Webster, *Shakespeare Today* (London: J.M.Dent, 1957), p.292.

'Good, but not immortal.'

Illustration 14 | Cartoon of Shakespeare by Al Ross.

(Courtesy of cartoonbank – the *New Yorker Magazine.*)

Bibliography

Arnott, Brian. *Edward Gordon Craig and Hamlet*. Ottawa, 1975

Artaud, Antonin. *The Theater and its Double*. Trans. Mary Caroline Richards. New York, 1958

Bablet, Denis. *Edward Gordon Craig*. Trans. Daphne Woodward. London, 1966

Barrault, Jean-Louis. *The Theatre of Jean-Louis Barrault*. Trans. Joseph Chiari, London, 1961

--------*Souvenirs pour demain*. London, 1972

Barton, John. *Playing Shakespeare*. London, 1984

Bartram, Graham and Anthony Waine (ed.). *Brecht in Perspective*. London, 1982

Bate, Jonathan and Russell Jackson. (ed.). *Shakespeare: An Illustrated Stage History*. Oxford, 1996

Benedetti, Jean. *Stanislavski: An Introduction*. London, 1982

--------(ed.). *The Moscow Art Theatre Letters*. London, 1991

Bentley, Eric. *In Search of Theater*. New York, 1953

--------*The Playwright as Thinker*. London, 1967

--------*The Brecht Memoir*. New York, 1985

--------*The Life of the Drama*. New York, 1991

Berry, Ralph. *Changing Styles in Shakespeare*. London, 1981

--------*On Directing Shakespeare*. London, 1989

Bloom, Harold. *Shakespeare: The Invention of the Human*. London, 1999

Boose, Lynda, E. and Richard Burt. (ed.). *Shakespeare, the Movie*. London, 1997

Boyd, James. *Goethe's Knowledge of English Literature*. Oxford, 1932

Bradby, David. *Modern French Drama 1940-1990*. 2nd edn. Cambridge, 1991

Bradby, David and David Williams. *Director's Theatre*. London, 1988

Braun, Edward (ed.). *Meyerhold on Theatre*. London, 1969

--------*The Director and the Stage*. London, 1982

--------*The Theatre of Meyerhold*. London, 1979

Brecht, Bertolt. *Brecht on Theatre: the Development of an Aesthetic* ed. and trans. by John Willett. 2nd edn. London, 1974

--------*Poems 1913-56*, ed. by John Willett and John Mannheim with the co-operation of Eric Fried. London, 1976

Brook, Peter. *The Empty Space*. London, 1968

--------'The Influence of Gordon Craig in Theory and Practice'. *Drama* No. 173 (1989): 40-1

--------*The Shifting Point: Forty Years of Theatrical Exploration 1946- 1987*. London, 1988

--------*There Are No Secrets: Thoughts on Acting and Theatre*.   London, 1993

--------*Threads of Time: a Memoir*. London, 1998

Brooking, Jack. 'Four Bare Walls and a Touch of Joy'. *Players* 41 (October 1964): 7

Carlson, Marvin. *The Theatre of the French Revolution*. New York, 1966

Capbern, August. 'Tyrone Guthrie: A Study of his Artistic Achievements in the U.S.A.' (unpub.) Ph. D. dissertation, University of California at Los Angeles, 1969

Clurman, Harold. *On Directing*. London, 1972

Clyman, Toby W. *A Chekhov Companion*. Westport, CT, 1985

Cole, Toby and Helen Krich Chinoy (ed.). *Directors on Directing: A Source Book of the Modern Theatre*. London, 1964

Coleridge, Samuel Taylor. *Lectures and Notes on Shakespere [sic] and Other English Poets* ed. by T. Ashe. London, 1885

Corrigan, Robert, W. *Theatre in the Twentieth Century*. New York, 1963

Craig, E. Gordon. *Books and Theatres*. London, 1925

--------*Henry Irving*. London, 1930

--------*On the Art of the Theatre*. London, 1957 [1911]

--------*The Theatre Advancing*. London, 1921

--------*Scene*. London, 1923

Croyden, Margaret. 'Peter Brook's *Tempest*', *The Drama Review*, 13 (Spring 1969)

Davies, Anthony. *Filming Shakespeare's Plays*. Cambridge, 1988

Daoust, Yvette. *Roger Planchon: Director and Playwright*. Cambridge, 1981

Delgado, Maria M., and Paul Heritage (eds.). *In Contact with the Gods? Directors Talk Theatre*. Manchester, 1996

Dieckman, Suzanne Burgoyne. 'Theory and Practice in the Total Theatre of Jean-Louis Barrault' [unpublished] Ph.D. dissertation, University of Michigan, 1975

Dulack, Tom. *In Love With Shakespeare: A Literary Memoir.* Lanham, Maryland, 2001

Eagleton, Terry. *Marxism and Literary Criticism.* London, 1989

--------*William Shakespeare.* Oxford, 1986

Eliot, T.S. 'Mr Craig's Socratic Dialogues.' *Drama* 173 (Dec. 1989): 36-37

Elsom, John (ed.). *Is Shakespeare Still Our Contemporary?* London, 1989

Esslin, Martin. *The Field of Drama: How the Signs of Drama Create Meaning on Stage and Screen.* London, 1987

Forsyth, James. *Tyrone Guthrie: a Biography.* London, 1976

Frayn, Michael. *Anton Chekhov: Plays.* London, 1988

Freud, Sigmund. *Two Short Accounts of Psycho-Analysis.* Trans. and ed. James Strachey. Harmondsworth, 1962

Friel, Brian. *Philadelphia, Here I Come!.* London, 1965

Fuegi, John. *The Life and Lies of Bertolt Brecht.* London, 1994

Gassner, John. *Directions in Modern Theatre and Drama.* New York, 1966

Gielgud, John. *Stage Directions.* London, 1963

Grass, Günter. *The Plebeians Rehearse the Uprising: a German Tragedy.* Trans. Ralph Mannheim. New York, 1966

Green, Amy S. *The Revisionist Stage: American Directors Reinvent the Classics.* New York, 1994

Guicharnaud, Jacques. *Modern French Theatre: from Giraudoux to Beckett.* New Haven, 1961

Guinness, Alec. *Blessings in Disguise.* London,1986

--------My *Name Escapes Me: the Diary of a Retiring Actor.* London, 1996

Guthrie, Tyrone. *Theatre Prospect.* London, 1932

--------'Hamlet and Elsinore'. *London Mercury*, 31 July 1937

--------'Is there Madness in the Method?' *New York Times Magazine*, 15 November 1957

--------*A Life in the Theatre.* London, 1987 [1960]

--------'Why and How They Play Hamlet.' *New York Times Magazine* 14 August 1960

--------'Dominant Director', *New York Times*, 21 August 1960, § 2

--------'The Star's The Thing'. *New York Times Magazine*, 23 October 1960

--------'So Long as the Theatre can do Miracles'. *New York Times Magazine*, 28 April 1963

--------*In Various Directions: A View of the Theatre*. London, 1965

Guthrie, Tyrone and Robertson Davies. *Twice Have the Trumpets Sounded: A Record of the Stratford Shakespearean Festival in Canada, 1954*. London, 1954

Hayman, Ronald. *Brecht: a Biography*. London, 1983

--------(ed.). *The German Theatre: a Symposium*. London, 1975

Heim, Michael Henry and Karlinsky, Simon. (eds.). *Anton Chekhov's Life and Thought*. Berkeley, Cal., 1973

Hoover, Marjorie L. *Meyerhold and his Set Designers*. New York, 1989

Houghton, Norris. *Moscow Rehearsals*. New York, 1936

Innes, Christopher. *Edward Gordon Craig*. Cambridge, 1983

Jones, Ernest. *Hamlet and Oedipus*. London, 1949

--------'The Death of Hamlet's Father' in *Psychoanalysis and Literature* ed. H.M. Ruitenbeek. New York, 1964

Kennedy, Dennis. Looking at Shakespeare: A Visual History of Twentieth-Century Performance. Cambridge, 1993

Kiernander, Adrian. *Ariane Mnouchkine and the Théâtre du Soleil*. Cambridge, 1993

Kinzer, Stephen. 'Shakespeare, Icon in Germany'. *New York Times* 30/12/95. pp.11 & 20

Knowles, Dorothy. *French Drama of the Inter-War Years 1918-1939*. London, 1967

Kott, Jan. *Shakespeare Our Contemporary*. Trans Boleslaw Taborski. 2nd edn. London, 1967

Kustow, Michael. 'Creating a Theatre of Real Life', *Theatre Quarterly* II, No. 5 (1972): 43-56

Leach, Robert. *Vsevolod Meyerhold*. Cambridge, 1989

Leiter, Samuel. *From Belasco to Brook: Representative Directors of the English Speaking Stage*. New York, 1991

--------*From Stanislavsky to Barrault: Representative Directors of the European Stage*. New York, 1991

Magarshack, David (ed.). *Stanislavsky on the Art of the Stage*. London, 1950

--------*The Real Chekhov*. London, 1972

Marowitz, Charles. *Prospero's Staff*. Indianapolis, 1986

Marshall, Norman. *The Producer and the Play*. London, 1975 [1957]

Miller, Jonathan. *Subsequent Performances*. London, 1986

Morgan, Joyce Vining. *Stanislavski's Encounter with Shakespeare : The Evolution of a Method*. Ann Arbor, Mich., 1984

Newman, L.M. 'Gordon Craig in Germany', *German Life and Letters* 40: 1 (October 1986): 11-33

Olivier, Laurence. *Confessions of an Actor.* London, 1989

Orwell, George. *Inside the Whale and Other Essays.* London, 1962

Osborne, John. 'From Political to Cultural Despotism: the Nature of the Saxe-Meiningen Aesthetic', *Theatre Quarterly* V, No. 17 (Mar.-May 1975): 40-54

Patterson, Michael. *German Theatre Today.* London, 1976

Pavis, Patrice. *Theatre at the Crossroads of Culture.* Trans. Loren Kruger. London, 1992

Poel, William. *Shakespeare in the Theatre.* London, 1913

Read, Leslie du S. 'Directing' in *The Cambridge Guide to Theatre* ed. Martin Banham. Cambridge, 1988

Rose, Enid. *Gordon Craig and the Theatre.* London: Sampson Low, Marston and Co., [n.d.]

Rossi, Alfred A. *Minneapolis Rehearsals: Tyrone Guthrie Directs 'Hamlet'.* Berkeley, 1970

--------Astonish Us in the Morning: Tyrone Guthrie Remembered. Detroit, 1980

Rouse, John. *Brecht and the West German Theatre: The Practice and Politics of Interpretation.* London, 1989

Rudlin, John. *Commedia dell'arte: an Actor's Handbook.* London, 1994

Rudnitsky, Konstantin. *Meyerhold the Director.* Ann Arbor, Michigan, 1981

Ryan, Kiernan. *Shakespeare.* London, 1989

Sayler, Oliver, M. (ed.). *Max Reinhardt and his Theatre.* Trans. Mariele S. Gudernatsch and others. London, 1968 [1924]

Senelick, Laurence. 'Chekhov on Stage' in *A Chekhov Companion* ed. Toby W.Clyman. Westport, CT, 1985

--------*Gordon Craig's Moscow 'Hamlet': a Reconstruction.* Westport, CT, 1982

--------(ed.). *National Theatre in Northern and Eastern Europe, 1746-1900.* Cambridge, 1991

Shaw, George Bernard. 'Granville Barker'. *Drama* No. 173 (Dec. '89): 30-32. (Originally printed as 'Barker's Wild Oats' in *Harper's Weekly.* 19 Jan. 1947)

Slonim, Marc. *Russian Theater: From the Empire to the Soviets.* London, 1963

Speaight, Robert. *Shakespeare on the Stage: An Illustrated History of Shakespearian Performance.* London, 1973

Speirs, Ronald. *Bertolt Brecht.* London, 1987

Stanislavsky, K.S. *My Life in Art.* London, 1980

--------*An Actor Prepares.* London, 1980

--------*Building A Character*. London, 1979

--------*Creating a Role*. London, 1981

--------*Stanislavsky Produces Othello*. Trans. Helen Nowak. London, 1948

Stein, Peter. 'The Theatre of Peter Stein', Interview by Roy Kift. *Drama* 164 (1987): 5-7

Steiner, George. *The Death of Tragedy*. London, 1961

Strasberg, Lee. 'Russian Notebook' (1934). *Drama Review* 17 (March 1973): 109

Styan, J.L. *The Shakespeare Revolution: Criticism and Performance in the Twentieth Century*. Cambridge, 1977

Taylor, Don. (ed.). *Sophocles: The Theban Plays*. London, 1986

Taylor, Gary. *Reinventing Shakespeare: A Cultural History, from the Restoration to the Present*. London, 1990

Terry, Ellen. *The Story of My Life*. 2nd edn. London, [n.d.]

Trewin, J.C. *Peter Brook: a Biography*. London, 1971

Tynan, Kenneth. *A View of the English Stage 1944-1965*. London, 1984

Vilar, Jean. 'Which One is the Creator: the Author or the Producer?' Trans. Heather Wilcock, from *Le Théâtre Service Public (et autres textes)*. Paris, 1975

Wells, Stanley and Gary Taylor. (ed.) *William Shakespeare: The Complete works*. Oxford, 1988

Whitton, David. *Stage Directors in Modern France*. Manchester, 1987

Wilcock, Michael Stewart (Ph.D) 'Shakespeare and the Director: A study of the emergence and changing role of the director in twentieth-century Shakespearean production.' Dublin, 1996

Willett, John. *The Theatre of Bertolt Brecht*. 3rd edn. London, 1967

Williams, David (ed.). *Peter Brook and 'The Mahabharata': Critical Perspectives*. London, 1991

Williams, Raymond. *Drama from Ibsen to Brecht*. London, 1968

Wilson, J. Dover. *What Happens in Hamlet*. 3rd edn. Cambridge, 1951 [1935]

Wilson Knight, G. *Shakespearian Production: With Especial Reference to the Tragedies*. London, 1964 [1936]

Index of Directors

Mike Wilcock lectures on Shakespeare and on directing at University College, Dublin. He has arranged courses on the challenges of transposing Shakespeare to cinema at both the Irish Film Centre and the UCD Centre for Drama Studies. In 1996, he completed a doctoral dissertation on 'Shakespeare and the Director' at University College, Dublin.

He has directed more than twenty theatre productions, including some of the major Shakespearean tragedies.

In the 1980s he ran the English Department at Newpark, Blackrock, and more recently was appointed an Assistant Principal.

CP

CARYSFORT PRESS

The Press aims to produce high quality publications which, though written and/or edited by academics, will be made accessible to a general readership. The organisation would also like to provide a forum for critical thinking in the Arts in Ireland, again keeping the needs and interests of the general public in view.

The company publishes contemporary Irish writing for and about the theatre.

Carysfort Press was formed in the summer of 1998. It receives annual funding from the Arts Council.

The directors believe that drama is playing an ever-increasing role in today's society and that enjoyment of the theatre, both professional and amateur, currently plays a central part in Irish culture.

Editorial and publishing inquiries to:

CARYSFORT PRESS

58 Woodfield, Scholarstown Road,
Rathfarnham, Dublin 16,
Republic of Ireland
T (353 1) 493 7383   F (353 1) 406 9815
e: info@carysfortpress.com
www.carysfortpress.com

NEW TITLES

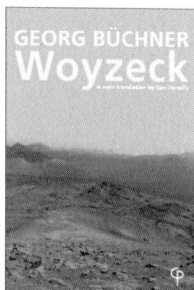

GEORG BÜCHNER: WOYZECK
A NEW TRANSLATION
BY DAN FARRELLY

The most up-to-date German scholarship of Thomas Michael Mayer and Burghard Dedner has finally made it possible to establish an authentic sequence of scenes. The wide-spread view that this play is a prime example of loose, open theatre is no longer sustainable.   Directors and teachers are challenged   to "read it again".

ISBN 1-904505-02-3
€18

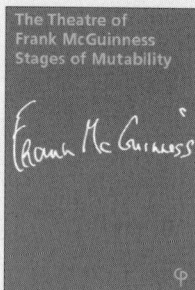

THE THEATRE OF FRANK MCGUINNESS
STAGES OF MUTABILITY
BY HELEN LOJEK

The first edited collection of essays about internationally renowned Irish playwright Frank McGuinness focuses on both performance and text. Interpreters come to diverse conclusions, creating a vigorous dialogue that enriches understanding and reflects a strong consensus about the value of McGuinness's complex work.

ISBN 1-904505-01-5
€15

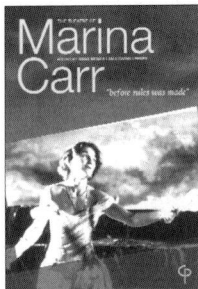

THE THEATRE OF MARINA CARR
"BEFORE RULES WAS MADE"
EDITED BY ANNA MCMULLAN
& CATHY LEENEY

As the first published collection of articles on the theatre of Marina Carr, this volume explores the world of Carr's theatrical imagination, the place of her plays in comtemporary theatre in Ireland and abroad and the significance of her highly individual voice.

ISBN 0-9534-2577-0
€15

HAMLET
THE SHAKESPEAREAN DIRECTOR
BY MIKE WILCOCK

"This study of the Shakespearean director as viewed through various interpretations of HAMLET is a welcome addition to our understanding of how essential it is for a director to have a clear vision of a great play. It is an important study from which all of us who love Shakespeare and who understand the importance of continuing contemporary exploration may gain new insights."

From the Foreword, by Joe Dowling,
Artistic Director, The Guthrie Theater,
Minneapolis, MN

ISBN 1-904505-00-7
€18

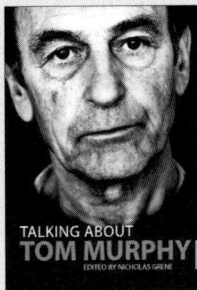

TALKING ABOUT TOM MURPHY
EDITED BY NICHOLAS GRENE

Talking About Tom Murphy is shaped around the six plays in the landmark Abbey Theatre Murphy Season of 2001, assembling some of the best-known commentators on his work: Fintan O'Toole, Chris Morash, Lionel Pilkington, Alexandra Poulain, Shaun Richards, Nicholas Grene and Declan Kiberd.

ISBN 0-9534-2579-7
€10

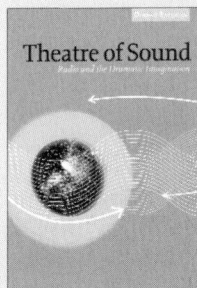

THEATRE OF SOUND
RADIO AND THE
DRAMATIC IMAGINATION
BY DERMOT RATTIGAN

An innovative study of the challenges that radio drama poses to the creative imagination of the writer, the production team, and the listener.

"A remarkably fine study of radio drama – everywhere informed by the writer's professional experience of such drama in the making…A new theoretical and analytical approach – informative, illuminating and at all times readable."

Richard Allen Cave

ISBN 0-9534-2575-4
€20

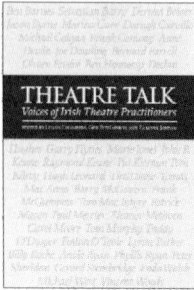

THEATRE TALK

VOICES OF IRISH THEATRE PRACTITIONERS

EDITED BY LILIAN CHAMBERS, GER FITZGIBBON & EAMONN JORDAN

"This book is the right approach - asking practitioners what they feel."

Sebastian Barry, Playwright.

"... an invaluable and informative collection of interviews with those who make and shape the landscape of Irish Theatre."

Ben Barnes, Artistic Director of the Abbey Theatre

ISBN 0-9534-2576-2
€20

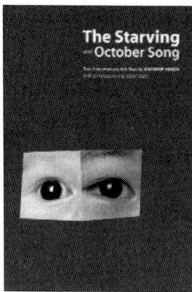

THE STARVING AND OCTOBER SONG

TWO CONTEMPORARY IRISH PLAYS

BY ANDREW HINDS

The Starving, set during and after the siege of Derry in 1689, is a moving and engrossing drama of the emotional journey of two men.

October Song, a superbly written family drama set in real time in pre-ceasefire Derry.

ISBN 0-9534-2574-6
€10

IN SEARCH OF THE SOUTH AFRICAN IPHIGENIE

BY ERIKA VON WIETERSHEIM AND DAN FARRELLY

Discussions of Goethe's "Iphigenie auf Tauris" (Under the Curse) as relevant to women's issues in modern South Africa: women in family and public life; the force of women's spirituality; experience of personal relationships; attitudes to parents and ancestors; involvement with religion.

ISBN 0-9534-2578-9
€10

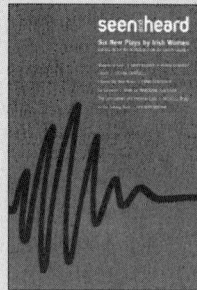

SEEN AND HEARD (REPRINT)

SIX NEW PLAYS BY IRISH WOMEN

EDITED WITH AN INTRODUCTION BY CATHY LEENEY

A rich and funny, moving and theatrically exciting collection of plays by Mary Elizabeth Burke-Kennedy, Síofra Campbell, Emma Donoghue, Anne Le Marquand Hartigan, Michelle Read and Dolores Walshe.

ISBN 0-9534-2573-8
€20

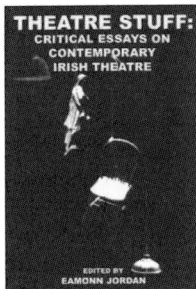

THEATRE STUFF (REPRINT)
CRITICAL ESSAYS ON CONTEMPORARY
IRISH THEATRE
EDITED BY EAMONN JORDAN

Best selling essays on the successes and
debates of contemporary Irish theatre at
home and abroad.

Contributors include: Thomas Kilroy, Declan
Hughes, Anna McMullan, Declan Kiberd,
Deirdre Mulrooney, Fintan O'Toole,
Christopher Murray, Caoimhe McAvinchey
and Terry Eagleton.

ISBN 0-9534-2571-1
€19

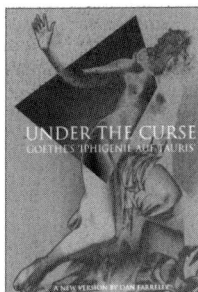

URFAUST
A NEW VERSION OF GOETHE'S   EARLY
"FAUST" IN BRECHTIAN MODE
BY DAN FARRELLY

This version is based on Brecht's irreverent
and daring re-interpretation of the German
classic.

"Urfaust is a kind of well-spring for German
theatre… The love-story is the most daring
and the most profound in German
dramatic literature." *Brecht*

ISBN 0-9534257-0-3
€7.60

UNDER THE CURSE
GOETHE'S "IPHIGENIE AUF TAURIS",
IN A NEW VERSION
BY DAN FARRELLY

The Greek myth of Iphigenie grappling
with the curse on the house of Atreus is
brought vividly to life. This version is
currently being used in Johannesburg to
explore problems of ancestry, religion, and
Black African women's spirituality.

ISBN 0-9534-2572-X
€20

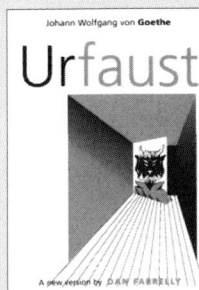

HOW TO ORDER
TRADE ORDERS DIRECTLY TO

CMD
Columba Mercier Distribution
55A Spruce Avenue
Stillorgan Industrial Park
Blackrock
Co. Dublin

T (353 1) 294 2560
F (353 1) 294 2564
E cmd@columba.ie

or contact
SALES@BROOKSIDE.IE